THE BUREAU OF INDIAN AFFAIRS

Westview Library of Federal Departments, Agencies, and Systems

Ernest S. Griffith and Hugh L. Elsbree, General Editors

†*The Library of Congress,* Second Edition, Charles A. Goodrum and Helen W. Dalrymple

†*The National Park Service,* Second Edition, William C. Everhart, with a Foreword by Russell E. Dickenson

The Forest Service, Second Edition, Michael Frome, with a Foreword by Carl Reidel and an Afterword by R. Max Peterson

†*The Smithsonian Institution,* Second Edition, Paul H. Oehser; Louise Heskett, Research Associate; Foreword by S. Dillon Ripley

The Bureau of Indian Affairs, Theodore W. Taylor, with a Foreword by Phillip Martin

†Available in hardcover and paperback.

THE BUREAU OF INDIAN AFFAIRS

Theodore W. Taylor

Foreword by Phillip Martin

Westview Press / Boulder, Colorado

Westview Library of Federal Departments, Agencies, and Systems

The photographs, unless otherwise attributed, were courteously provided by the Bureau of Indian Affairs.

Published in 1984 in the United States of America by
Westview Press, Inc.
5500 Central Avenue
Boulder, Colorado 80301
Frederick A. Praeger, President and Publisher

Library of Congress Cataloging in Publication Data
Taylor, Theodore W.
The Bureau of Indian Affairs.
(Westview library of federal departments, agencies, and systems)
Bibliography: p.
Includes index.
1. United States. Bureau of Indian Affairs.
2. Indians of North America—Government relations.
3. Indians of North America—Tribal government.
I. Title. II. Series.
E93.T265 1983 353.0081'497 83-2480
ISBN 0-86531-315-6

Printed and bound in the United States of America

CONTENTS

ILLUSTRATIONS

Tables

Figures

Photographs

(The photo section appears following page 104.)

FOREWORD

It is difficult for anyone who has not grown up on a reservation to understand the terribly complex set of legal circumstances with which Indian people must deal every day, the plethora of government agencies, the questions of who, if anyone, has legal jurisdiction. It is difficult for those who have grown up on reservations as well!

Central in all the complexity is the Bureau of Indian Affairs, which Ted Taylor in this book has fully described and, perhaps more importantly, placed in the full context of governmental dealings with the Indian people. To us, the situation with the bureau is often that "we can't live with it and we can't live without it." This book goes a long way toward explaining why that is.

This book contains one of the best summaries of Indian policy options that I have ever encountered, not just because the whole range of issues are addressed, but also because the Indian viewpoint and the viewpoint of the general American citizenry are both present. As Ted points out, the "Indian business," like the "agency view," can be confining, and most of the information we tribal leaders receive is based totally on premises unknown to the average non-Indian citizen.

My tribe, the Mississippi band of Choctaw Indians, is presently on the horns of a major policy dilemma, which Ted describes: the conflict between the "special relationship" with the federal government and tribal "self-sufficiency." Over the past four years, the Choctaw tribe has succeeded in creating nearly 500 "private sector" jobs in tribal enterprises as the result of a self-sufficiency strategy—which has been especially helpful at a time when the federal budget cutbacks have been forcing a decline in the dollar aspect of the "special relationship." Although helpful in the short run, what will continued success in the economic realm mean for the "special relationship," for the treaty obligations of the national government, for the preservation of Indian cultures and languages?

This book discusses this and other issues that Indians and other Americans must address if Indian policy is to be both reasonable and fair. I believe this book will be of great aid in seeing that reason and fairness will characterize the ongoing debate.

Phillip Martin
Chief, Mississippi band of Choctaw Indians
President, National Tribal Chairmen's Association

ACKNOWLEDGMENTS

S. Lyman Tyler, American West Center, University of Utah, reviewed the entire first draft of the manuscript and made many valuable suggestions. His encouragement helped keep the project going. John C. Ewers, ethnologist emeritus, Smithsonian Institution; Francis Paul Prucha, author of much Indian historical material; and S. Lyman Tyler all reviewed and criticized the original draft of Chapter 1. It is much improved as a result. Kenneth L. Smith, assistant secretary, U.S. Department of the Interior, with jurisdiction over Indian affairs, suggested the inclusion of a chapter on tribal government when he reviewed the original outline. This suggestion was adopted, and Chapter 4, "Tribal Government," is one of the most informative and important chapters in the book. Kenneth Payton, as acting assistant secretary in charge of the operations of the Bureau of Indian Affairs, gave counsel and wrote to the governors of the states for information on their Indian programs. Without this information an important aspect of the Indian environment would have been omitted. Joseph W. Gorrell, director, Office of Budget for the Department of the Interior, obtained information on Indian activities and funding for other bureaus and offices of the department. Officials of the Indian Health Service provided budget and program information.

Tim Vollmann, of the Office of the Solicitor, Interior Department, and Peter Taylor, on the staff of the Senate Select Committee on Indian Affairs, helped the author through the policy process that resulted in the settlement of the Maine land claims. Dennis Tiepelman, Alaska Federation of Natives; Bradley H. Patterson, on the White House staff at the time of the Trail of Broken Treaties; and Cecil Hoffmann, on Assistant Secretary Smith's staff, reviewed material and suggested improvements. Some of the material concerned had to be omitted because of space limitations.

Ralph Sabers, deputy assistant director for financial management, BIA, provided budget information on program activity and funding. Sam Adams, Division of Management Research and Evaluation; Irene Fischer, personnel officer; Don Asbra, Contracts and Grants; and Raymond V. Butler assisted with organizational information. Roger Boyd and George Lynn, BIA statisticians, were of great assistance in furnishing 1980 census data as rapidly as it was available. The Division of Tribal Government Services received the letters from the governors, reviewed parts of the manuscript, and patiently answered questions.

Officials in all of the program divisions were helpful in obtaining basic material and in reviewing the early drafts. Howard Piepenbrink and Shirley M. Crosby were often the anchor persons on realty matters; Elizabeth Holmgren, on education; and Theodore C. Krenzke and Raymond V. Butler (both serving as acting commissioner for short periods), for the Office of Indian Services.

Throughout the effort of preparing this book Thomas Oxendine and his public information staff were always ready to assist. Hugh Elsbree commented on the organization of material and made suggestions as to tone and content. At Westview Press, Kathy Jones, Alice Levine, Jeanne Remington, and copy editor Megan Schoeck capably contributed to the quality of the book.

My life partner, Jean Shippey Taylor, patiently edited and proofread countless pages, and Mary Anne Sigler struggled successfully in typing the various drafts of the manuscript. In short, the assistance received from many people has been indispensable. Of course, what appears in the book is the author's responsibility.

Theodore W. Taylor

INTRODUCTION

Francis Paul Prucha has urged that the goal in studying Indian history be to understand events and their impacts and not to praise or condemn the actors involved.[1] All authors have their own views and biases, and the present author is no exception. However, the intent of the author in this book is to present as balanced an account as possible of events, alternative policies, and the various views of different persons and groups concerning such policies. Some description is given of different programs and their supporting organizational structures, as well as of the behavior of specialist personnel and organizations.

As one reviews the historical record or current actions it is well to ask the question, What options were or are available? The answer requires an understanding of the forces present in each situation. Once these forces are understood, the reader may believe that a better option might have been selected, but he or she probably will be more sympathetic to the option chosen and the reasons for it. For example, what were the possible alternatives to the removal of the Five Civilized Tribes from southeastern United States or to the 1876 agreement with 10 percent of the Sioux and the congressional enactment of the agreement as law in 1877? Of the various possible options which ones were politically feasible? What would have been the results of the feasible options had they been chosen? This kind of review may temper the impulse for emotional judgment.

Persons working in an institutional environment with an "institutional" or "agency" view may consider the discussion of other views and the questioning of the "agency" or "tribal" view as being critical of current policies and their proponents. This is not the intent of this book. The objective is to raise questions and explore options on the assumption that improvements are possible. A more complete understanding of the complexities of and challenges in Indian affairs may be the result.

It is easy to feel outrage at certain results of policy, such as the transfer of land from Indians to non-Indians or the idleness and rural slum conditions that exist on some reservations today. On the other hand the improvement of many tribal governments, the great increase in the academic achievement of Indians, and the successful participation in the work, business, and professional worlds by many Indians are pluses that also can be interpreted to some extent as policy outcomes.

In Part One, Chapter 1 presents a brief history of Indian policy to provide background on the main interactions between the Indian and white cultures and to point out the primary policies applied by governments to Indians from colonial times to the present. It also indicates the forces that resulted in the development of a government agency, the Bureau of Indian Affairs, to implement Indian policy. A short organizational history of the Bureau of Indian Affairs follows in Chapter 2.

The present federal functions and organizations responsible for Indian programs and services are listed in Chapter 3 (Tables 3.1 and 3.2), along with a brief discussion of the Indian Health Service and the Department of Justice. Tribal government, which plays a key part in formulating and executing Indian policy, is the subject of Chapter 4.

Part Two concentrates on the interrelationships and involvement of the various participants in Indian policy discussed in Part One. Chapter 5 presents the Maine land claims issue and how policy concerning that issue evolved. Chapter 6 summarizes various aspects of the Indian affairs environment and the policy process in Indian affairs.

Part Three presents trends that are likely in the future and some of the policy options that have grown out of the past. Chapter 7 stresses the ever-increasing pace of change and its effect on the challenge facing Indian and all other citizens in the formation and execution of Indian policy. The chapter then presents some policy issues and optional approaches.

Part One

THE CHALLENGE

1

BRIEF HISTORY OF INDIAN POLICY

Early Contacts

History records the migrations, conquests, and shifting of peoples and cultures along with the creation of successive empires such as the Babylonian, Egyptian, Persian, Athenian, and Roman and such later empires as the Portuguese, French, Spanish, and English. In the New World, the English, though arriving later than the Spanish or the French, succeeded in colonizing parts of North America with their own people who brought their own culture and economy. "Unlike the Spaniards and other empire builders, the English succeeded in founding a new state, which became vast in extent, independent in government, and basically European in stock. That achievement is one of the capital facts of world history."[1] Today the United States is one of two superpowers and regarded as a world leader by much of humanity.

There were people in the New World before the European empire builders arrived. The current theory is that the inhabitants of the New World came across the Bering Strait, and the immigration may have gone on for centuries. These early people were divided into hundreds of groups and varied in physical appearance and language. Those in Central and South America were more numerous and most advanced. These southern groups developed corn, built fantastic cities of stone, devised a calendar with no leap year, and had strong governments and a division of labor. Harold Driver states that the Maya "were the most intellectually advanced of all Indian peoples." They exceeded the Greeks and the Romans in their knowledge of mathematics and astronomy, but they had only an "ideographic glyph stage" of writing.[2] Spaniards demolished the Mayan civilization in the name of Christianity, plundered for gold, and along with Indian survivors, became the basis of the present Latin American nations after the revolution against Spain (about 1810 to 1830).

North of Mexico the Indians contacted by the first European invaders were less advanced than the Indians in Central and South America (Figure 1.1). However, the pueblos in Southwestern United States and the mounds further east indicate that higher forms of culture had existed and declined. The Temple Mound culture existed from A.D. 700 to 1700 and reached its highest form in the Mississippi valley. About 1540 Spanish explorer Hernando de Soto found substantial fields of maize and large mounds with temples and palaces and "witnessed the arrival of male and female chiefs on litters carried on the shoulders of commoners."[3] At the time of European contact many Indians north of Mexico grew corn or other vegetables, but others relied on berries, wild grass seeds, nuts, fish, and game for their food.[4]

Many of the estimated 800,000 to 2,000,000 inhabitants of what is now the United States[5] were seminomadic Indian bands with individual leaders. Others resided in villages and adobe pueblos. Frederick Hodge states that "the social, political, and religious institutions of the tribes of North American Indians differed in both kind and degree" but that the "organic units" and the "social fabric were based on kinship and its interrelationships and not on territorial districts or geographical areas."[6] Larger and more complex governmental forms existed in the Powhatan confederacy in Virginia, the Creek confederacy in the Gulf plains, and in the League of the Iroquois, which included the five Iroquois tribes and later the Tuscarora. The Iroquois League, a federal union formed about 1570, "attained the highest form of governmental organization reached by any people north of the valley of Mexico."[7]

The Iroquois example was cited by Benjamin Franklin in his 1754 proposal for a union of the colonies, and Alvin Josephy states that "in such forms and methods by which Senate and House conferees work out bills in compromise sessions, for instance, one may recognize similarities to the ways in which the Iroquois League functioned."[8]

Edward Spicer points out that beginning in the middle of the sixteenth century, when the first European invasions occurred, "the struggle for dominance continued for nearly three centuries" among the various European powers. The Indians did not know what the future held, but until the late 1870s "the view of most of the Indians seems to have been that some kind of a balance of power might be struck among the warlike Europeans and themselves."[9]

The encounter of the Indian and European cultures altered both.[10] The relationship between the various groups of Indians and the people and governments of the colonies and later the United States is as an important a part of the history of the United States as it is of the history of the Indian peoples.

There were several motives for the invasion of North America by the Europeans. First, the initial explorations sought an ocean passage to the Orient for the rich cargoes that otherwise had to go overland. Second, since the Spanish had found much gold in Central and South America, many other Europeans were spurred by the hope they too would find treasure in North America. Third, many of the English settlers were fleeing religious and other conditions they did not like in their homeland. Fourth, the Europeans were also interested in trade; if it could not be oriental cargoes, they would settle for furs.

The English tended to consider themselves and their way of life superior to the aboriginal people they encountered, and they expected that such persons and societies would see the logic of adopting English ways. But such was not to be the case.

The difference in the Indian and English views of land use and ownership caused much trouble over the years. Indians did not have the concept of land ownership according to metes and bounds, with an individual owner's having exclusive control of the use of the land. Indians thought in terms of general territorial areas. If no one was using an area, it was proper for anyone to use it. (Of course, some tribes drove others from favorite hunting grounds when they had the power to do so, and intertribal wars were frequent.) Land was not owned by individuals but was for communal use. Thus, there often was difficulty on the part of both non-Indians and Indians in understanding what the other party meant when a treaty provided for the cession of a given area of land. With a sparse population and a great deal of acreage the Indian concept worked fine. With increased population density and European farming practices it did not work so well. The Europeans cut trees, plowed fields, and drove the game away.

Even though Driver indicates that farming was practiced by eastern Indians, many Indians, especially the men, were not particularly receptive, to European farming practices. Thomas Jefferson spoke to the chiefs of the Shawnee nation in 1807 and encouraged them to engage in agriculture and learn civilized ways,[11] but providing the Indians with farmers, blacksmiths, teachers, and carpenters, which was specified in many treaties and done in many instances without treaty requirements, often did little good. The European concepts of such artisans and teachers often did not coincide with the culture, including the values and lifestyles, of the Indians. In general, the Indians thought their way of life was better.

With the increasing number of settlers ways to obtain land for the increased numbers of non-Indians and ways to maintain the peace

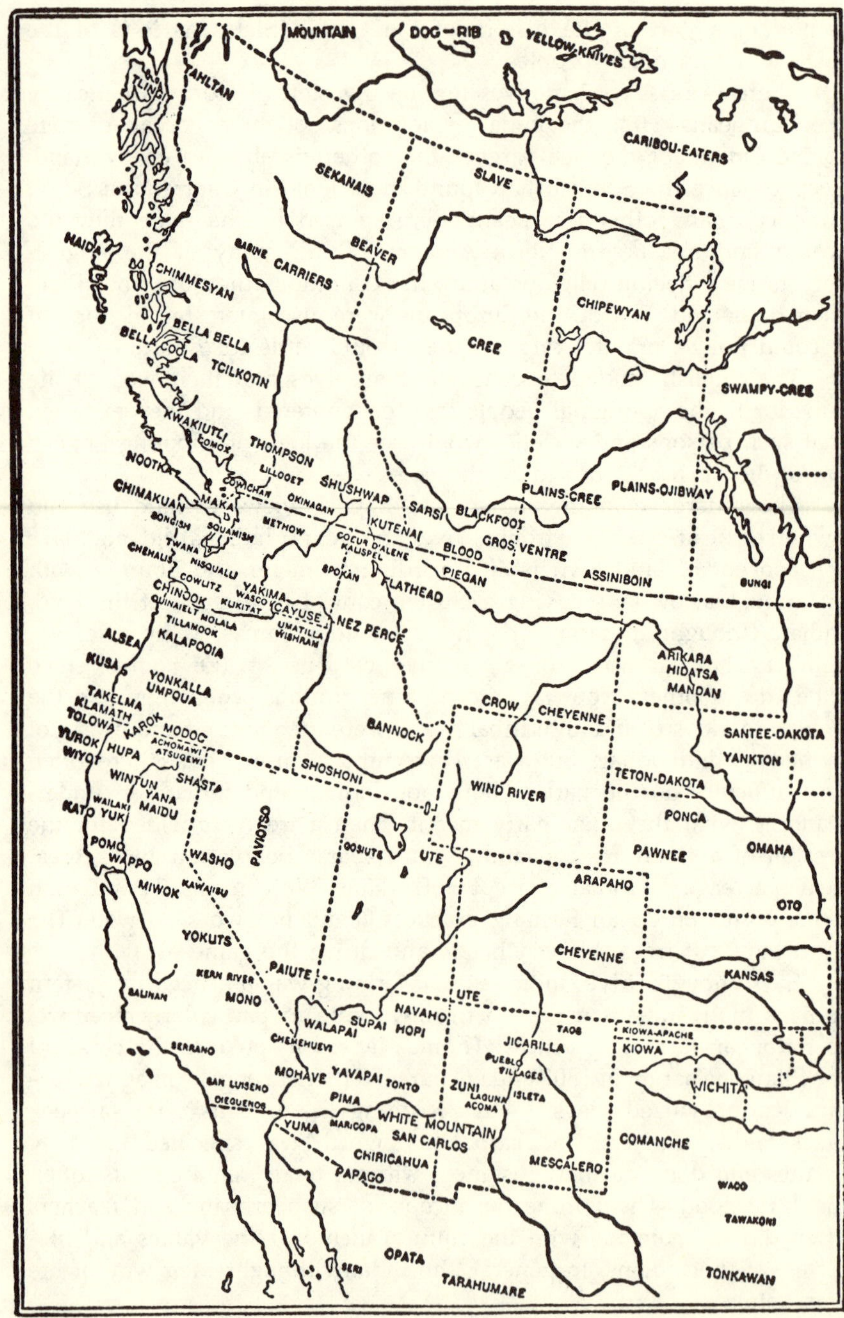

Figure 1.1 Probable location of Indian tribes north of Mexico about A.D. 1500. (Source: Clark Wissler, *Indians of the United States* [New York: Doubleday and

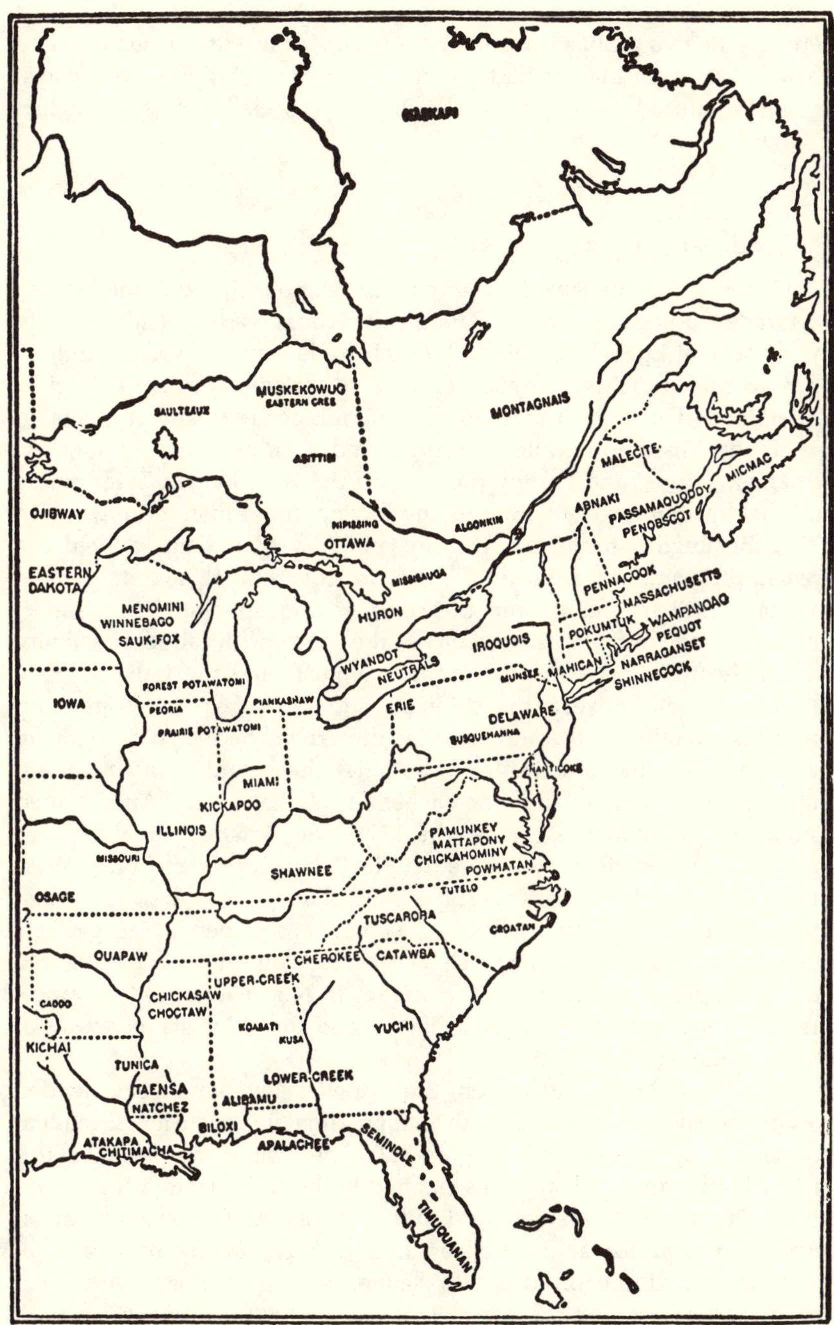

Co., n.d.]; distributed by the BIA along with two other maps to the interested public.)

between the two groups became high priorities. Since it was increasingly obvious that most Indians had no intention of adopting European ways, a general attitude of hostility developed, especially on the English frontier.

Trade and Rivalry

One of the Europeans' most important relationships with the Indians was trade—especially for furs. Uniform practices were difficult to apply by the several English colonies, and their trade was not well controlled. Encroachments on Indian land resulted in periodic attacks on English settlements. The French sent forth both missionaries and trappers to search the Mississippi valley for souls and furs, and they established settlements, forts, and trading posts along the way. Lyman Tyler points out that in conference with Indians during the Albany Congress in 1754, the English found out that the majority of Indians favored the French program. As a result the British government sought to take control of Indian affairs from the colonies and appointed two superintendents, one in the north and one in the south, with full responsibility for "all relations between the English colonists and the Indians."[12]

As tensions between the colonists and the crown grew stronger, the British reminded the Indians that the crown had tried to regulate trade and treat the Indians fairly but that the colonists often abused the trade relationship and encroached on Indian land. After armed conflict began with the English in 1778, the British sent a force of loyalists and Iroquois to attack settlers in Pennsylvania and New York. In 1779 General John Sullivan and 4,000 colonial troops moved against the Iroquois, demolishing brick and stone houses; destroying gardens of corn, beans, and melons as well as orchards; and in general "blighted one of the most advanced Indian societies in North America."[13] France, the traditional enemy of Great Britain, aided the colonists as a way of attacking England.

In 1783, after the Revolution, the United States boundary extended west to the Mississippi River, north to approximately the current Canadian border, and south to Florida (Figure 1.2). The area of the present states of Mississippi and Alabama was claimed by both the United States and Spain. Florida and the region west of the Mississippi River were Spanish territory, except for a disputed area, now occupied by the states of Washington and Oregon, that was claimed by Russia, Spain, and Great Britain. Russia claimed the coast of Alaska. In 1800 Napoleon acquired the Louisiana Territory from Spain, and Jefferson bought it from France in 1803.

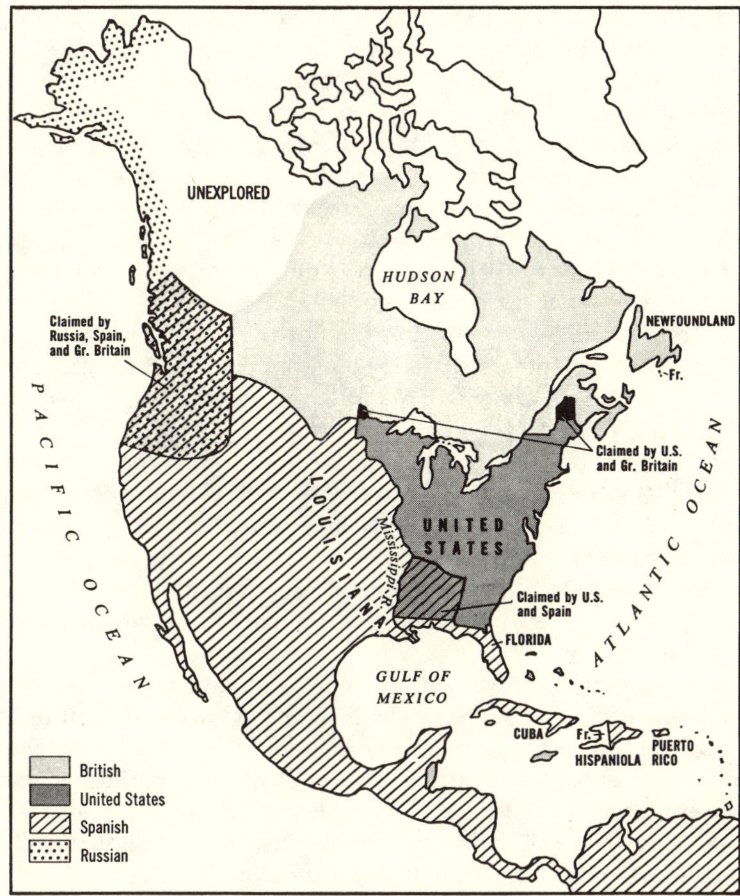

Figure 1.2 North America in 1783. (Reproduced by permission of Harcourt Brace Jovanovich, Inc., from John M. Blum, et al., *The National Experience: A History of the United States* [New York: Harcourt Brace Jovanovich, Inc., 1963], p. 116.)

Continental Congress and Constitutional Convention

Article 9 of the Articles of Confederation gave the Continental Congress responsibility for regulating trade and managing Indian affairs "provided that the legislative right of any State within its own limits be not infringed or violated." This proviso meant, as a practical matter, that the states controlled Indian policy within their boundaries and the central government had control only in the territory west of the states' boundaries. Congressional statements providing for the protection of Indian territory, including the Northwest Ordinance of 1787, were generally ignored by the settlers, land speculators, trappers, and hunters. As a forerunner of the trade and intercourse laws to come later Congress provided in 1783 that title to Indian land outside of state jurisdiction could only be obtained under the authority of Congress, and "any purchase or cessions made without such authority were declared null and void."[14] This legal restriction is the basis of the current federal trust responsibility for tribal land and is now expressed in volume four of the U.S. *Statutes at Large*, p. 730.

The representatives to the Constitutional Convention were determined to eliminate some of the weaknesses of the Articles of Confederation, and the new Congress was given full power over Indians with no exception. "The Congress shall have Power. . . . To regulate Commerce with foreign Nations, and among the several States, and with Indian Tribes."[15] Since many Indian tribes were regarded as independent groups they were dealt with through the machinery used for foreign relations, the war department, and diplomacy—including treaty making. These were federal, not state, functions under the Constitution. The Constitution, the laws of the United States, and treaties "shall be the supreme Law of the Land."[16]

The Constitution was somewhat ambivalent, however. Some Indians were citizens of the United States, and some paid taxes. Not all Indians were to be considered as members of separate or semi-independent groups. "Representatives and direct taxes shall be apportioned among the several States . . . , according to their respective Numbers, which shall be determined by adding the whole Number of free Persons . . . , and excluding Indians not taxed, three-fifths of all other Persons."[17]

Removal

Indian policy from colonial times to the present has involved three basic approaches: (1) removal of Indians to Indian country based on the belief that there was room and sufficient resources for all and that in the separation of Indians from non-Indians there would be little conflict and no need to be concerned over the Indians' problems; (2) assimilation of the Indians into the European-oriented society—expressed by Jefferson, some early treaties,[18] and attempts to educate and train Indians in European ways; and (3) assigning Indians to reservations to eliminate conflict with the advancing white population. As can be seen from the early history both assimilation and removal policies have operated at the same time, but the march of events contributed to the separation of the Indians and the whites.[19]

Jefferson suggested to Congress the possibility of removal in 1803 and succeeded in incorporating a provision for exchange of Indian lands in the act organizing the Louisiana Territory in 1804. Thus, Jefferson championed both assimilation and removal. When some of the Cherokee expressed a preference to stay on individualized land and obtain citizenship in 1808 Jefferson "insisted on removal," and the Cherokee began selling and migrating under pressure; 2,000 had moved to Arkansas by 1811.[20] Numerous treaties that provided for removal were negotiated between 1815 and 1830. Secretary of War John C. Calhoun favored removal, and President James Monroe approved. President John Quincy Adams "was in general agreement but hampered by scruples."[21]

Removal was also assisted by other factors. Alexis de Tocqueville, visiting the United States in 1835, pointed out that trade with the Indians for furs put a double pressure on game as the Indians hunted not only for food but for sufficient furs to buy guns, ardent spirits, and iron. It is estimated that 50 million deer were reduced to 500,000 between 1825 and 1915.[22] The bison (buffalo) were practically exterminated, too, which changed a recently acquired culture of many of the Plains Indians.

If the westward movement of the Indians' following the receding game animals did not keep ahead of the advancing settlers, government envoys pointed out that the game was gone but that there was adequate game beyond the mountains. As a further inducement they would offer "fire-arms, woolen garments, kegs of brandy, glass necklaces," and other articles. If the Indians still were reluctant to move the envoys would inform them that the government would not have the power to protect them if they remained where they were.[23]

Of the hunting tribes Tocqueville wrote that many of the Indians who had formerly inhabited the coastal areas ranging west to the mountains—such as the Narraganset, Mohican, Pequot, and Lenape—had no existence "but in the recollection of man."[24] Some Indians continued on in reduced numbers under state jurisdiction, such as the Seneca and Onondaga in New York, the Penobscot in Maine, and the Pamunkey in Virginia.

The agricultural Pueblo Indians in the Southwest survived the Spanish invasion in the 1500s and still exist today. One of the obvious reasons is that they were not subjected to the same economic pressures as the hunters in the East and on the Great Plains. The Pueblos lived in tightly knit agricultural communities and thus were not dependent on game. Neither was their desert land as attractive to Europeans in the early days. They were surrounded but not obliterated. Nor, generally, were they forced to move.

Under severe pressure from the whites and deprived of their accustomed source of food, as Tocqueville puts it, the southern tribes "were placed between civilization and death." Thus, they took to agriculture and the Cherokee "created a written language, established a permanent form of government," and even set up a newspaper.[25] So some Indians could adapt to European and white ways. Even though many Indians in the Five Civilized Tribes (Cherokee, Choctaw, Seminole, Creek, and Chickasaw) did adapt, the states still wanted them out.

The federal government had succeeded in obligating itself to two conflicting commitments. The compact of 1802 provided that Georgia would cede land (now part of Alabama and Mississippi) and the United States would extinguish Indian title within that state's limits. On the other hand, treaties with various tribes provided for their exclusive use and control of land described in the treaties, some of it the same land. Georgia enacted laws "to harass and make intolerable" the life of the Eastern Cherokee. Chief Justice John Marshall held these laws unconstitutional in *Worcester* v. *Georgia* (1832), but this decision had little effect on the state and federal executives. Supported by President Andrew Jackson, Congress had passed the Indian Removal Act (4 Stat. 411) in 1830, and proposed amendments to this act that provided respect for treaty rights and protection for Indians were defeated. This act gave the president authority to negotiate for removal, and the Indians were advised that refusal "meant the end of Federal protection and abandonment to State Laws." Thus coerced, a faction of the Cherokee signed the Treaty of New Echota in 1835 (7 Stat. 478), which ceded all land east of the Mississippi in return for $5 million and some 7 million acres west of the Mississippi; the latter was never to be included in any state or territory without the consent of the Cherokee.

Most of the tribes moved as a result of persuasion, bribery, or threats, but some, such as the Seminole, had to be moved forcibly at great cost, and not all of them were caught.[26] William T. Hagan describes the woeful and disgraceful treatment of the Winnebago through numerous removals.[27] Complicating the removal was the fact that other Indians' territory was being invaded—which often resulted in wars between Indians[28]—and the impact of the nearly 100,000 removed Indians on the balance between wildlife and man. Many of the "removed" Indians were located in Indian territory, now known as Oklahoma (Figure 1.3).

From the beginning of the new U.S. government to the present time, "moral indignation over the plight of the red men varied with the distance from him." Frontiersmen who wanted land and were afraid of Indian raids were "inclined to classify him as subhuman and devoid of rights." People not on the frontier often "detected great potential in the Indian."[29]

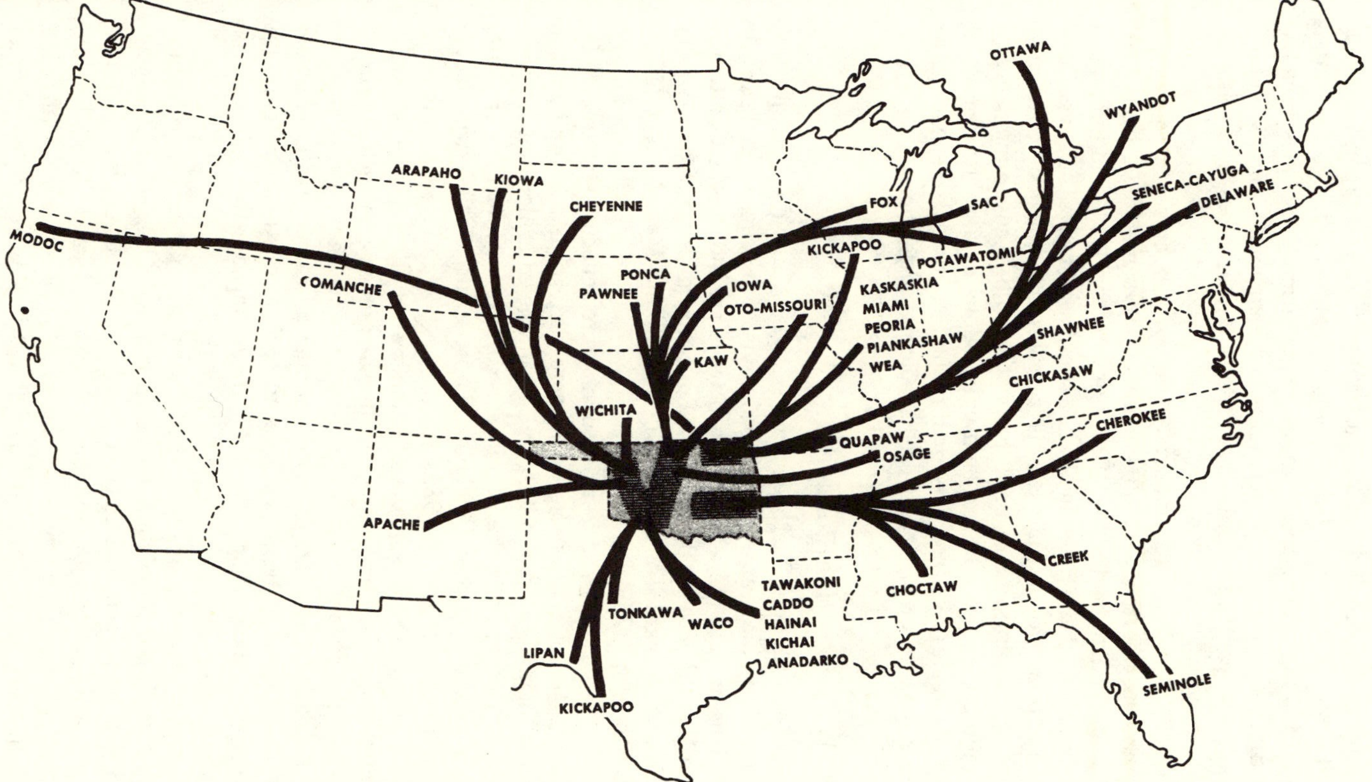

Figure 1.3 Movement of Indian tribes into Oklahoma. Some of the tribes—such as the Kiowa, Arapaho, Cheyenne, and Comanche—moved on their own volition; others were pressured to move; and some, such as the Seminole, were forcibly moved. (Courtesy U.S. Public Health Service, Division of Indian Health)

Complications in Indian administration during the removal period were the result of agents' being politically appointed, fighting among missionaries for Indian souls, tribal factionalism, and tribes invading other tribes' territories, disagreements between mixed bloods and full bloods, and treaty and nontreaty factions within tribes as a result of removal negotiations.[30]

In 1824 the Bureau of Indian Affairs was organized, and in 1832 Congress recognized the small bureau and designated its head commissioner of Indian affairs.[31] In 1834, a new Indian Trade and Intercourse Act became law, and it redefined Indian country and gave the government authority to control intruders. This act was the lineal descendant of earlier acts limiting Indian trade to people with a government license and limiting the sale of Indian land unless done by a public treaty with the United States.[32] Those acts in turn had continued the pattern set by the ordinance of 1786 and earlier colonial legislation.

Early Civilization Policy

Treaties with the Cherokee and Delaware and the government's willingness to place carpenters, blacksmiths, and other specialists with the Indians to train them in European ways are indications of attempts to absorb and live with the Indians. Education of Indian youth was an objective of Harvard College (1650), William and Mary College (1691), and Dartmouth (1769).[33]

These early actions and inclinations were reflections of one of the basic impulses of the people who were displacing the Indians. The concept of helping Indians adjust and obtain the education and resources necessary to compete in the non-Indian culture that was then engulfing them and has now surrounded them did not die out. It is the government's basic Indian policy in the 1980s.

Opposition to European ways remained strongly embedded in Indian culture. Tocqueville commented on Indian groups in which the men's role was hunting and war as follows: "he [the Indian] considers the cares of industry as degrading occupations; he compares the plowman to the ox that traces the furrow; and in each of our handicrafts he can see only the labor of slaves. War and hunting are the only pursuits that appear to him worthy of a man."[34]

At the time of the arrival of Europeans in what is now the United States, the Indian population was an estimated 800,000 to 2,000,000. By 1872 it had decreased to an estimated 300,000, excluding Alaska. War, disease, and famine had taken their toll, and the "vanishing American" became the view of the day. Treaty making with tribes ceased in 1871 as Congress realized that tribes were no longer independent and the House of Representatives wanted to participate in Indian policy.

Reservation Policy

Attempts at "civilization" had limited success, and the removal policy was doomed to failure. Under the banner of "manifest destiny" the Americans moved west to the Pacific Ocean. Former Indian territories, which were not supposed to be breached by non-Indians, were violated. There was not enough land and game for all, and the idea that Indians could live in their traditional way in a designated Indian territory proved to be an illusion.

The discovery of gold took adventurers to California in 1849, to Colorado in the 1850s, and to South Dakota in 1875. They and the people who followed killed game and overran Indian country. Occasionally Indians retaliated by attacking wagon trains and settlements, and a period of sporadic armed conflict ensued. Railroads were pushed west after the Civil War and provided support for the subjugation of "nonpeaceable" Indians. White hunters almost exterminated the buffalo in a few years.

Federal reservations as we now know them were gradually instituted by treaties and executive orders as the advancement of the whites made such a policy necessary. These reservations differed from the concept of Indian territory at the time of the removal of the Five Civilized Tribes in the early 1800s. These reservations were generally smaller, had specific boundaries, and were frequently established for one tribe or group. Indian agents were assigned one or more reservations. After the Civil War, as more whites moved west, Indians frequently were required to stay on their reservations, and non-Indians were supposed to remain outside, in order to avoid friction between the two groups. Not all Indians were confined to reservations in the West until the latter part of the nineteenth century, and now, of course, Indians are free to move about like any other citizen.

In a sense, the establishment of reservations was similar to the concept of removal. At first there may have been the idea that the Indians would be self-sufficient and run their own affairs on a reservation, but the reservations did not provide adequate resources for self-sufficiency for those Indians who depended upon hunting for their subsistence. Many Indians on reservations were issued food rations, and the Indian agent took over many governmental functions—dealing with individual Indians rather than working through Indian governments.

The early reservation experience was undoubtedly traumatic for the hunting Indians. The men could not pursue their practices of hunting and raiding other tribes. Their movements were restricted, they could not support themselves, and they tended to drift toward a subsidized existence of idleness in many cases. The pueblo farming communities and some of the fishing economies in the Northwest were not affected in the same way or to the same extent as their subsistence bases were less vulnerable to destruction.

Indian agents and missionary groups made sincere efforts to train Indians in mechanical and agricultural pursuits; efforts were also made for religious and secular education. The lack of results from these efforts was largely due to cultural differences. The Indians continued to view their way of life as superior and were thus not inclined to abandon it for European ways, even though the basis for their traditional life was being seriously eroded.

Various treaties establishing reservations or providing for cessions of land called for specific services to be provided by the federal government. Although the Navajo treaty of 1849 made no provision for education or training, federal laws were to be applied in respect to trade and peace; the Navajo were to be under the jurisdiction of the United States; U.S. citizens were to have free passage through Navajo territory under rules of the United States; the U.S. government was to have the authority to establish military posts, trading houses, and agencies as it saw fit; and the U.S. government was to have the authority to establish territorial boundaries.[35] The Navajo treaty of 1868 provided for a warehouse, an agency building, a carpenter shop, a blacksmith shop, seeds and agricultural implements, articles of clothing or raw materials, and the purchase of 15,000 sheep and goats. Since the treaty provided for the removal of the Navajo from the Bosque Redondo Reservation to the area now occupied by the Navajo (boundaries specified by treaty), a purchase of 500 beef cattle and a million pounds of corn was authorized for relief of the needy during the following winter. The obvious purpose of these provisions was to encourage the Navajo to take up farming and stock raising so that they could support themselves. Article 6 provided:

> In order to insure the civilization of the Indians entering into this treaty, the necessity of education is admitted, especially of such of them as may be settled on said agricultural parts of this reservation, and they therefore pledge themselves to compel their children, male and female, between the ages of six and sixteen years, to attend school; and it is hereby made the duty of the agent for said Indians to see that this stipulation is strictly complied with; and the United States agrees that, for every thirty children between said ages who can be induced or compelled to attend school, a house shall be provided, and a teacher competent to teach the elementary

> branches of an English education shall be furnished, who will reside among said Indians, and faithfully discharge his or her duties as a teacher.
>
> The provisions of this article to continue for not less than ten years.[36]

The Omaha were dealt with in a treaty of July 15, 1830—along with many other groups—which provided for cession of lands and payment therefor, an annuity for education for ten years, and a reservation for Omaha, Iowa, and Otoe "half-breeds." The Otoe, Missouria, and Sauk tribes covered in this treaty received a blacksmith and necessary tools for agricultural purposes.[37] A further treaty on October 15, 1836, modified the treaty of 1830 by ceding more land, with reimbursement, and providing for the plowing of 100 acres for the Omaha at the new site to which they agreed to move.[38] On March 16, 1854, more land was ceded, and the Omaha living on the ceded land moved; provision was made for the assignment of lots to Indians; and the Omaha were promised a grist mill and a sawmill and provisions for its repair, a blacksmith, and an experienced farmer to instruct them for a period of ten years. The Omaha agreed to the construction of necessary roads and railroads with appropriate compensation for rights-of-way.[39] Another treaty with the Omaha on March 6, 1865, provided for further cession of lands from the Omaha for use by the Winnebago, division of tribal land into plots for individual Indians, an Omaha reservation, and repurchase of the ceded land on the same terms if the planned location of the Winnebago thereon should prove detrimental.[40]

As another example, a treaty with the Nez Percé in 1855 provided for cession of land and payment therefor; a reservation; schools, blacksmith shops, gunsmith shops, a carpenter's shop, a wagonmaker and plowmaker's shop; the employment of farmers for instruction; a sawmill; a hospital and physician; and the fact that the president could assign lands to individuals if he wished.[41] An 1855 treaty with the Blackfeet provided that the Nez Percé and other tribes could use Blackfoot territory as a common hunting ground.[42] An 1863 treaty with the Nez Percé provided for an additional cession of lands and payment therefor and the division of farming land into lots on which families could choose to settle—the remainder of the land was to be held in common. There were to be two schools, a hospital, a blacksmith's shop; matrons, teachers, mechanics, millers; and other provisions.[43] In 1868 the foregoing treaty was amended to say that if Indians on an allotment in the ceded areas could not be placed on an allotment within the reservation, they could remain in the ceded area if the land did not exceed twenty acres for each male person twenty-one years of age or over. Tribal timber was to be protected by the United States, and school moneys not used in previous years—either not spent or used for other purposes—were to be reimbursed to the tribe and held in trust by the United States with interest being paid to the tribe for the support of teachers.[44]

These examples of treaty provisions indicate how the United States acquired Indian land; how reservations and boundaries were established; the removal of Indians; the methods to introduce Indians to white men's farming, trade, and educational practices; and in some instances, the policy of land ownership by the individual rather than in common. These developments increased the workload of the Bureau of Indian Affairs, which was the main government agency charged with carrying out the treaty provisions.

The states were a problem. Since the federal constitution assigned some responsibility for dealing with the Indians to the national government, the states did not regard Indians as their responsibility during much of the nineteenth century. Indian reservations were not subject to state law except by permission of the federal government. Indian land, which was held in trust by the federal government, could not be taxed by the state or its localities. The citizens of the various states often considered Indians as "outcasts," "intruders," and "normal prey for anybody strong or cunning enough to defraud them." Indian Commissioner Edward P. Smith stated in 1875 that the "most potent and sure remedy for this evil will be found in committing the Indians at the earliest day possible to the care of the state.[45]

Emphasis on Indian Individuals Rather Than Tribes

Allotment of land to individuals began in the early part of the eighteenth century, and by 1885 over 11,000 patents (certificates of ownership) had been issued to individual Indians under the authority of various treaties and laws. This practice was accelerated, and the period from 1865 to 1900 has been called a time of "American Indian policy in crisis,"[46] a crisis that began after the Civil War because of the "vast tides of migration of whites from the east and west, crushing the Indians between them." The period was characterized by interest groups that were convinced that "Americanizing" the Indian was the only solution to placing the Indians on an equal plane with other citizens. Beginning in 1883 these "friends of the Indian" met on an annual basis at a resort in Lake Mohonk, N.Y., which belonged to Albert K. Smiley, a member of the Board of Indian Commissioners. Attending were representatives of Indian rights organizations, missionary leaders, Indian Bureau representatives, educational leaders, protestant clergymen, newspaper editors, and others. Francis Prucha describes their efforts:

> The reformers put their faith principally in three proposals: first, to break up the tribal relations and their reservation base and to individualize the Indian on a 160 acre homestead . . . ; second, to make the Indians citizens and equal with the whites in regard to both the protection and restraints of law; and third, to provide a universal government school system that would make good Americans out of the rising generation of Indians.[47]

All of these objectives were pressed for vigorously, and the result was the General Allotment Act of 1887.[48] This act marked the beginning of a comprehensive school system set up by the Bureau of Indian Affairs, attempts to stamp out tribalism and "Indianness," and the breaking up of tribal government through the assumption of many governmental functions on Indian reservations by the Bureau of Indian Affairs and its reservation superintendents or agents. All these changes were aimed at enforced acculturation. Civilization through education and agriculture would "finally enable the Government to leave the Indian to stand alone."[49] To prevent the sale of land by the Indian owner, alloted land was to be held in trust by the United States for a period of twenty-five years, during which time permission of the Indian agent was required for alienation of the land.

Individualizing the ownership of land, when it occurred, did not achieve the results expected by the policy's supporters because of the conflict in values between the Indian and non-Indian views. Most Indians leased their land or sold it to non-Indians rather than working it themselves.[50]

Increased Responsibilities of Federal and State Governments

Citizenship for Indians had been conferred by treaty to specific groups as early as 1817.[51] Indians who received an allotment of land became citizens, and in 1924 Congress conferred citizenship on all other Indians born within the territorial limits of the United States.[52] The Fourteenth Amendment to the Constitution, ratified on July 9, 1868, provided that all citizens of the United States were also citizens of "the state wherein they reside." Thus, Indians were state citizens and, if they met the same qualifications as other voters, could vote in state and local elections. Not all Indians lived on trust land, and those that did not were generally subject to state laws in the same manner as any other citizen.

Since the Indian agent and his staff were carrying out many government functions on Indian reservations, and increasing sums of money for support of such activities were being requested, substantive (authorizing) legislation was adopted by the Congress in 1921.[53] This act, often referred to as the Snyder Act, stated the objectives of the Bureau of Indian Affairs for which funds were authorized: to provide for the general support and civilization of the Indians and to be responsible for education, welfare, health, and industrial assistance; improvement in irrigation; administration of land; employment of superintendents, matrons, farmers, physicians, Indian police, Indian judges, and other employees; and the necessary buildings, grounds, and incidental expenses connected with the administration of Indian affairs.

A Reversal: Promotion of the Tribe and Indian Culture

Surveys of the Indian condition and the appointment in sequence of Charles J. Rhoads (1929) and John Collier (1933) to the post of commissioner of Indian affairs, along with the Great Depression, reversed the emphasis on breakup of the tribes, selling Indian land, and immediate absorption of Indians into the non-Indian culture. In 1926 Secretary of Interior Hubert Work, in response to pressures for reform in Indian affairs,[54] requested the Institute for Government Research to conduct a survey of economic and social conditions of Indians. Financed by John D. Rockefeller, Jr., the study was headed by Lewis Meriam, and its results were published in 1928.[55] A report on Indian irrigation was also completed in 1928 and is known as the Preston-Engle Irrigation Report.[56] Public and congressional interest in Indian affairs resulted in the launching in 1928 of an exhaustive survey by the Senate Committee on Indian Affairs.[57]

The Meriam report suggested effective education to enable Indians to take advantage of the opportunities in the non-Indian world, preparing Indians to make contributions in service and taxes for the maintenance of government, preparing white communities to receive the Indian, working out systems of taxation with local and state governments, and adopting state law and order procedures when the Indians were economically self-sufficient, willing to accept state law and order, and willing to work with the non-Indian community.[58] Meriam also emphasized the problem of unearned income as a disincentive to work. Rations had become regarded as a right, income was received from the sale or lease of allotments, sales of complicated heirship properties brought other income, and Indians expected revenues from claims against the government. Many Indians had "developed a pauper point of view."[59]

Tyler points out that the Meriam study was not revolutionary as earlier surveys, studies, reports, and recommendations to Congress by the Bureau of Indian Affairs and other groups had voiced similar ideas.[60] However the report clearly broke with the forced acculturation philosophy of the earlier "civilization" period. It recommended a program based on an understanding of the Indian point of view and a recognition of the good in Indian economic, social, religious, and ethical concepts, and it sought "to develop . . . and build on . . . rather than crush out all that is Indian."[61] The Senate's survey ran from 1928 to 1944, and Senate hearings had an impact in the 1930s even though a report had not been prepared.

President Franklin D. Roosevelt appointed Harold L. Ickes as secretary of the Interior and John Collier as commissioner of Indian affairs in 1933. John Collier had been involved in Indian reform for ten years as executive secretary of the Indian Defense Association and was editor of the magazine, *American Indian Life.* Working together Ickes, Collier, and Roosevelt managed to get Congress to pass the Indian Reorganization Act of 1934 (IRA).[62] In contrast to the 1887 Allotment Act, the IRA provided authority for the purchase of additional land for Indians, not disposal of Indian land; the establishment of tribal organizations and government, not their destruction; a loan fund for individual and tribal businesses; and an extension of the trust on Indian lands, not an emphasis on removing the trust (such as occurred from 1917 to 1920).

There were three important factors, in addition to the Meriam and Senate surveys, that affected the development of Indian policy in the early 1930s. First, a change in national philosophy was taking place. From colonial times through most of the nineteenth century Americans believed in the doctrines of expansion, exploitation, and speculation—let the devil take the hindmost. This outlook was reflected in such events as insurance scandals, ruthless competition, destruction of resources without regard for the future, and a general exploitation of all citizens, including the Indians. Since the turn of the century—and especially in more recent years—social responsibility and concern for the worker and the underprivileged, as well as for conservation of natural resources, have been more highly valued. Regulation of predatory business practices, social service programs (especially in the areas of health and welfare), education, and the conservation of resources have been aspects of society in general as well as of programs for the Indian.

Second, the Great Depression not only accelerated the acceptance of increased social responsibility on the part of the government (e.g., the collapse of the Insull utility holding company empire helped spur the creation of the Securities Exchange Commission), but it increased economic distress in the society in general and among the Indians in particular. There were 90,000 landless Indians. The Depression decreased their options for earning a livelihood, so unemployment was widespread among Indians. Therefore, Collier emphasized subsistence farming and animal husbandry for the Indians and an avoidance of competition with white industrial labor or white commercial agriculture.[63]

The third factor was the influence of Commissioner Charles J. Rhoads and his Assistant Commissioner J. Henry Scattergood (1929–1933). Each had a deep interest in the Indians and they laid the groundwork for implementing the Meriam recommendations. Their work paved the way for John Collier (1933–1945).

The reaction of some segments of society to the excesses of an unrestrained competitive economy is reflected to some extent in John Collier's view. He believed the Pueblo Indians had a society that blended the building of personality with social institutions. He not only thought the Indian value system had much to offer the larger white society but, as Lawrence C. Kelly put it, he believed "the preservation of Indian culture was essential to the survival of western civilization." Or as Dr. Kenneth Philp stated, Collier hoped to "create a utopia where tribal communities offered a model of communal living for individualist-oriented American society."[64]

Reduction of Federal Responsibility

An 1855 treaty stated that "the Wyandotte Indians having become sufficiently advanced in civilization, and being desirous of becoming citizens . . . are hereby declared to be citizens of the United States." It also provided that those Wyandotte Indians who opted for citizenship "shall in all respects be subject to the laws of the United States, and to the Territory of Kansas in the same manner as other citizens of said Territory."[65] Efforts to terminate special federal relationships to Indians, such as having trust responsibility for their land, generally led to an assumption of those responsibilities by the tribes, states, or individual Indians. The Board of Indian Commissioners stated in 1899: "We have entire faith that before many years . . . the Indians . . . will be better off under the general laws of our States and Territories, and by incorporation with the great body of our American citizens."[66] In removing the federal trust over individual Indian land, during the so-called forced patent period (1917–1921), special federal relationships were discontinued with Indians who were already competent to handle their own affairs, and more assistance was provided to those who were not so they would more "speedily achieve competency."[67]

The Senate Committee on Indian Affairs issued a report in 1943 in which it was stated that instead of the original aim "to make the Indian a citizen," the aim now "appears to be to keep the Indian an Indian" and attempt to help him "recapture his ancient, worn-out cultures," which are but a "vague memory" and not applicable to the present world. Non-Indians, said the committee, do not try "to recapture our glamorous pioneer culture," even though that past could be regained more easily than the Indians' could. The committee felt that government policy was "segregating the Indian from the general citizenry" and "condemning the Indian to perpetual wardship."[68] In the following year the House Select Committee on Indian Affairs agreed that the goal of Indian policy was to help the Indian "take his place in the white man's community on the white man's level and with the white man's opportunity and security status," but the committee concluded that the Indians were not ready to be "turned loose."[69]

In 1947, with a reduction of federal expenditures in mind, the Senate Post Office and Civil Service Committee requested that Acting Commissioner William Zimmerman provide a list of tribes that could be separated from federal jurisdiction as well as a draft of legislation to accomplish that objective. The list was presented along with drafts of legislation to incorporate the Klamath, Osage, and Menominee tribes, to establish state control of Indians in California and North Dakota, and a bill that would permit individuals to withdraw from a tribe.[70]

In 1949 the Hoover Commission recommended "progressive measures to integrate the Indians into the rest of the population."[71] Dillon S. Myer stated in 1951 that the two long-range objectives of the Bureau of Indian Affairs were "(1) a standard of living for Indians comparable with that enjoyed by other segments of the population, and (2) the step-by-step transfer of Bureau functions to the Indians themselves or to the appropriate agencies of local, state or federal government."[72]

House Report No. 2503, largely compiled by BIA staff members in 1952, is a compendium of data on Indians: the readiness of tribes for withdrawal of federal services; negotiations with tribes and states in process; and tables of information on population, education, income, degree of blood, assets, taxable value of trust land, and BIA expenditures by tribe and state. The House committee indicated that Indian legislation should be directed toward ending the trust status of Indian land (as that status was "not acceptable to the American way of life") and "the assumption by individual Indians of all the duties, obligations, and privileges of free citizens" to the end that "the Indians be assimilated into the Nation's social and economic life."[73]

On March 13, 1953, Assistant Secretary of the Interior Orme Lewis wrote to the Senate and House Indian affairs subcommittees indicating that "federal responsibility for administering the affairs of individual Indian tribes should be terminated as rapidly as the circumstances of each tribe will permit."[74] This recommendation was followed on August 1, 1953, by House Concurrent Resolution 108 (HCR 108), adopted by both the House and Senate, which stated that the policy of Congress was, as rapidly as possible, "to make the Indians . . . subject to the same laws and entitled to the same privileges and responsibilities as are applicable to other citizens." This was the high point of the so-called termination policy.

Twelve termination acts were passed from 1954 to 1962 dealing with the Alabama and Coushatta tribes of Texas, California rancherias and reservations, the Catawba tribe of South Carolina, the Klamath tribe of Oregon, the Menominee tribe of Wisconsin, the Ottawa tribe of Oklahoma, the Paiute Indians of Utah, the Peoria tribe of Oklahoma, the Ponca tribe of Nebraska, the Uintah and Ouray Ute mixed bloods of Utah, western Oregon bands (600 of them), and the Wyandotte tribe of Oklahoma. Later some of these actions were reversed, and the following have been restored to federal status: the Menominee tribe of Wisconsin (1973), the confederated tribes of Siletz Indians in Oregon (1977), the Ottawa tribe of Oklahoma (1978), the Peoria tribe of Oklahoma (1978), the Wyandotte tribe of Oklahoma (1978), the Paiute tribe of Utah (1980), and four rancherias in California—Big Lagoon, Hopland, Robinson, and Upper Lake.[75]

"Undoubtedly, the termination program, had it continued unabated, would have reached its goal."[76] There was general acceptance, or at least resignation to the inevitability, of the termination program by both Indians and the states in the beginning.[77] The forces bringing about a reversal of attitude on termination would be an intriguing field of study. Price is cautious but believes that the Office of Economic Opportunity (OEO) "was . . . a major transforming event" in bringing about that reversal and in the placing of less emphasis on integration and more emphasis on separateness and support for cultural minorities. He states:

> Its funds and its policy of maximum feasible participation of the subject populations in the management of their progams clearly enunciated a return to the policies of the 1930's, the strengthening of the collective or tribal entity. The Bureau of Indian Affairs was drastically reduced in influence. The concept of advocacy, particularly the power of submerged groups to gain representation and use the power of newly defined rights, became part of reservation culture as it did the culture of the urban poverty areas. And the entire focus of federal funds changed as well. Where the financial incentives in Indian policy in the 1950's was to encourage Indians to leave the reservation to obtain jobs in urban areas, substantially greater federal funds were used to create an abundance of new employment opportunities on the reservation, and for the first time there were many jobs that were at the executive level. These jobs made it possible and legitimate to seek economic security as well as leadership in reservation affairs.[78]

The jobs, of course, were subsidized and not necessarily on a sound economic base, so one could question Price's use of the word "legitimate."

The OEO funds totaled $27 million to Indian tribes in 1971,[79] and the jobs provided by the funds were often attractive enough to encourage Indians who had left the reservation to return. Peter MacDonald had been working as an engineer with Hughes Aircraft, but he returned to Navajo in 1963 and was appointed head of the OEO program there in 1965. Through the OEO he gained the recognition and momentum that enabled him to run for tribal chairman in 1970 and win.

Another Reversal: Emphasis on Special Status for Indians

Secretary of Interior Stewart Udall's task force concluded in 1961 that the emphasis on termination affected the willingness of many tribes to embark on new programs that might make them more self-sufficient. Under Commissioners Philleo Nash (1961–1966) and Robert Bennett (1966–1969) there was no mention of termination. Instead, the emphasis was on Indian economic, social, and governmental development and Indian involvement in such development. Legislation enacted during the Kennedy and Johnson years included the Elementary and Secondary Education Act, the Education Professions Development Act, the Vocational Education Act, the Higher Education Act, the Economic Opportunity Act, and increased funds for the above programs as well as for housing assistance, manpower training, and economic development. The number of federal programs and funds channeled to Indian reservations by various agencies under this legislation constantly increased during the 1970s, and jobs and programs on many reservations are dependent on a continuance of these subsidies. Whether or not any real economic development is occurring to improve the reservation economy as a result of these subsidies probably varies from reservation to reservation, and the question is often debated.[80]

In 1967 the Bureau of Indian Affairs proposed an economic development bill, but it was attacked by the National Congress of American Indians (NCAI) because it gave authority to tribes to mortgage trust land to obtain capital for economic development. It was also claimed that the proposal was prepared without Indian consultation. Even though the proposal was introduced on Capitol Hill and hearings were held, it died without action.[81]

Commissioner Bennett regarded the BIA as an advocate of the Indian cause, which was a change from the earlier posture of the BIA's representing the dominant society in its dealing with Indians as well as helping the Indians adjust to their new circumstances. From 1966 on BIA policy was pro-Indian in the same manner as the Department of Agriculture is pro-farmer and the Department of Labor, pro-labor.

With this change in philosophy came reversals of earlier actions that had been based on "getting the feds out of the act." California reversed its position taken in the 1950s and under Governor Ronald Reagan sought the return of federal funds and federal services for Indians. Nebraska had assumed civil and criminal jurisdiction over Indian reservations in 1953, but, in 1969 that state authorized a retrocession to U.S. jurisdiction except for motor vehicle operation on roads and highways.[82] The Governor's Interstate Indian Council (GIIC) moved from cautious support of HCR 108 in the early 1960s to opposition in 1970.

Presidents Johnson and Nixon both issued presidential messages on Indian policy.[83] The philosophy in both messages was similar: a rejection of the termination policy; the need for Indian involvement; develop Indian leadership; expand credit; improve schools and Indian participation in their operation; and emphasize the transfer of control and responsibility from the federal government to Indian communities rather than to state or local government, but with continued federal responsibility for funding, services, and technical assistance. President Johnson said the Indians should have the "right to freedom of choice and self-determination," and the government must see to it that the "special relationship between the Indian and his government grow and flourish."

President Nixon's message included several items that have been important in subsequent federal policy: a request for the repeal of HCR 108 and an affirmative declaration by Congress of the federal government's Indian responsibility; a request to empower tribes with final decision and authority on whether to take over administration of Indian service programs of the Interior Department or the then Department of Health, Education and Welfare; a proposal to establish an Indian Trust Counsel Authority as an Indian advocate on trust matters such as land and water to avoid conflict of interest within Interior and Justice; and the creation of the position of an assistant secretary for Indian and territorial affairs in the Interior Department. In his preelection statement Nixon expressed the current philosophy of pluralism: "We must recognize that American society can allow many different cultures to flourish in harmony and we must provide an opportunity for those Indians wishing to do so to lead a useful and prosperous life within an Indian environment.[84]

During the 1970s the Alaska Native Claims Settlement Act,[85] the Indian Financing Act of 1974,[86] the Indian Self-Determination and Education Assistance Act,[87] Procedures for Establishing That an American Indian Group Exists as an Indian Tribe,[88] and the Education Amendments Act of 1978[89] were adopted. These actions were based on the philosophy of the two presidential messages and were the result of the strong support of Indian leadership by Indian pressure groups and rigorous work on the part of the BIA and Indian committee staffs and chairmen of committees on Capitol Hill who advocated obtaining all the traffic would bear for Indians.[90]

In 1977 the congressionally appointed American Indian Policy Review Commission (AIPRC) based its conclusions and recommendations on the theses of a separate tribal sovereignty and a special trust relationship between the tribes and the United States. "The concept of sovereignty and the concept of trust are imperative to the continuation of the Federal-Indian relationship."[91] The AIPRC proposed expanding the federal trust to include not only Indian land but other services provided by the Bureau of Indian Affairs and the Public Health Service. The Alaska Native Claims Settlement Act of 1971 and the Maine Indian Claims Settlement Act of 1980[92] established some innovative relationships among the tribes, the states, and the federal government.

Indian Population Today

Compared to the estimated 800,000 to 2,000,000 Indians who lived in what is now the United States when the Europeans arrived, the commissioner of Indian affairs estimated that there were only about 300,000 Indians in 1872. The 1970 census indicated about 827,000 Indians (including Eskimos and Aleuts), and the 1980 census counted 1,418,000 Indians (including Eskimos and Aleuts), of which the BIA served or had some connection with 734,895, or 52 percent. The last figure indicates that many Indians have moved into the general population and are served by the same governments as other citizens. Since the estimated natural increase of Indians is only about 2.5 percent per year, the increase in the census count raises a question. One of the reasons for the higher count, other than natural increase, may be the improved image of and pride in being an Indian. As a result, a higher percentage of the estimated 10 million to 20 million[93] persons in the general population with some Indian blood may have identified themselves as Indian in 1980 than in the 1970 census. Improved census procedures also may have contributed to a more accurate count. However, many persons with some Indian blood have largely lost their identity as Indians.

Comparing the census count of Indians with the total U.S. population indicates that Indians constituted 0.41 percent (less than one-half of 1 percent) of the total in 1970. For 1980 the U.S. total was 226,500,000 and the Indian total 1,418,000 or 0.63 percent (about two-thirds of 1 percent) of the total population.

Table 1.1
Indian Population and Land by State, 1980

State	Population								Trust Land (Acres)	
	Total	Indian	% Ind.	BIA Connected	% Respon. BIA	% Respon. State	BIA Con. 16+ able to work	% Unem-ployed	Tribal	Individual
	1	2	3	4	5	6	7	8	9	10
US Total	226,504,825	1,418,195	.6	734,895	52	48	325,104	46	41,856,465	10,033,480
Alabama	3,890,061	7,561	.2	-	-	100	-	-	-	-
Alaska	400,481	64,047	16.0	64,047	?	?	25,941	62	86,759	341,004
Arizona	2,717,866	152,857	5.6	152,145	100	-	69,491	59	19,555,053	252,254
Arkansas	2,285,513	9,411	.4	-	-	100	-	-	-	-
California	23,668,562	201,311	.8	19,946	10	90	10,621	57	500,136	72,450
Colorado	2,888,834	18,059	.6	2,624	15	85	994	56	752,086	3,838
Connecticut	3,107,576	4,533	.1	-	-	100	-	-	-	-
Delaware	595,225	1,330	.2	-	-	100	-	-	-	-
Florida	9,739,992	19,316	.2	1,881	10	90	942	37	79,014	-
Georgia	5,464,265	7,619	.1	-	-	100	-	-	-	-
Hawaii	965,000	2,778	.3	-	-	100	-	-	-	-
Idaho	943,935	10,521	1.1	6,953	66	34	2,925	36	460,318	333,653
Illinois	11,418,461	16,271	.1	-	-	100	-	-	-	-
Indiana	5,490,179	7,835	.1	-	-	100	-	-	-	-
Iowa	2,913,387	5,453	.2	695	13	87	275	52	4,164	-
Kansas	2,363,208	15,371	.6	2,165	14	86	987	17	5,664	22,522
Kentucky	3,661,433	3,610	.1	-	-	100	-	-	-	-
Louisiana	4,203,972	12,064	.3	550	5	95	226	8	416	-
Maine	1,124,660	4,087	.4	2,326	57	43	1,032	46	-	-
Maryland	4,216,446	8,021	.2	-	-	100	-	-	-	-
Massachusetts	5,737,037	7,743	.1	-	-	100	-	-	-	-
Michigan	9,258,344	40,038	.4	5,551	14	86	2,555	44	12,080	9,166
Minnesota	4,077,148	35,026	.9	16,511	47	53	6,375	52	712,125	50,903
Mississippi	2,520,638	6,180	.2	4,914	80	20	1,679	33	17,478	19
Missouri	4,917,444	12,319	.2	-	-	100	-	-	-	375
Montana	786,690	37,270	4.7	27,463	74	26	12,548	49	2,175,548	3,037,153
Nebraska	1,570,006	9,197	.6	3,097	34	66	1,582	55	22,395	42,531
Nevada	799,184	13,304	1.7	7,361	55	45	3,657	46	1,067,877	78,408
New Hampshire	920,610	1,352	.1	-	-	100	-	-	-	-
New Jersey	7,364,158	8,394	.1	-	-	100	-	-	-	-

State	1	2	3	4	5	6	7	8	9	10
New Mexico	1,299,968	104,777	8.1	106,840	100	-	55,543	33	6,464,373	676,466
New York	17,557,288	38,732	.2	10,626	27	73	4,763	54	-	-
North Carolina	5,874,429	64,635	1.1	5,664	9	91	2,407	43	56,461	-
North Dakota	652,695	20,157	3.1	20,044	99	1	7,389	52	203,791	646,934
Ohio	10,797,419	12,240	.1	-	-	100	-	-	-	-
Oklahoma	3,025,266	169,464	5.6	156,501	92	8	60,789	24	86,172	1,136,162
Oregon	2,632,663	27,309	1.0	4,777	17	83	1,895	35	617,797	140,362
Pennsylvania	11,866,728	9,459	.1	-	-	100	-	-	-	-
Rhode Island	947,154	2,898	.3	-	-	100	-	-	-	-
South Carolina	3,119,208	5,758	.2	-	-	100	-	-	-	-
South Dakota	690,178	45,101	6.5	41,321	92	8	19,090	65	2,600,238	2,490,870
Tennessee	4,590,750	5,103	.1	-	-	100	-	-	-	-
Texas	14,228,383	40,074	.3	-	-	100	-	-	-	-
Utah	1,461,037	19,256	1.3	6,649	35	65	3,105	55	2,249,771	33,823
Vermont	511,456	984	.2	-	-	100	-	-	-	-
Virginia	5,346,279	9,336	.2	-	-	100	-	-	-	-
Washington	4,130,163	60,771	1.5	41,233	68	32	19,624	59	2,005,943	489,164
West Virginia	1,949,644	1,610	.1	-	-	100	-	-	-	-
Wisconsin	4,705,335	29,497	.6	17,106	58	42	7,237	42	328,736	80,876
Wyoming	470,816	7,125	1.5	5,705	80	20	1,432	53	1,792,071	94,547

Notes on columns 1 through 10:

1 U. S. total and state population, all races, 1980 census (Advance Reports PHC80-V-1). U. S. total includes 637,651 in District of Columbia.

2 U. S. total and state population, Indian (American Indian, Eskimo, and Aleut), 1980 census. U. S. total includes 1031 in District of Columbia.

3 Indian percent of total population, U. S. total and each state.

4 BIA Connected: "Indians living on federal reservations or nearby and who are eligible for services from the Bureau of Indian Affairs" - from "Local Estimates of Resident Indian Population and Labor Force Status; December 1981" issued by BIA January 1982 (Appendix A); hereafter cited as BIA Census 1981. U. S. total includes 200 in District of Columbia.

5 Percent Responsibility, BIA: Percent of Indians for which the BIA has some responsibility compared to total number of Indians.

6 Percent Responsibility, State: Percent of Indians not eligible for BIA services and subject to state governments. States provide services to federally connected Indians, too, in many instances.

7 BIA Connected, 16 + years of age and able to work: Of the 480,961 (65% of BIA Connected) 16 years of age or older, 65,686 are students, and 90,171 have to care for children or are disabled, retired, or too old; this leaves a total of 325,104 that are 16 or older and able to work. BIA Census 1981.

Table 1.1, concl.

8 Percent Unemployed: Dividing the number of unemployed by the total 16+ years of age able to work. Columns for the number of employed and unemployed are omitted to save space.

9 Acres of tribally owned land in trust under the jurisdiction of the Bureau of Indian Affairs as of September 30, 1980, from "Annual Report of Indian Lands," September 30, 1980, published by the BIA; hereafter cited as BIA Land Report 1980 (figures rounded). This column does not include the forty million acres transferred to Alaska natives under the Alaska Native Claims Settlement Act of 1971 and amendments (85 Stat688) since that land is not in trust. Maine Indian land placed in trust as a result of the Maine Indian Claims Act of 1980 94 Stat. 1785) is not included in this column. The Maine act authorized the purchase of three hundred thousand acres to be placed in trust. Although New York reservation land, other than the Poospatuck and Shinnecock reservations, cannot be alienated without federal approval it is not included in the BIA Land Report 1980. New York reservation acreage was a little over one hundred thousand acres in 1970 (Theodore W.Taylor, *The States and Their Indian Citizens* (Washington, D.C.: Department of the Interior, Bureau of Indian Affairs, 1972), p. 176.

10 Acres of trust land under the jurisdiction of the BIA owned by Indian individuals (BIA Land Report 1980).

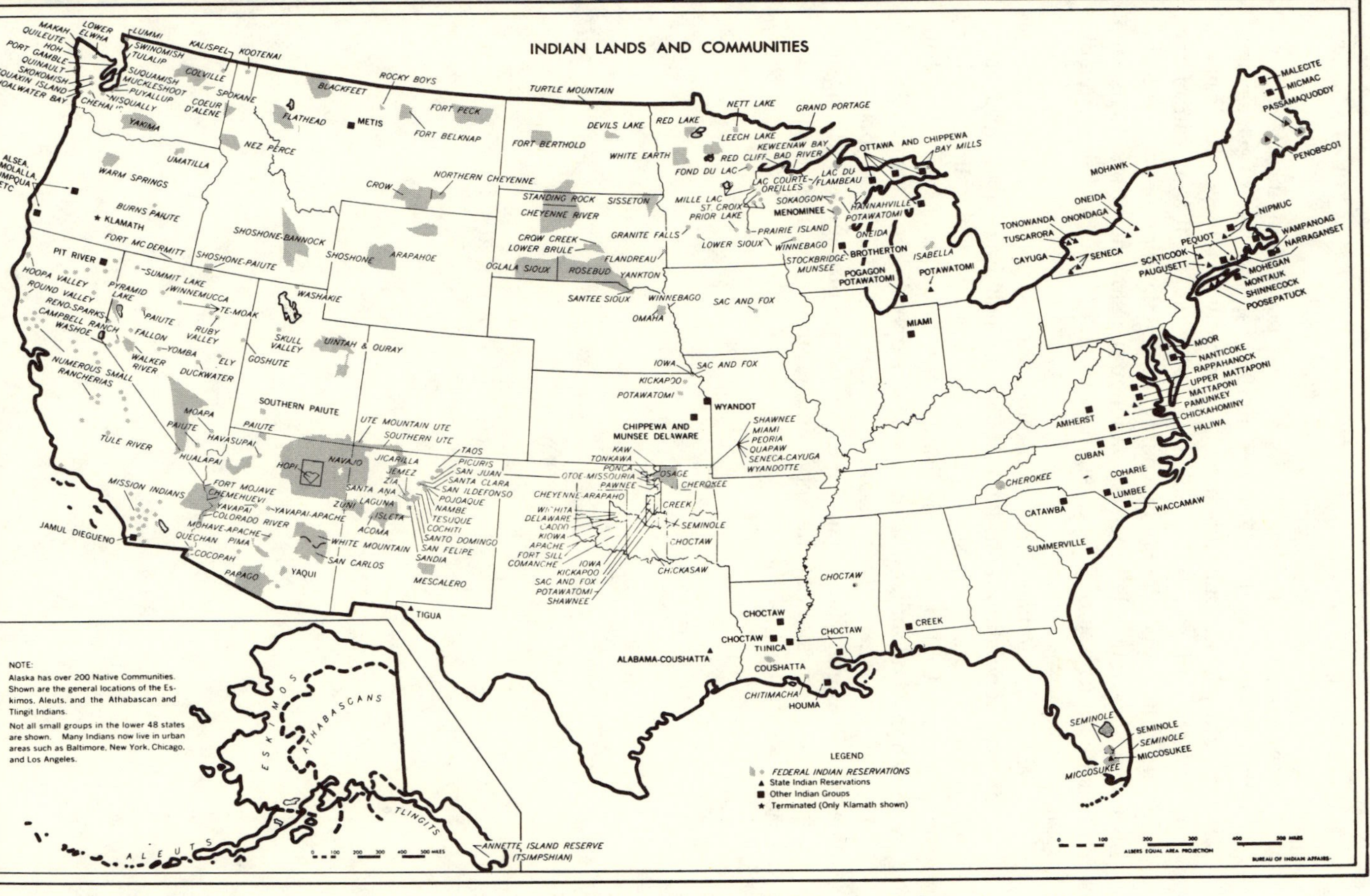

Figure 1.4. Indian lands and communities. (Source: BIA publication, Haskell Junior College Press, 1971.)

The Bureau of Indian Affairs service population increased from about 477,000 in 1970 to 734,895 in 1980, an increase of 54 percent. Bureau officials attribute this increase primarily to four possible causes: (1) better reporting by the Indian agencies and by the Bureau of the Census in its Indian counts by county, (2) immigration of some Indians who had previously left the reservation and a slowing of out-migration, (3) natural increase of 2.5 percent a year, and (4) more-effective health programs.

Table 1.1, "Indian Population and Land by State, 1980," presents summary population and land statistics, including labor force and employment data. Figure 1.4, "Indian Lands and Communities," is a map of the United States indicating the location of federal Indian reservations and other Indian groups. Appendix A, "Indian Service Population and Labor Force Estimates," presents 1981 Indian population data by BIA area office, state, reservation, and BIA agency. The agency figures are indicators of the approximate number of Indians of various tribes served by the BIA.

2

ORGANIZATIONAL HISTORY OF THE BUREAU OF INDIAN AFFAIRS

Early Organization

Since the population of the colonies and the United States in the late 1700s and the early 1800s was relatively small and since the Indian tribes were in a comparatively strong position, the president, his cabinet, and Congress gave considerable attention to Indian matters. All pertinent agencies of government were involved, and the president appointed envoys and other representatives to work with the Indians. The Continental Congress set up three departments to deal with Indian matters rather than the two that had existed under the British. The northern department included the Iroquois confederacy and the Indians to the north; the Cherokee and other neighboring tribes were under the southern department; the middle department included those tribes that lived between the other two major areas.[1]

Secretary of War Henry Knox was placed in charge of Indian matters in 1786, and he continued to formulate and carry out Indian policy under President Washington. In 1796 government trading houses for Indians were established under the direction of the president, but they were discontinued in 1822. The office of superintendent of Indian trade was established in 1806, and money to carry out its functions was appropriated.

The utilization of U.S. courts for Indians and non-Indians on reservations who broke the law was established by statute in 1817, and in 1819 the president was authorized to employ agricultural instructors, teachers, and other skilled people to instruct the Indians.[2] Many of the "civilization" efforts were in the hands of missionary organizations in the first half of the nineteenth century, so appropriations of government funds were made to such groups for the education of Indian children and the construction of schools.

Territorial governors often served as ex officio superintendents of Indian territory and Indian matters with the hope that in this way they could help coordinate contacts between the frontiersmen and the original inhabitants. These governors had Indian agents to assist them but had to depend on local marshals and the territorial courts to enforce the trade and intercourse laws. Agents, some of whom reported to superintendents and others to the central office in Washington, were generally assigned to one or more tribes. Army officers were sometimes assigned as Indian agents, and often the Indian agent had to get help from the nearest military post to enforce the liquor law, drive intruders off Indian land, and control lawless behavior.

Each territorial governor reported to the secretary of state in connection with his territorial functions but to the secretary of war in regard to his Indian functions. Territorial governors were often key figures in negotiating treaties and clearing land titles. For example, S. Lyman Tyler noted that William Henry Harrison, when he was governor of Indiana Territory, was the leader in formulating fifteen treaties between 1800 and 1812 through which the land was obtained for most of what today is Illinois, Indiana, and portions of Ohio, Michigan, and Wisconsin.

The military was important in regard to Indian relations throughout most of the nineteenth century, but, as might be expected, the relations between civilian agents and army officers were often strained. By 1818 there were fifteen agencies and ten subagencies administering Indian affairs and reporting to the secretary of the army.

In 1824 Secretary of War John C. Calhoun created the Bureau of Indian Affairs, and Thomas L. McKenny, formerly superintendent of Indian trade, became its first head. Assisted by two clerks, these three formed an Indian secretariat within the War Department. Their duties included being in charge of appropriations for annuities, approving all vouchers for expenditures, administering the funds appropriated to "civilize" the Indians, deciding on claims arising between Indians and whites under the trade and intercourse acts, and handling correspondence dealing with Indian affairs.[3] In 1832 statutory authority for an Office of Indian Affairs within the War Department was obtained,[4] and in 1849 the Office of Indian Affairs was transferred to the new Interior Department.

Since religious institutions were still active in Indian affairs after the Civil War President Ulysses S. Grant turned many Indian agencies over to superintendents who were nominated by religious groups. By 1871 sixty-seven of the seventy-four Indian agencies were headed by such nominees.[5] "Sectarian rivalry, narrow-minded denominationalism and church jealousies provoked bickerings, recriminations, and bad

Table 2.1
Total Number of Employees in Bureau of Indian Affairs by Date

Date	Number of Employees
1852	108
1888	1,725
1911	6,000
1933	5,000
1934	12,000
Since 1934	11,000 to 16,000

Source: Theodore W. Taylor, "The Regional Organization of the Bureau of Indian Affairs." (Ph.D. dissertation, Harvard University, December 1959, p. 98)

feeling."[6] The procedure of having superintendents nominated by religious organizations was abandoned in the 1880s.

Phenomenal Growth

As is obvious, the implementation of federal Indian policy has required personnel and organization, and from a very small beginning the organization has become one of the largest civilian bureaus in the government.

In terms of number of employees the growth is indicated in Table 2.1, but changes in policy and growth are also illustrated by the number of specialized personnel. The budget request for 1852 was for 14 employees in the central office and 94 employees in the field—consisting of agents, subagents, interpreters (55), and clerks. The number of field employees increased tenfold in twenty years; in 1872 there were 987 field employees including twenty-one different types of specialists such as physicians, teachers, farmers, blacksmiths, carpenters, millers, shoemakers, teamsters, gunsmiths, wagonmakers, and plowmakers. In 1915 about half of the approximately 6,000 employees were in education. The effects of the Allotment Act were showing up as there now were an irrigation service and an allotment service, inheritance examiners, and probate attorneys. After 1928 modern specialities were gradually added to the bureau staff such as soil scientists, extension specialists, credit specialists, and the like.[7]

A few statistical generalizations help clarify the condition of the Indians and the responsibilities of Indian agents in 1872. The number of Indians, exclusive of Alaska, was estimated to be approximately

Table 2.2.
Condition of Indians in 1872

Means of Support:	
Supporting themselves on reservations, receiving nothing from the government except interest on their own funds or annuities pursuant to treaties	130,000
Entirely subsisted by the government	31,000
In part subsisted by the government	84,000
Subsisting by hunting, fishing, roots, berries; begging or stealing	55,000
Connection with the government:	
On reservations under complete control of agents	150,000
Visited agency at times for food or gossip, but generally roaming on or off their reservations, engaged in hunting or fishing	95,000
Never visited agency, and over whom government exercised practically no control, but most of whom were inoffensive	55,000
Treaties and reservations:	
Had treaties with the government, 92 reservations	180,000
No treaties, but 15 reservations with agents in charge	40,000
No treaties, no reservations, but were more or less under the control of agents appointed for them and received more or less subsistence	25,000
No treaties, no reservations, practically no government control	55,000
Degree of "Civilization" (with no degree of assurance):	
Civilized	97,000
Semi-Civilized	125,000
Wholly barbarous	78,000

Source: Commissioner of Indian Affairs, Annual Report (Washington, D.C.: Government Printing Office, 1872, pp. 15, 84).

300,000, and the commissioner's *Annual Report* classified this Indian population as indicated in Table 2.2 (terminology is as in the *Annual Report*).

After passage of the Curtis Act in 1898,[8] which authorized allotments of land to members of the Five Civilized Tribes, the BIA had two duties of great magnitude. One was the preparation of a roll of the members of the tribes. Applications for membership numbered 250,000, and the BIA reviewed these carefully. The final roll consisted of "approximately 101,000—one-fourth full blood, one-half mixed blood or intermarried whites, and one-fourth freedmen."[9] The other big job was to classify and determine the value of over 19 million acres of land, divided into 40-acre tracts. Then, bureau employees had to remove intruders, survey 308 towns, place allottees on their land, sell the surplus land, and divide the proceeds of a sale among tribal members. This type of work may, in part, help explain the increase in the number of BIA employees from 1,725 in 1888 to 6,000 in 1911.

Organizational Changes: Expansion of Functions and Professionalism

As indicated in Chapter 1, the individualizing of Indian land, the granting of citizenship to Indians, the restricting of Indians to reservations, and the necessity of providing rations and other aid to them resulted in the Indian agent and his staff largely replacing Indian government. In the last quarter of the nineteenth century, the bureau engaged in many specialized functions—irrigation, forestry, law enforcement, health, and construction—as a result of its increasing responsibilities and the inability of most Indian groups to provide these services for themselves.

In some of the treaties quoted in Chapter 1, education in the white man's way was much on the minds of the treaty makers. In 1879 the first off-reservation boarding school was established at Carlisle in Pennsylvania, and it was followed in the next five years by the Chemawa Indian School in Oregon, Haskell Institute in Kansas, and the Chilocco Indian School in Oklahoma.

In 1907 Commissioner Francis E. Leupp, believing that education would resolve the Indian problem, replaced many Indian agents with school superintendents and farmers. As he viewed the situation, an Indian agent had been needed at an earlier stage, but since the tribes were being broken up as land was assigned to individual Indians, and since the children were learning non-Indian ways in school, the bureau was now dealing primarily with Indians as individuals rather than as members of a group. Small groups of Indians were assigned to "a bonded day-school teacher or farmer" who reported directly to the commissioner's office. "In the course of time the Indian day schools are expected to merge into the local common school system, and then . . . they [the Indians] will have been absorbed into the general body politic and become like all other Americans, except as to origin and ancestry."[10]

However, the Snyder Act of 1921[11] still gave legislative authority for a wide range of activities to be supervised by agents on reservations, and in 1927 Laurence Schmeckebier indicated BIA functions under the following headings: allotting land; issuing patents in fee and certificates of competency; supervising land, including determination of heirs, approval of wills, distribution of property, the sale and leasing of land, granting rights-of-way and easements, and the administration of forest lands; custody of Indian money, both tribal and individual; education; furnishing medical relief; promoting industrial advancement, including the construction of irrigation, water supply, and drainage systems, the advancing of money, the promotion of agriculture and stock raising, and the obtaining of employment; promoting home economics; supporting Indians; policing reservations and punishing offenses; suppressing liquor traffic; controlling Indian traders; supervising attorney contracts, and aiding missions. Each of these functional activities is described in Schmeckebier's book in detail.[12]

Schmeckebier then described the organization, manned by 5,000 employees, that was to carry out the above mentioned functions: commissioner of Indian affairs; chief clerk; Inspection Division; Administrative Division (supervision of agencies, schools, law and order, promotion of industry and agriculture), headed by the general superintendent of Indian affairs who was assisted by a supervisor of home economics (health education, institutional living conditions, instruction in home economics), and nine district superintendents; Medical Division; Purchase Division; Probate Division; Finance Division; Land Division; Irrigation Division; and Forestry Division. The basic delivery of services to Indians was through the agencies, which were headed by superintendents. There was also a special attorney for the Pueblo Indians and a special commissioner who carried out advisory duties in connection with the affairs of the Navajo and the Pueblo, as well as the Board of Indian Commissioners. The commissioner of Indian affairs was required to consult with the board about the purchase of supplies. A description of each of these organizational components is found in Schmeckebier's book,[13] and a detailed outline of organization is also presented there.[14] Statistics relating to the 262,000 Indians who were under the jurisdiction of the Indian Service in 1927 are presented by tribe, agency, and blood quantum.[15] The total number of Indians counted by the Indian office in 1920 was 336,379; the Census Bureau counted 244,437. Since there was no definition of an Indian, Schmeckebier pointed out that it would be impossible to reconcile the two figures.[16]

The Meriam report of 1928[17] recommended improved professionalism in agriculture, teaching, the operation of dormitories, and other services in order to increase the effectiveness of the bureau's programs. Improved educational qualifications for agency personnel have been required since the 1930s.

Establishment of Area Offices

The growth of BIA responsibilities increased the number of personnel at the agencies, and with improved transportation and communication many decisions were made in Washington. The correspondence was so voluminous, and the central office so far removed from the local situation, that area or regional offices were superimposed on the agency structures after World War II to decentralize some of the work. The entire government, in fact, was experiencing similar organizational problems, and other agencies in the Interior Department and other departments were regionalizing at about the same time. This change was not without pain, as the central office functional office heads, the agents, and Indians bitterly fought the regional move and succeeded in delaying it for several years until 1949,[18] but the three-level organization continues today.

Dispersion of Functions

In 1943 Commissioner John Collier, because of the recommendations of the Meriam report and congressional pressure, urged agents to evaluate all possibilities for the transfer of bureau functions and activities to tribal, state, county, or municipal governments "such as law and order, health, and education."[19] As an example of the result of this policy, in 1950 Congress authorized a joint county-Indian hospital in Albuquerque to serve both Indians and non-Indians. In 1955 Indian health responsibility was transferred from the BIA to the Public Health Service,[20] and from the 1940s to the 1960s many functions were transferred to the states.[21]

Increased Stature of Indian Function

Prior to 1976 the BIA was under an assistant secretary in the Interior Department whose responsibilities covered territories, Indians, and other land management activities. The general pattern, not only in Interior but in other departments, was to assign several different bureaus or activities to each assistant secretary. Indians pushed for more clout, some even recommending that the BIA be placed directly under the president. President Lyndon Johnson created the National Council on Indian Opportunity—chaired by the vice-president, half of the members of the council were Indian, and the other members were of cabinet rank[22]—but the council was phased out under President Richard Nixon.

After the forcible occupation of the BIA building on Constitution Avenue in Washington, D.C., by the AIM (American Indian Movement)-led Trail of Broken Treaties in 1972, the BIA headquarters organization was disbursed to various locations in Washington, and the bureau's top organization was also restructured. The BIA was removed from the jurisdiction of the Interior Department's assistant secretary for public land management and placed under a special assistant to the secretary for Indian affairs; Marvin Franklin, former chief of the Iowa tribe and an official of the Phillips Petroleum Corporation, was appointed to this post. The number of personnel in the bureau's central office was reduced from 1,318 to 715 (only 300 people were affected because of many vacant positions), former top officials were fired and transferred, and emphasis was placed on functions being carried out by the area offices and reservation agency offices of the bureau. The titles of the key staff offices in Washington were changed from assistant commissioner to office director, and the office directors were to have only staff functions. The position of commissioner was not filled until 1973 when a new commissioner, Morris Thompson, was appointed, and he reported directly to the secretary of the Interior Department; the position of special assistant to the secretary for Indian affairs was phased out.

The 1975 the Indian Self-Determination and Education Assistance Act (PL 93-638, January 4, 1975) implemented the "self-determination" policies that had been stressed by Presidents Johnson and Nixon. This act has had a significant impact on the BIA and Indian Health Service organizations as it has encouraged tribes to operate government programs for themselves under government contracts or grants.

In 1977, Cecil Andrus, the new secretary of Interior, decided to assign an assistant-secretary slot to Indian affairs; he did not fill the position of commissioner. The assistant secretary, Forrest Gerard, and two deputies—one responsible for program operations and the other for administration—managed the BIA. The headquarters office directors and field area directors reported through both deputies to the assistant secretary. A task force to study the recommendations of the American Indian Policy Review Commission resulted in the appointment of a commissioner of Indian affairs, William Hallett, in 1978 and the abolishing of one of the two deputy assistant-secretary positions.

Education achieved some separation from control of BIA generalists as a result of the Education Amendments Act of 1978 (Title 11, PL 95-

561, November 1, 1978), which established a direct line of authority from the assistant secretary to the director of education to the education personnel in the field. The education specialists and administrators on the central, area, and agency levels were removed from the authority of the commissioner, area director, and the agency superintendent. However, administrative operations and maintenance services for schools continued to be provided by the commissioner, area directors, and agency superintendents.

After the 1980 election there was a return to having an assistant secretary with two deputies and no commissioner. However, the functions of the two deputies were different than in the 1977 arrangement. One deputy was assigned the responsibility of administering the BIA, and the other was to have an "outward facing policy role in which an attempt would be made to have more impact on Indian affairs policies" throughout the federal government.[23]

Indian Preference

Giving Indians preferences in employment in the BIA was prescribed by the Indian Reorganization Act of 1934.[24] Up until the 1970s preference was limited to entry positions; after employment, merit governed transfers and promotions. In the early 1970s Commissioner Louis Bruce and Secretary of the Interior Rogers C.B. Morton applied Indian preference to all personnel actions, and this policy was upheld by the courts as being authorized by law. Indians have made up a majority of the BIA's personnel since before 1950 and in 1982 constituted approximately 75 percent of that force.

The broadened Indian preference has had an impact on the morale of non-Indians since they have been, for the most part, frozen in their positions. This freeze sometimes has resulted in persons with less experience and ability filling key technical and administrative positions with a resultant lessening of organizational efficiency in serving the Indians. The opposite has sometimes occurred when very bright and able Indians have moved rapidly from one job to another, in and out of the BIA, with a resultant lack of continuity and stability in the functions affected. This latter situation has been in evidence at the assistant secretary, commissioner, and office director levels in some instances since the early 1970s. The continuity and ability to perform bureau functions that has existed under this situation has been provided by career civil servants—both Indian and non-Indian.[25]

Change from Direct Operation to Grants and Contracts

Since Commissioners Francis E. Leupp (1907) and John Collier (1933) the emphasis has been on transferring functions to the Indians themselves or to states and localities. The Indian governments established subsequent to the Indian Reorganization Act were to take over as much of the governmental responsibility that had been performed by the BIA as possible. In the 1950s an effort was made to transfer functions to tribes and states, with the most drastic action being termination of federal trust and services in several instances. This termination philosophy was rejected and the so-called self-determination philosophy ushered in in the 1970s. The Indian Self-Determination and Education Assistance Act of 1975 gave a further impetus to tribes to take over functions performed by the BIA and the IHS (Indian Health Service), and federal funds were to be supplied to carry out those functions. This process is accomplished through contracts or grants to tribes for the functions that are being assumed by the tribes.

Thus, the movement is toward transforming the BIA from a direct operating and direct service agency, as it was to a large extent in the last quarter of the nineteenth and first quarter of the twentieth centuries, to a contracting or granting agency. This is a change of major magnitude. In many ways achieving program results through the contracting or granting process is more difficult than through direct operation. It certainly requires a different organizational emphasis and expertise.

There has been difficulty in developing the necessary understanding in the BIA and among the tribes for the smooth operation of grants and contracts. A September 10, 1981, comptroller general's report indicated that in fiscal years 1978 through 1980 the bureau awarded $726 million in grants and contracts to Indian tribes. Deficiencies noted were retroactive awards of contracts and grants; lack of performance measurement and criteria; inadequate monitoring; poor cash management; weak tribal financial management; and questionable practices such as unauthorized use of expired appropriations, increasing funding without requests from the tribes, the use of funds for unauthorized purposes, etc.[26]

In 1977 the Congress adopted legislation that distinguished between grant and contract, or procurement, relationships.[27] Contracting was for the purpose of purchase of property or services for the direct benefit or use of the government—for example an automobile. Grants were to accomplish a public purpose of support or stimulation with no substantial involvement of the executive agency awarding the grant in the performance of the activity for which funds were provided. This grant definition fits the objective of the self-determination act much more closely than the contract process and will be emphasized by the BIA in the future. Another process, the cooperative agreement, will also be used when there is to be substantial involvement of BIA personnel with the tribe or other groups in carrying out the contemplated activity. Assistant Secretary for Indian Affairs Kenneth L. Smith announced a proposed realignment of BIA organization and process in February 1982, which aimed at pinpointing responsibility and emphasizing an increased "transfer to" or "sharing with" tribes of BIA activities.[28]

3

THE BUREAU OF INDIAN AFFAIRS TODAY

Introduction

The two main functions of the Bureau of Indian Affairs through most of its history have been (1) to help Indians adjust to the society that gradually surrounded and engulfed them, or to help them live in the presence of that society on a self-sufficient basis, and (2) to exercise trust responsibility for Indian land and resources as long as that was required by law.

Classroom education, emphasized in many treaties, has had a major role in helping many Indians become self-sufficient in their new and ever-changing environment. In addition, however, all of the BIA's activities have an educational purpose: Agriculturists teach and demonstrate agricultural practices; range managers show individual owners of cattle or sheep how to care for and manage their animals; soil conservationists demonstrate conservation practices to tribal and individual owners of land; foresters help tribes and individuals understand sustained yield management of timber resources; social service workers help the Indians learn how to use county and state social services or how to organize a tribal social service program; tribal operations personnel and BIA agency superintendents work with tribal leaders and staff to develop governmental skills; and economic development personnel help tribes and individual Indians attract private sector investment, organize and operate individual or tribal enterprises, and further cooperative relationships with state and federal economic development programs. The history of the BIA has been largely oriented toward the concept of a transfer of BIA responsibilities to the Indians themselves and toward helping the Indians use the services of local, state, and federal governments. Even before the Allotment Act, one of the underlying concepts was for the BIA "to work itself out of a job."

However, in the 1970s the view developed of a special Indian–federal government relationship as a basic principle, without end, as well as an indefinite continuance of the federal government's trust responsibility for Indian land. Whether this viewpoint is a temporary deviation from the historical trend or a change in direction of Indian policy only time will tell. If it is a change in direction, the BIA or its equivalent may continue for a long time.

Once a direction or goal is established, it does not automatically result in action toward the desired goal. All administrative agencies affect a policy in its execution, and broad legislative policy directives and authorization must be made specific for action. Thus, the BIA drafts its section of the Code of Federal Regulations, initiates rules and procedures for publication in the Federal Register, and maintains a BIA manual with even more detailed guidance and procedures for each area of the bureau's activity. How these regulations and guidelines are written determines the specifics of policy direction. How area directors, superintendents, and their staffs actually implement the regulations also controls what is done. In Indian affairs, as in any other program, what is actually done in the field becomes the policy as far as the persons being served are concerned, whether or not the action bears close relationship to written statements of policy or procedure. It is next to impossible to cover every contingency in drawing up regulations and procedures, and unwise to try. Human conditions and situations vary, and flexibility to take the action that seems best to achieve the desired objective is required. Background, expertise, and judgment are important ingredients in deciding among optional actions. Therefore, the federal organization for dealing with Indians is critical to Indian policy and to that policy's implementation.

In 1950 the BIA was the repository of most federal Indian functions. Today that situation is no longer the case. Since 1966 Indian advocates have pushed hard for special provisions relating to Indians in all legislation providing services or grants to the general public. Advocates who help develop legislative policy in this manner include the BIA, staffs of the House and Senate committees on Indian affairs, Washington-wise Indian lobbies, aggressive tribal leaders, and Washington representatives retained by individual tribes. This drive has been largely successful, as is amply illustrated by specific references to Indians in statutes authorizing funding and services. In the early 1960s Commissioner Philleo Nash pushed for the application of federal resources to the Indian community. During this period, for example, the Department of Labor agreed to apply the Manpower Development and Training Act to Indians, and Congress approved considering Indian reservations as communities in the war on poverty legislation.[1] The Elementary and

Table 3.1
Indian Funding by Agency ($ in Millions)

Agency	1980 Actual	1981 Est.	Carter 1982 Est.	Reagan 1982 Est.
Interior	1023	1048	1079	1004
Housing and Urban Development (HUD)	884	843	740	34
Health and Human Services (HHS)	655	717	806	663
Education	231	276	284	256
Labor	198	157	203	102
Agriculture (USDA)	36	45	53	53
Commerce	26	19	26	0
Treasury (Revenue Sharing)	10	11	11	11
Total	3063	3116	3202	2123

Source: From a fact sheet prepared by the Office of Management and Budget, dated March 20, 1981. Included as attachment 3 in a "Memorandum to Tribal Leaders," March 31, 1981, from James F. Canan, acting deputy assistant secretary, Indian Affairs, Interior Department. Fact sheet does not include Indian participation in federal programs generally available to all U.S. citizens and, therefore, excludes funding for such items as Social Security, Food Stamps, Unemployment Compensation, Home Energy Assistance, Aid to Families with Dependent Children, and Supplemental Security Income.

Secondary Education Act of 1965 was amended a year later to include Indians in BIA schools as beneficiaries.

The Bureau of Indian Affairs is still the largest administrative organization dealing with Indians, and it has the greatest variety of activities as well. Tables 3.1 and 3.2 indicate the funding by agency and program for 1980 (actual) and estimates for fiscal years 1981 and 1982. Services provided by the BIA are available only to federally recognized Indians in contrast to some agencies that provide services to Indians without requiring federal recognition.

Relationships within Department Structures

The Bureau of Indian Affairs as an organizational entity appears to be in a state of transition. As indicated in Chapters 1 and 2, statutory law provides for a commissioner of Indian affairs as well as specifying the functions of the bureau.[2] However, for a time no commissioner was appointed by President Carter or by President Reagan.

Prior to 1973 the BIA was one of several offices or bureaus reporting to an assistant secretary, who frequently settled conflicts between the

Table 3.2
Indian Funding by Program and Agency ($ in Millions)

	1980 Actual	1981 Estimate	1982 Carter Budget	1982 Reagan Budget
Education................	484	528	536	492
Interior...........	(270)	(274)	(282)	(266)
Education..........	(214)	(254)	(254)	(226)
Health Services/Nutrition	583	652	708	680
HHS................	(547)	(607)	(655)	(627)
USDA...............	(36)	(45)	(53)	(53)
Housing..................	867	829	727	18
Interior...........	(19)	(23)	(24)	(18)
HUD................	(848)	(806)	(703)	(0)
Social Services..........	121	124	130	118
Interior...........	(87)	(90)	(96)	(90)
HHS................	(34)	(34)	(34)	(28)
Employment...............	250	203	249	136
Interior...........	(52)	(46)	(46)	(34)
Labor..............	(198)	(157)	(203)	(102)
Economic Development.....	88	84	92	62
Interior...........	(26)	(28)	(29)	(28)
Commerce...........	(26)	(19)	(26)	(0)
HUD................	(36)	(37)	(37)	(34)
Natural Resources.......	74	87	87	86
Interior..........	(74)	(87)	(87)	(86)
Trust Activities.........	51	45	48	48
Interior...........	(51)	(45)	(48)	(48)
Management & Facilities..	131	141	151	151
Interior...........	(131)	(141)	(151)	(151)
Construction.............	251	247	319	194
Interior...........	(160)	(149)	(172)	(156)
HHS................	(74)	(76)	(117)	(8)
Education..........	(17)	(22)	(30)	(30)
Other Interior Funds.....	153	165	144	127
Revenue Sharing..........	10	11	11	11
TOTAL FEDERAL FUNDS......	3,063	3,116	3,202	2,123
INTERIOR TRUST FUNDS.....	969	511	465	465
TOTAL FEDERAL/TRUST......	4,032	3,627	3,667	2,588
Est. Federal funds per capita	$4,400	$4,450	$4,600	$3,000

Source: From a fact sheet prepared by the Office of Management and Budget dated March 20, 1981.

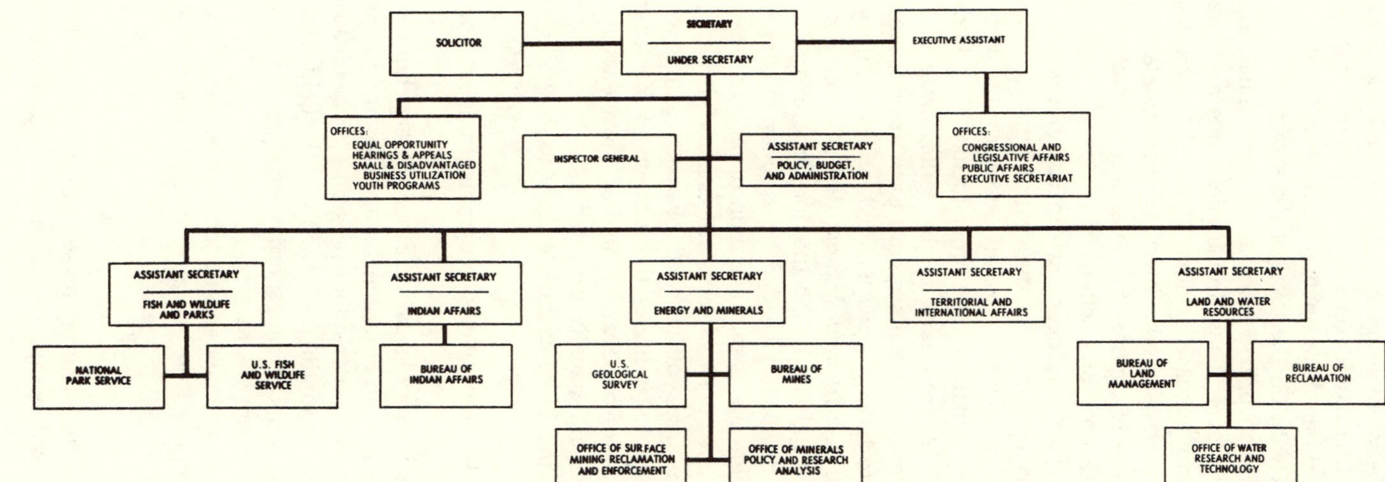

Figure 3.1. Department of the Interior organization chart. (Source: *The United States Government Manual 1981/1982*, Office of the Federal Register, National Archives and Records Service, General Services Administration [Washington, D.C.: Government Printing Office, May 1, 1981], p. 832.)

bureaus. Further, an assistant secretary with several bureaus or activities cannot be a full-time advocate for only one of the bureaus. Now conflicts between Indian and other departmental activities, if not resolved by negotiation, are dealt with on the level of the secretary of the Interior. The current structure also provides for a full-time Indian advocate on the assistant secretary level. Thus, Indian programs are in a position of higher visibility and increased status. Figure 3.1 indicates that the other four assistant secretaries in the Interior Department are responsible for two to four activities in contrast to the assistant secretary for Indian affairs who deals with only one activity.

If the present "acting" arrangement can continue and perhaps be recognized in statutory language, the duplication implicit in having both a commissioner and a deputy assistant secretary for Indian affairs (operations) could be eliminated in the superstucture. Should this change not be politically feasible, returning to the earlier arrangement of the BIA's being one of several bureaus reporting to an assistant secretary might be preferable to having a two-layered superstructure.

The United States Government Manual 1981/82 described the responsibilities for Indian affairs in the Interior Department.[3] As will be noted in Figure 3.2, the BIA is headed by a commissioner (or deputy assistant secretary) who directs the operation of programs through area and agency offices. There are twelve area offices and eighty-two agencies. Appendix A lists the area offices and agencies along with Indian population data; Figure 1.4 indicates the location of the federal Indian reservations. Most BIA personnel are located on the agency level, where programs and services are actually executed.

The functions of the BIA headquarters are to

1. develop bureauwide policies, programs, budgets, and justifications;
2. develop bureauwide legislative programs and reports;
3. provide a liaison with other federal agencies and national Indian organizations regarding Indian programs and bureau activities;
4. monitor and evaluate the performance of the field establishment;
5. participate in periodic and specific management and program reviews of field operations; and
6. advise the commissioner and the director of the Office of Indian Education Programs on bureau programs, policy matters, regulations, and related matters.

Day-to-day operations and program service delivery are the functions of the bureau's field, rather than central office, organization.[4]

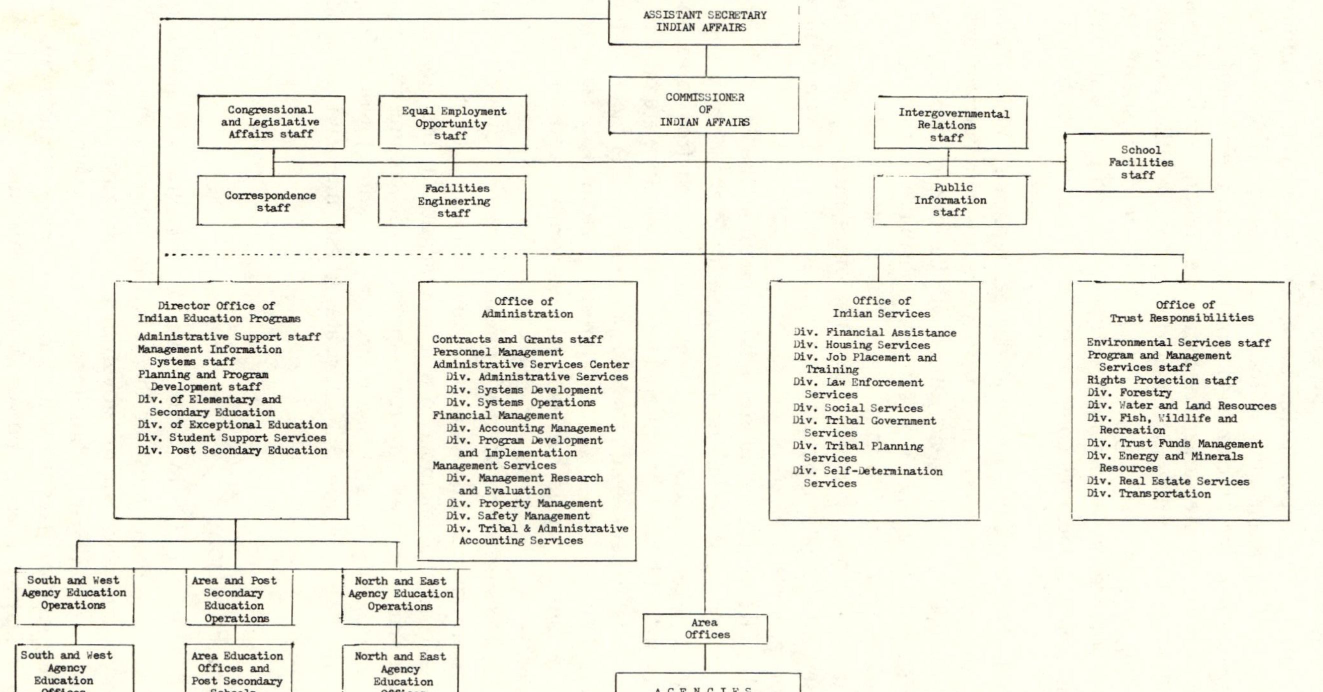

Figure 3.2. Bureau of Indian Affairs organization chart. In 1983 no commissioner had been appointed, and the commissioner's function was being performed by a deputy assistant secretary. (Source: Based on chart approved March 15, 1982, U.S. Department of Interior, *Departmental Manual*, chap. 130, p. 2.)

The commissioner is assisted by staff offices: Congressional and Legislative Affairs, Correspondence, Equal Employment Opportunity, Intergovernmental Relations, Public Information, School Facilities, and Facilities Engineering. The functional staff offices under the commissioner of Indian affairs in the headquarters office are Indian Services, Trust Responsibilities, and Administration. The director of the Office of Indian Education Programs in Washington, D.C., reports to the assistant secretary's office but receives its personnel, budget, contracting, procurement, management services, facilities construction, and maintenance from the bureau.

Area and agency offices, to some degree, replicate the functional activities at the national level. That is, if there are commercial forests under the jurisdiction of an agency, there will be forestry personnel on the agency staff. If an agency's forestry responsibility is so small that it would not be cost effective to assign a forester to the agency staff, a forester from another agency or the area office might provide the necessary service. Irrigation personnel are assigned only where there are irrigation projects, and so on.

Since 1949 all functions in an area have been under the line authority of the area director and under the line authority of the agency superintendent at the agency level. Education was removed from area and agency direction in 1978. Technical guidance and assistance are provided through functional experts—e.g., forestry personnel at BIA headquarters advise area forestry personnel, and area forestry personnel advise agency foresters. If a conflict occurs between an area forester and an agency superintendent—i.e., the latter disagrees with the technical direction from the area forester to the agency's forester—the area director steps in and settles the matter. Likewise, if technical direction from a Washington professional staff member to a functional staff at the area level did not meet with the area director's approval, the commissioner (or at present, the deputy assistant secretary for operations) would have to resolve the issue. Figure 3.3 illustrates these line and guidance relationships.

Program Functions

When I joined the BIA in 1950 it was a government in miniature as it fulfilled for Indians most of the functions normally handled by local, county, state and federal governments for other citizens. Responsibilities of the BIA regarding Indians included education; health; social services; land management; forestry; soil conservation; regulation of grazing; irrigation; electric power; tribal government support; law and order; loans; business, agricultural, and industrial development;

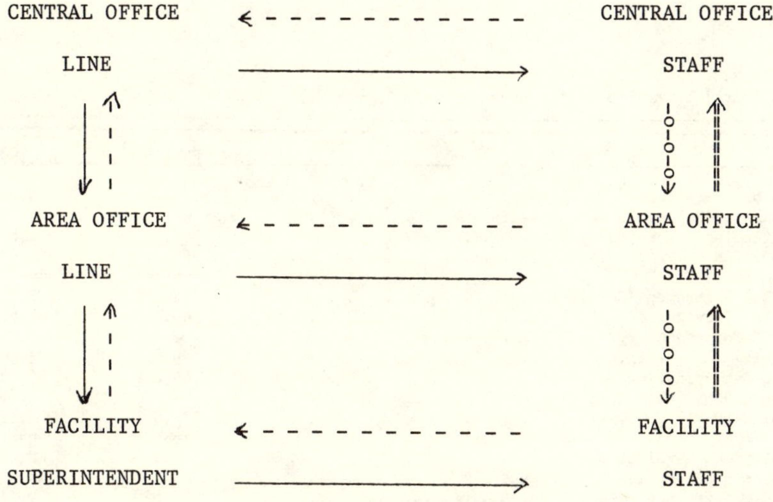

LEGEND:

——— LINE RESPONSIBILITY: Supervision, Orders, Directions, Suggestions, Information, Consultation.

\- - - SUBORDINATE LINE OFFICE AND STAFF OFFICE RESPONSIBILITY TO A LINE OFFICE: Operational and Policy Recommendation, Consultation, Reports, Information.

STAFF RESPONSIBILITY TO OTHER STAFF GROUPS:
-o-o- Down: Technical Guidance, Consultation, Information.
===== Up: Information, Requests for Technical Assistance, Suggestions, Consultation.

Figure 3.3. Chart illustrating relationships, Bureau of Indian Affairs. (Source: Theodore W. Taylor, "The Regional Organization of the Bureau of Indian Affairs" [Ph.D. dissertation, Harvard University, December 1959], p. 220)

tourism; employment and relocation; construction, operation, and maintenance of necessary facilities such as hospitals, schools, irrigation works, and roads; management of trust responsibilities for Indian land and Indian funds in the U.S. Treasury; and many more functions.

Today the Indian Health Service is in the Department of Health and Human Services (HHS), and agricultural extension services are performed by the Department of Agriculture (USDA), although they are funded by BIA appropriations. In addition, many expanded services for Indians have developed in other government departments. For those

Table 3.3
BIA Fiscal Year 1983 Budget Request ($ in Thousands)

	FY 1982*	FY 1983
School Operations	176,106	179,841
Johnson O'Malley Education Assistance	25,954	25,954
Continuing Education	52,446	50,877
EDUCATION	254,506	256,672
Tribal Government Services	23,789	26,339
Social Services	90,351	98,664
Law Enforcement	32,515	36,041
Housing	29,810	23,289
Self-Determination Services	49,222	56,882
Navajo-Hopi Settlement Program	4,178	3,899
INDIAN SERVICES	229,865	245,114
Employment Development	27,120	28,410
Business Enterprise Development	8,136	16,046
Road Maintenance	17,628	22,117
ECONOMIC DEVELOPMENT AND EMPLOYMENT PROGRAMS	52,884	66,573
Forestry and Agriculture	71,165	70,989
Minerals, Mining, Irrigation and Power	13,578	16,214
NATURAL RESOURCES DEVELOPMENT	84,743	87,203
Indian Rights Protection	18,516	18,248
Real Estate and Financial Trust Services	27,350	28,957
TRUST RESPONSIBILITIES	45,866	47,205
FACILITIES MANAGEMENT	83,380	93,381
Management and Administration	49,465	56,698
Employee Compensation Payments	4,161	4,582
Program Management	4,350	7,822
GENERAL ADMINISTRATION	57,976	69,102
GENERAL COST REDUCTION (Overhead)	-0-	-16,000
OPERATION OF INDIAN PROGRAMS (Total)	809,220	849,250
INDIAN EDUCATION ASSISTANCE (Total)	71,597**	51,119
Irrigation Systems	46,192	45,900**
Building and Utilities	47,436	60,100
Land Acquisition	-0-	-0-
CONSTRUCTION (Total)	93,628	106,000
IMPACT AID: SCHOOL CONST. AFFCTG. IND. LANDS (Total)	9,000**	838
ROAD CONSTRUCTION (Total)	47,160	43,585
TOTAL FEDERAL FUNDING	1,030,605	1,050,792

*1982 figures include actual appropriations and pending supplemental request.
**Programs included in the Department of Education in FY 1982, including recission proposed in FY 1982.
***Includes Ak Chin Irrigation Project proposed for later transmittal.

Source: BIA Press Release, February 8, 1982.

functions within the jurisdiction of the assistant secretary for Indian affairs, the funding for 1982 and requested for 1983 is indicated in Table 3.3.

Office of Indian Education

A review of Table 3.3 shows that education receives the most money; it also requires the greatest number of personnel. "School operations" involves the direct operation of BIA schools, with a 1983 estimate of approximately 31,000 Indian students, and contract schools operated by various tribes, approximately 8,000 students.[5] These operations receive the largest portion of the education budget. Under the Johnson-O'Malley Act of 1934—which authorized the secretary of the Interior to enter into contracts with states for Indian education, medical attention, agricultural assistance, and social welfare—payments are made to states for supplemental education programs for approximately 181,000 Indian children in public schools who are living on trust land or who are otherwise federally recognized (basically, federal Indian reservation children). Approximately 75 to 80 percent of reservation Indian children are educated in state public schools; only about 2 percent are in schools under contract with Indian tribes. Public schools generally operate under the direction of elected school boards, and many Indians are serving on school boards for their communities.

BIA-operated schools are generally in isolated geographic locations. Some are full-time boarding schools that serve Indians who live too far from other school facilities, and others are day schools on reservations. Off-reservation boarding schools serve three groups of students: (1) those living in isolated areas without a school near their home, (2) those with family or home problems, and (3) those with learning or behavioral problems.

Increasing numbers of Indian children are graduating from high school; 20,000 college scholarships were awarded Indian students in 1980, and 17,000 were estimated for 1983. Other Indians go to college on non-BIA scholarships or use their own funds. The BIA also directly supports some tribally operated postsecondary institutions and offers continuing education programs in many communities. It is estimated that there are 40,000 Indians who are engaged in postsecondary school education, and there were 18,500 adult education enrollments in 1980.

Many people—including Commissioner Luepp in 1907, Lewis Meriam in 1928, and Indian leaders today—view education as the main process for helping Indians achieve economic, social, and political self-sufficiency. A considerable number of Indians have already attained that goal and are performing important roles both on and off the reservation.

Office of Indian Services

Division of Tribal Government Services. Aid to tribal governments involves giving funds and expert assistance to tribes to improve their governmental operations, to modify governing documents, to conduct elections, to prepare membership roles, to review and approve tribal attorney contracts, and to perform necessary operations in carrying out judgment awards—such as processing detailed plans for the utilization of judgment funds and preparing descendancy rolls of judgment award beneficiaries and handling enrollment appeals. These functions are concerned with those activities in which the tribal government is acting as a government per se rather than when it is functioning as the manager of service programs for its members; the self-determination program provides assistance to improve managerial capacity. This is a difficult distinction to understand, and the 1982 budget justification furnished the following example: the Division of Tribal Government Services might work with a tribe in drafting an amendment to the tribe's constitution to permit tribal contracting and then assist, if necessary, in the process of tribal adoption of the amendment. Funding appropriated to the division of Self-Determination Services could then be used by the tribe to acquire the necessary expertise or training to successfully operate a contract.

The Division of Tribal Government Services also does the research on and the processing of petitions for federal acknowledgment of Indian groups not currently recognized by the bureau. Four such groups were recognized in 1981—the Paiute, Grand Traverse, Tunica-Biloxi, and Jamestown Clallam.

Funds have been provided by the BIA to the Department of Agriculture for 4-H and home extension services and the operational direction of the Youth Adult Conservation Corps (YACC) and Youth Conservation Corps (YCC) camps located on Indian reservations. Under the Maine Indian Claims Settlement Act the provision of Indian services to certain Maine Indians is a part of the function of the Division of Tribal Government Services.

The Judicial Services Branch is engaged in improving the judicial capacities of Indian tribes. In 1982 this branch provided technical assistance to 108 tribal courts and 28 courts of Indian offenses (Code of Federal Regulations [CFR] Courts) operated on reservations (see Chapter 4, section on "Tribal Courts," for further discussion). Assistance is provided for the technical aspects of establishing and maintaining Indian courts and for helping them achieve due process and equal protection for the individuals appearing before them. This assistance includes reviewing tribal ordinances and helping tribes upgrade law

Table 3.4
Social Services Cases and Costs for 1982 ($ in Thousands)

	Cases per Month or Year	1982 Estimates
General Assistance	57,750 per month	$ 54,863
(TWEP)	(4,300) per month	(2,838)
Child Welfare Assistance	3,500 per month	13,000
Miscellaneous Assistance	1,325 per year	1,137
Indian Child Welfare Act Grants	------	10,000
		79,000

Source: Bureau of Indian Affairs, "Budget Justification for FY 1982" (January 1981).

and order codes. Tribal court cases were expected to increase from 132,000 in 1982 to 141,000 in 1983.

Division of Social Services. Welfare assistance grants are provided to tribal members living on or near reservations only if the recipient establishes need and cannot obtain assistance from state or local public welfare agencies. State assistance standards are used in determining the amount of the grants.

There are four types of grants or contracts—the number of people and costs involved are indicated in Table 3.4.

1. *General Assistance*: consists of (a) direct financial assistance for living expenses to families and individuals whose income is below state standards, (b) nonmedical institutional or custodial care for incapacitated adults, and (c) contracts with tribes to operate a Tribal Work Experience Program (TWEP). That innovative program replaces welfare with work experience, and those Indians who work on tribal projects receive $45 per month over their welfare entitlement.

2. *Child Welfare Assistance*: provides for care of abandoned, neglected, or handicapped children through foster homes, small group care, or institutions.

3. *Miscellaneous Assistance*: pays for burial expenses for the indigent without families or those whose survivors cannot afford funeral expenses. This fund also helps tribes with storage and distribution costs of federally provided food and with disaster emergencies.

4. *Indian Child Welfare Act Grants*: grants funds to tribes and Indian organizations to operate Indian child and family services programs such as licensing or regulating Indian foster and adoptive homes and providing facilities for counseling and temporary custody of Indian children,

homemaker services, day care, afterschool care, recreational activities, employment and training of tribal court personnel, adoptive subsidies, legal representation, and other services.

Other social services include the administration of the above programs, provision of professional counseling services to Indian individuals and families, and assistance to tribes to help develop social services programs.

Division of Law Enforcement Services. The BIA and Indian tribes provide law enforcement and detention services in areas where tribal governments have the authority to adopt and enforce tribal criminal and civil laws. One hundred and sixty-three reservations have this authority in twenty-three states. In 1980 there were 381 BIA and 878 tribal law enforcement officers serving approximately 475,000 Indians and patrolling 105,000 square miles of Indian country in 779 patrol vehicles, each averaging 24,000 miles of patrolling a year. Tribes were also serviced by sixteen BIA and ninety-five tribal and contract jails, and sixteen local units of government provided temporary confinement facilities without cost.

Estimates for 1982 were:

Complaints investigated	240,000
Nonenforcement responses	675,000
Prisoners detained per day	. 650

The cost of this program for 1983 was projected to be $36 million. (See Chapter 4, section on "Law and Order," for further discussion.)

Division of Housing Services. The great bulk of new housing for Indian reservations has been financed by the Department of Housing and Urban Development (HUD)—see Tables 3.1 and 3.2—although funds from HUD were greatly reduced in FY 1982. One of the functions of the BIA's Division of Housing Services has been to help tribes obtain federally funded housing from HUD and the Farmers Home Administration (FmHA).

This division also provides funds for new homes or for repair of existing homes to tribal members who cannot qualify for the housing programs of other federal agencies. The division also provides counseling and training for tribal housing staffs and tenants so that maximum benefit is obtained from the housing provided.

A survey in 1980 indicated the following statistics in regard to Indian housing needs.

Service population (families)	165,000
Less existing dwellings in standard condition	76,800

Families needing housing assistance	88,200
Houses suitable for renovation to standard	30,200
New homes required	58,000

Division of Self-Determination Services. The Indian Self-Determination and Education Assistance Act (PL 93–638) authorized the BIA to make grants to tribal governments to increase their ability to operate federal programs under contract. It also authorized and directed the contracting of such programs by the BIA when requested by the tribes. (See Chapters 2 and 4 for related discussions.)

As of 1980, 480 tribes had received BIA grants to improve management in such areas as personnel, finance, and property management and to sponsor community meetings and the establishment of branch offices. Also in 1980, 370 tribes contracted with the BIA for the operation of $200 million worth of programs. It should be noted that there are added costs to cover the overhead expenses of the tribes in administering these contracts, which amounted to an estimated $35 million in 1981. Bureau costs were not reduced because the bureau had to administer programs not contracted, so this self-determination contractual initiative costs the federal government more money. The justification is that it is an educational and a training process that will help tribes become self-sufficient over time. The activities of the Division of Self-Determination Services are intended to complement the aid to tribal governments program.

The tribes and the BIA are having difficulties in following the guidelines for money control and monitoring contracts and grants under this program (see Chapter 2). If this situation is not corrected some of these contracts and grants will be destructive to the goals of increasing the Indians' ability for self-government and improving their self-sufficiency.

A new proposal, called the "Small Tribes Management Initiative," was introduced in the BIA budget request for 1983. Its purpose is to provide small tribes (1,500 and less population) with a core-management capability and to enable them to function as stable and competent tribal governments. It is estimated that approximately 200 tribes are in need of this assistance. Additional financial funds might be obtained from self-determination grants and contracts. It was projected that fifteen consortiums might develop involving tribes with a population of fewer than 400 and that eighty tribes with between 400 and 1,500 population might make advances in tribal government under this program. This initiative is an effort to meet the question of tribal size and resources in relation to economic and political viability.

Navajo-Hopi Settlement Program. Not all fights or differences of opinion are between Indians and non-Indians. One of the bitterest and toughest issues to face the BIA and Congress has been the dispute between the Hopi and the Navajo over jurisdiction in the approximately 2.5 million-acre reservation set aside in 1882 by President Chester Arthur for the Hopi and "such other Indians as the Secretary of the Interior may see fit to settle thereon."[6] Approximately 300 Navajo were living in the area at the time of the order; by 1930 there were an estimated 3,300 Navajo there. In 1962 a U.S. district court decided (*Healing* v. *Jones*) that Grazing District No. 6 was Hopi, and that the two tribes had an undivided and equal interest in the remainder of the 1882 reservation. The basic problem was that Navajo were using much of the 1882 area outside of District 6. The Hopi wanted the area divided (partitioned) and the Navajo moved from the area assigned to the Hopi.

In 1974 Congress passed the Navajo-Hopi Land Settlement Act,[7] which provided for a mediator to be appointed by the director of the Federal Mediation and Conciliation Service, an interagency committee, and a tribal negotiating team to work on the partition problem. In 1977 the U.S. district court issued a judgment of partition, basically following the recommendation of the mediator. Congress passed another statute in 1980[8] setting deadlines for the division of the disputed area between the Hopi and the Navajo, for the transfer of 250,000 acres of land from the Bureau of Land Management (BLM) to the Navajo tribe to replace land lost from the 1882 reservation, for funds to assist in the necessary relocation of individuals, for life estates from some individuals, and for court resolution of issues arising because of the act. In 1981 the Relocation Commission presented its plan and report to Congress for completing relocation as required by law. In 1982 the main issues were conflicts with both tribes on stock reduction efforts and completion of the partition fence. The staff and resources of the Joint Use Office, established in 1972, are being transferred to the Phoenix and Navajo area offices, and those offices were directed to support the legislative intent and not be advocates for their respective tribes.

The actions taken by the Joint Use Office were significant. In summary, 160,000 sheep units were reduced, 76,000 acres of range were restored, 287 miles of boundary fencing and 765 miles of interior fencing constructed, 98 water sources were developed, and law enforcement and court programs were provided to ensure compliance with grazing regulations. The first year of reducing costs was 1982 when stock reduction and range restoration neared completion.

Through 1981 the Flagstaff Administrative Office (Joint Use Office), which was in charge of the Navajo-Hopi Settlement Program, reported to the commissioner of Indian affairs and was indicated on some BIA organization charts, including the one in the BIA budget justification for FY 1982.

Economic Development and Employment Programs

Employment Development. Employment programs for Indians consist of adult vocational training, job placement, work experience, and on-the-job training. Adult vocational training[9] and job placement provide the following assistance to individuals.

Transportation to training or employment locations
Weekly subsistence for those in training and subsistence until the first check is received by persons placed in jobs
Medical costs, including glasses
Purchase of necessary tools for training or employment
Rental and utility deposits
Shipment of household goods to training or employment location
Allowances for purchase of clothing, furniture, etc.
Tuition and related costs for training
Child care costs

Vocational training may be in any recognized vocation or trade, apprenticeship, or on-the-job training program. Any recognized school or other activity at any reasonable location may be utilized. The objective, of course, is to promote economic self-sufficiency skills. The utilization of these employment programs is indicated in Table 3.5. Some tribes have established training programs in cooperation with community colleges, federal agency staffs, and the staffs of various BIA activities, and funds are provided to help with these tribal efforts.

Work experience and on-the-job training in construction, management, and agricultural pursuits are provided through various BIA field programs.

Business Enterprise Development. This program involves promoting commercial, business, industrial, and tourism enterprises. In recent years this program has played a role in the establishment of 264 manufacturing and commercial activities, which employ over 15,500 workers and have an annual payroll in excess of $113 million. The BIA staff works with the tribes to get private firms to locate on reservations, obtain grants and contracts from other agencies, and gather data on which economic development decisions can be based. There is some question as to the cost-effectiveness of this program and the actual percentage of successes.[10]

The September 30, 1981, budget revision eliminated commercial enterprise development funds, and that program has been abolished. A new initiative was proposed for 1983—$10 million for a grant program

Table 3.5
Adult Vocational Training and Job Placement

Program	FY 1980	FY 1981	Est. FY 1982
Adult Vocational Training			
In training at start of year	2,469	2,492	2,391
New entries during year	4,101	3,800	4,084
Total number in training	6,570	6,292	6,475
Completions	2,307	2,202	2,266
Discontinued from training	1,771	1,699	1,748
Carryover to next FY	2,492	2,391	2,461
Average cost per trainee*	$4,105	$4,094	$4,049
Adjusted participation rate for FY	(4,068)	(3,810)	(4,100)
Discontinued from training is approximately 27%			
Placed in employment after completion of training is approximately 90%			
*Average cost per trainee is based on adjusted participation rate for FY.			
Employment Assistance			
Total participants	8,974	6,951	6,198
Average cost per participant	$1,556	$1,725	$1,867

Source: Bureau of Indian Affairs, "Budget Justification for FY 1982" (January 1981). The September 30 revision recommended elimination of funds for direct employment.

to help tribes obtain financial assistance or investment from private-sector sources to develop natural resources and strengthen economic enterprises on Indian reservations. Compared to previous Economic Development Administration efforts this proposal is lilliputian, but it does continue a long line of endeavors by the BIA to help Indian tribes make a breakthrough on the tribal self-sufficiency front.

Credit and Financing. Credit for financing business development is important, particularly to help Indian tribes, Indian organizations, and individual Indians and Alaska Natives utilize their own resources. The Office of Credit and Financing can make business and economic development loans (with resources made available by Congress) and assist Indian individuals and groups in obtaining financing from other sources.

In 1980 loans totaling $19.2 million were made by the BIA, and assistance and servicing for approximately 125 guaranteed loans with a face value of over $72.7 million were projected for 1982. It was estimated that there would be 12,500 BIA-supervised direct loans outstanding in 1982 with a value of $190 million.

Indian Arts and Crafts Board. The Indian Arts and Crafts Board promotes the development of Native American arts and crafts both to improve the native economy and to continue the vitality of a valuable American heritage. The board also operates three museums.

Road Construction and Maintenance. Road construction and maintenance on reservations are managed by the Division of Transportation and paid for with BIA funds. The replacement cost for the approximately 18,000 miles of improved roads on the BIA system has been estimated to exceed $2 billion. Road maintenance is not only to provide for public safety and convenience but to protect this investment. The September 30, 1981, budget for FY 1982 proposed over $44 million for improving and replacing roads and bridges and over $18 million for road maintenance.

Natural Resources Development

Forestry, Agriculture, and Water Programs. Eighty-three Indian agencies have natural resource programs that deal with agriculture; range, irrigation, and power operations; forestry, fish, and wildlife; recreation; and environmental quality. The BIA's objective is to use each of the 52 million acres of Indian land in such a way as to maximize its productiveness and income to the owners while using sound conservation practices to protect the resources.

Many Indian owners do not farm their land themselves, but for those that do, technical assistance in sound agricultural practices, soil analysis, establishing animal unit capacities, animal husbandry, water development, and pest control is provided by BIA professionals.

The BIA also helps maximize Indian productivity of 5.6 million acres of Indian forest by intensifying forest development and supervising an annual allowable cut of 1.05 billion board feet. The BIA supervises the sale of stumpage and subsequent harvesting and processing following modern forestry concepts. Protection from fire, insects, disease, and trespass is provided. Some tribes have forestry enterprises, and BIA foresters provide technical advice for these tribal operations. Forestry activities were estimated to have generated over 10,000 jobs in 1982.

Water is a valuable asset, particularly in the West. The BIA reviews Indian water entitlements and assists in conserving, developing, and using water resources. The review includes, for 274 reservations, history of reservation water rights, identification and inventory of available resources, identification and inventory of existing water uses, and identification of future water needs and development potentials.

Fish and wildlife resources—valued for their aesthetics, cultural significance, and economic potential—are important to Indians. Many tribes, through funding contracts with the BIA, are involved in developing, managing, and enhancing these resources. Approximately twenty tribes in the Pacific Northwest operate fish hatcheries, which release over 40 million salmon and trout fry annually. Inland fisheries in the Rocky Mountain Region and the Southwest provide well over 100,000 days of recreational fishing. The BIA's Division of Fish, Wildlife and Parks (established May 1980) is attempting to be more directly responsive to Indian fish and wildlife resource conservation and management needs. The tribes are increasingly interested in developing and protecting these resources, and the BIA, tribes, and state and other federal agencies are cooperating in the management of fish and game populations. The Pacific Northwest is the scene of much of this activity as a result of federal court decisions as well as the general importance of fisheries in the area.

Minerals and Mining. The high market demand for energy-producing minerals has greatly expanded the opportunities of many tribes as well as increased the workload of the BIA. Indian mineral resources are a significant portion of the U.S. total and may amount to 25 percent of the total mineral wealth of the United States. *Forbes* magazine estimated that Indian reservations contain "nearly 5% of U.S. oil and gas, one-third of its strippable low-sulfur coal, one-half of its privately owned uranium." The same article pointed out that mineral royalties were a "larger source of tribal revenue than either farming or ranching, yielded the tribes nearly $180 million last year (1980), not counting bonuses. Of that sum, $160 million came from oil and gas, much of it (37.5 percent) from the Osage reservation, the rest mainly from the Navajo, Jicarilla, Wind River and Uintah and Ouray reservations. Another $20 million was derived from hard minerals, mostly uranium and coal, largely from the Navajo, Crow, Laguna and Spokane reservations.[11]

The establishment of the BIA's Central Office Division of Energy and Mineral Resources in Lakewood, Colorado was designed to improve the bureau's ability to coordinate with and assist the U.S. Geological Survey and the Bureau of Mines in all phases of Indian mineral resource development. The historical practice of the use of realty personnel for mineral leases because of a limited number of mineral specialists is described as follows.

> It is physically impossible for the people assigned to this program (Minerals and Mining) to perform all the ministerial functions associated with over 20,000 mineral leases. For many years, personnel in BIA Area and Agency Realty offices have assumed these administrative tasks as part of their duties. Considering the fact that most of these people have little or no formal training in mineral development, they have performed extremely well. However, it is recognized that some form of training for these people is urgently needed. It is the intent of the newly established Central Office Division of Energy & Minerals to take the lead in providing training sessions for the Realty personnel.[12]

Table 3.6
Irrigation Construction Projects

Project	Amount
Ak Chin	$ 27,100,000
Cocopah (400 Indians)	1,250,000
Ft. McDowell	500,000
Ft. Mojave	2,200,000
White Mountain Apache (Cayon Day Unit)	1,500,000
Omaha (Blackbird Bend Unit)	900,000
Fallon	4,000,000
Navajo Irrigation Project	5,116,000
Standing Rock Sioux (Ft. Yates Unit)	1,000,000
Cheyenne River Sioux (Moreau River Unit)	500,000
Crow Creek Sioux (Tribal Farm Unit)	550,000
Lower Brule Sioux (Grass Rope Unit)	2,600,000
Safety of Dams	7,200,000
Engineering and Supervision	2,390,000

Source: Bureau of Indian Affairs, "Budget Justification for FY 1982" (January 1981).

Irrigation Construction, Operation, and Maintenance. There are eighty-three Indian irrigation projects that range in size from over 100,000 acres to scattered units of a few acres each. The BIA operates and maintains fifteen major projects, including those whose water delivery systems serve both Indian and non-Indian land. Tribes are assisted in the maintenance of smaller systems, especially when heavy equipment is required. The estimated cost of operation and maintenance in 1982 was $18.2 million, of which $11 million was to be collected from water users. Non-Indian users pay their full pro rata share of the operation and maintenance costs, but certain Indian users are subsidized: (1) those financially unable to pay their assessments, (2) those relieved of charges because of law or court decree, and (3) owners of small garden tracts. This subsidy covers about 94 percent of the operation and maintenance costs attributable to Indian lands.

The repayment of the large sums required for construction costs is not even considered.[13] President Carter zeroed in on uneconomic water projects, and irrigation projects, both Indian and non-Indian, frequently can be classed in this category. The Yuma irrigation project has been rebuilt several times, is not used by Indians, but does yield a subsidized income. The Colorado River Reservation has a few successful Indian operators, but most of the irrigated land is leased to non-Indians. The Navajo irrigation project seems to be having great difficulties. See Table 3.6 for a list of construction projects.

Office of Trust Responsibilities

Real Estate and Rights Protection. The core legal responsibility of the secretary of the Interior, exercised through the BIA, is that of acting as trustee for Indian land. Thus, all aspects of title, land ownership, land acquisition, disposal, land use, and resources connected with the land (water, minerals, range, forest) are involved in this trust responsibility. As indicated earlier, education may be the most important program leading to Indian individual and tribal group self-sufficiency, but the basic trust responsibility is with the Indian land base. Any inadequate exercise of this trust responsibility for tribal land subjects the government to suit for damages.

Examples of inadequate performance are excessive grazing on trust land, which endangers the land's productivity; inefficient land title services; and the almost impossible fragmentation of land ownership of individually owned trust land. BIA staff members are not necessarily culpable for these deficiencies—Indian tribes, pressure groups, and Congress bear equal shares of responsibility—but the secretary of Interior is legally responsible, and the Treasury must pay any award resulting from legal suits on these matters. The approximately 52 million acres of Indian trust land constitute a multibillion-dollar estate for which the secretary of Interior is legally responsible as long as the land is held in trust by the federal government for the Indian owners.[14]

The Division of Real Estate Services has historically been short of funds. This area is not glamorous like soil conservation, education, or vocational training, and the division has always had huge backlogs of work. Real estate services are provided through the eighty-five agency and field offices, the twelve area offices, and the central office. In addition to BIA statutes, real estate services must be responsive to federal statutes such as the National Environmental Policy Act, the Historic Preservation Act, the Archaeological Antiquities Act, and the Archaeological Resources Protection Act.

Major activities of realty personnel in the agencies and area offices include surface and subsurface leasing and modifications, rights-of-way grants and permits, land acquisition, land disposal, partitions and exchanges of interest in lands, the operation and maintenance of a systematic land-title ownership records system, lease and land contract compliance monitoring, appraisal of land and land evaluation services, land use planning, boundary surveys, land management counseling services, land resource inventory evaluation, and condemnation actions. The aim of these interrelated activities is to provide landowners with the essential data and assistance for the management and development of their energy, mineral, and land resources.

Leases supervised by realty personnel yielded over $198 million in 1979, including farm, business, oil and gas, and other mineral leases. In addition, landowners increase their land values through the land improvement and conservation stipulations in the lease documents. Technical advice to tribes and realty personnel from mineral, farm, forestry, and other specialists is utilized in making decisions and drawing up the provisions of lease documents.

The so-called heirship problem is dramatically illustrated in the following.

> Land ownership record keeping becomes more complicated each day because of the heirship problem and segregated surface and sub-surface ownership. There are over 200,000 surface tracts of individually owned trust land with an average tract ownership of 10 undivided interest owners. This means there are over 2,000,000 separate undivided interests to keep track of. Ownership in some tracts is so complicated that owners own an undivided interest in which the common denominator is in the quintillionths. If such tracts were leased, some undivided-interest owners would receive a fraction of a penny. This kind of ownership either makes it impossible to develop such tracts or severely restricts the development since all owners have to be contacted.[15]

Boundary surveys, called cadastral surveys, are performed by the Bureau of Land Management for the BIA. Recent funding budgeted by the BIA has resulted in approximately 700 miles of such surveys annually. Surveys are done on a priority basis, and those concerned with energy-related mineral development receive emphasis at present.

The Maine Indian Claims Settlement Act provided for the acquisition of 300,000 acres of land, and realty personnel will purchase the land selected by the tribe, provide records of title, and carry out other required realty services. Also, the issuance of trust patents to Alaska Native applicants as a result of recent legislation will require real estate services.

Other Office of Trust Responsibilities functions are related to environmental quality and the protection of Indian rights. The National Environmental Policy Act (NEPA) requires that all proposed major federal actions that may significantly affect the quality of the human environment be preceded by an environmental impact statement. The BIA carries out the intent of NEPA and other acts concerning the environment by examining proposed actions on Indian lands for their impact, such as the effects of mining and oil and gas exploration. When a significant impact is apparent, an environmental impact statement (EIS) is prepared so that the Indian people and the trustee (secretary of the Interior) are aware of the effects before proceeding. Funds have been transferred to the National Park Service for provision of archaeological clearance services prior to a contemplated land use, but the BIA was expected to perform these clearances beginning in 1983.

The Indian rights protection activity concerns those rights guaranteed Indian tribes through treaty, statute, or executive order and those actions required of a prudent trustee of Indian land. Since Indians are U.S. citizens, their rights as citizens are also involved. Citizenship, of course, involves responsibilities as well as rights, but there is not much emphasis on this aspect in BIA literature or functional statements. The emphasis in the organization manual, budget justification documents, speeches, and literature is on the responsibilities of the Congress and the government in general to Indians.

Significant areas involving important Indian rights are water rights, which are largely unquantified and for which there are many claimants, and hunting and fishing rights. "The majority of the tribes are not financially able to undertake the programs necessary to protect their rights and resources."[16]

Financial Trust Services. This BIA activity provides for the accounting for and the disbursing of tribal and individual Indian moneys deriving from the sale or lease of tribal resources such as land, timber, minerals, and water; the disbursing of per capita payments, judgments, awards, and claims; the preparation of trust fund histories, research projects involving special fiscal problems, special financial reports for use in litigation cases, trust fund data for legislative acts, and recommendations for the execution of the acts; investing the various revenues so as to maximize returns while still protecting the security of the funds; and, through an automated accounting system, monthly reports for the appropriate tribe and individual. As of September 30, 1980, there were $1,153 million invested with annual earnings of $121.4 million. Services were provided for 225 tribes and 230,000 individual accounts.

Personnel authorized to collect and disburse funds for land and property held in trust are stationed at most Indian agencies.

Facilities Management

The facilities engineering staff and the school facilities staff are located in Albuquerque, New Mexico. The facilities engineering staff provides architectural, engineering, construction management, contract, facilities management, and other technical services related to the construction of new facilities. This staff also coordinates any major rehabilitation, alterations, improvement, and maintenance of existing buildings, utilities, grounds, and other facilities. Design, construction, and technical assistance is also provided to Indians and Alaska Natives.

The BIA spent about $400 million in facility improvement and repair costs and about $160 million in replacement costs in 1982. Small amounts for new school construction were included in the original 1982 budget, as well as three noneducational structures.

The school facilities staff provides advice on the planning, design, construction, equipping, and evaluation of BIA, public, and tribally operated school facilities. The objective is to have building layout and equipment meet educational needs in the most effective way. The facilities engineering staff utilizes this information in the design and construction of school facilities, as do the tribes and—it is to be hoped—the states when they build schools primarily for Indians with federal funds.

Office of Administration

The Office of Administration is responsible for providing staff support to the commissioner and administrative support services to the director of Indian Education Programs. The following functions are involved: system development, automatic data processing, budget preparation, energy conservation, finance and accounting, management research and evaluation, personnel management, procurement, property management, contracting, program development and implementation, and safety management. The Administrative Services Center in Albuquerque, New Mexico, provides centralized information systems planning and development, automatic data processing (ADP) operations and support for the bureau, fiscal accounting, a centralized payroll, and automated personnel records systems.

The program development and budget function is in many ways similar to the budget and program evaluation offices of other agencies, but there are some additional complexities because of the need to meld tribal priorities and tribal comprehensive plans into the bureau's program development and budget requests. The contracting function includes negotiations with the tribes, as a result of the self-determination act, to help them perform functions formerly carried out by the BIA.

In an agency the size of the BIA the administrative workload is heavy; Table 3.7 gives some indication of the magnitude.

Other Interior Bureaus

Although the BIA is the central organization for Indian affairs in the Department of the Interior, other Interior bureaus are also involved. Indian-related activities carried out by these bureaus are funded in two ways: reimbursement, primarily by the BIA or a tribe, or directly from each bureau's own appropriation. Table 3.8 presents a summary of Indian services by these other U.S. Department of Interior bureaus and offices for fiscal year 1981.

Table 3.7
Selected Workload Factors--Adminstrative Services

Selected Workload Factor	U/M	FY 1980	FY 1981 (Estimate)	FY 1982 (Estimate)
I. Fiscal Transactions Processed [1]	No.	8,350,000	8,350,000	8,700,000
II. Procurement Actions Completed [2]	No.	70,234	74,000	77,000
III. Contracts Negotiated:				
1. Program Contracts P.L. 93-638 (Self-Determination)	No.	1,554	1,600	1,700
2. Service Contracts [3]	No.	2,900	3,000	3,200
IV. Grants Administered				
1. P.L. 93-638	No.	620	620	650
2. Child Welfare Act	No.	60	60	62
V. Personnel Actions Completed [4]	No.	46,000	45,000	47,000
VI. Property Inventory Items Maintained [5]	No.	175,000	175,000	182,000
VII. Volume of Records Maintained [6]	Cu. Ft.	124,529	125,000	130,000
VIII. Pieces of Franked Mail Dispatched [7]	No.	5,000,000	5,500,000	5,700,000

[1] Includes all types of intra- and inter-Bureau transactions processed during the year such as allotments, allocations, obligations, disbursements, collections, refunds, etc.

[2] This number takes into account procurement requests for acquisition of supplies, materials, property, utilities, space and other similar services used in the conduct of Bureau operated programs.

[3] Includes consultant software, construction contracts, and other program performance and service contracts.

[4] Processing of personnel actions such as accessions, promotions, separations, etc., requiring completion of SF-50.

[5] Includes only personal property items which are maintained on the property management inventory system and are accountable to an organization element.

[6] Figure represents total volume on hand including volume created during the year, less volume transferred to Record Center or destroyed.

[7] Based on semi-annual sampling data.

Source: Bureau of Indian Affairs, "Budget Justification for FY 1982" (January 1981), p. 115.

Table 3.8
Services for Indians, Interior Activities Other Than Bureau of Indian Affairs, 1981 ($ in Thousands)

Bureau, Service or Activity	Reimbursable	Non-Reimbursable
Fish and Wildlife Service		
Fish and game activities on various reservations	$ 1634.4	$ 3121.6
Geological Survey		
Conservation, geologic, water resource and mapping services; technical assistance for oil, gas, coal etc. on Indian reservations	4315.6	3075.8
Bureau of Land Management		
Realty conveyances, realty records and cadastral surveys on Indian land	1300.0	7960.0
Bureau of Mines		
Assessment of mineral potential on Indian reservations	1547.0	--
Office of Surface Mining		
Abandoned mine land restoration programs	--	520.9
National Park Service		
Archeological, cultural and recreational assistance to Indian groups	897.6	1160.1
Bureau of Reclamation		
Navajo irrigation construction	11480.0	--
Construction, operation and maintenance of various Indian projects	--	31546.0
Office of the Secretary		
Board of Indian Appeals	--	236.0
Indian Probate	--	1118.0
Office of Solicitor--legal work and counsel on Indian matters	40.0	3500.0
Total	$21214.6	$52238.4

Source: Information from bureaus and activities in response to a memorandum dated November 20, 1981, from the director, Office of the Budget, Department of the Interior, requesting programs and funds for Indians for fiscal year 1981.

The U.S. Fish and Wildlife Service provides technical assistance to tribes in the preparation of fish management plans and in the implementation of such plans, especially concerning fish hatchery operations and fish stocking for Indian reservations. It also advises on predatory animal and prairie dog control and wildlife management planning, including inventory and management plans for deer and other big game.

The U.S. Geological Survey (USGS) conducts inspections, reviews permits or lease plans, and makes environmental assessments for oil and gas, coal, and other energy programs on Indian reservations. This assistance includes help in monitoring royalty accounting for the Indians' share of income from oil and gas production. The USGS also carries out field geologic and geophysical investigations of the mineral potential of Indian reservations; conducts water resource investigations, including quantitative and qualitative studies; and prepares aerial topographic and other maps for Indian reservations.

Cadastral surveys and the issuance of land patents for the transferal of land to Alaska Natives (under the Alaska Native Claims Settlement Act), in Maine, and to other recipients are performed by the Bureau of Land Management. The Bureau of Mines helps determine the mineral potential on Indian reservations. For example, the Office of Surface Mining worked with the Navajo and Crow tribes on land recovery plans related to surface mining in 1981.

The archaeological investigations by the National Park Service help both the BIA and the tribes. The Park Service also advises on facilities such as the Navajo fairgrounds and the Yakima cultural center, tribal park and recreation facilities, and the rehabilitation of Hopi villages. It also has investigated approximately 4,000 native historic sites and cemeteries under the provisions of the Alaska Native Claims Settlement Act. The service also provides technical assistance to tribes on ranger, park, and museum activities.

The Bureau of Reclamation is constructing the waterworks for the Navajo irrigation project with reimbursable funds from the BIA. With its own appropriated funds, the Bureau of Reclamation worked with approximately fifteen tribes in 1981 on various stages of irrigation and water projects including, in some instances, their impacts on fishery and wildlife resources. Many of these projects may help support Indian claims to water rights.

In addition to the assistant secretary for Indians affairs, the Office of the Secretary of Interior includes the Office of Hearings and Appeals and the Office of the Solicitor. The Office of Hearings and Appeals is in charge of Indian probate hearings, claims under the Alaska Native Claims Settlement Act, and administrative appeals on Indian matters. The Office of the Solicitor provides legal advice and counsel regarding Indian affairs.

The special expertise and organizational capability of the various agencies in the Interior Department are utilized for services to Indians when appropriate. However, the various bureau programs are not always in harmony with BIA objectives—this aspect of Interior bureau relationships is discussed in Part Two of this book.

Other Federal Government Indian Activities

As indicated in Chapter 2, many agencies and offices of government have had various responsibilities in connection with Indian policy and services over the years. Federal funding for Indian reservation programs in fiscal year 1970 totaled approximately $600 million of which $309 million, about 50 percent, was administered by the Bureau of Indian Affairs. The breakdown by department was Agriculture, $22 million; Commerce, $22 million; Defense, $2 million; Office of Economic Opportunity, $33.5 million; Health, Education and Welfare, $170 million; Housing and Urban Development, $22.5 million; Interior, $314 million; Labor, $6.5 million; and the Small Business Administration, $4.5 million.[17]

Tables 3.1 and 3.2 indicate the more recent funding history of federal agency Indian programs. The total funding for FY 1980 and FY 1981 was over $3 billion for each year, of which the BIA accounted for approximately $1 billion. Other agencies accounted for the other $2 billion annually. Expenditures for 1982 and 1983 were reduced.

Indian Health Service (IHS)

Of those programs in other government agencies that specifically relate to Indians, the most important is the Indian Health Service (IHS), a bureau within the Health Services Administration of the Public Health Service. IHS-operated health facilities in FY 1982 included 48 hospitals, 99 health centers, and 300 smaller health stations and satellite clinics. In addition to the IHS and tribal health delivery systems, the IHS operates a contract health care system for services not available in IHS or tribal facilities. Maximum utilization of health resources for Indians is achieved through many direct and indirect cooperative programs operated by the IHS, the tribes, and various state agencies.

Some tribes choose to operate directly major portions of the health care system using IHS funds. For example, in 1981 fully functioning health programs were being operated by the Seneca nation of New York, the Menominee tribe of Wisconsin, the Norton Sound Health Corporation, and the Bristol Bay Area Health Corporation of Alaska. Hospitals were being operated by the Creek nation in Oklahoma, the Navajo Health Foundation in Arizona, and the Norton Sound and Bristol Bay organizations.[18]

The IHS also coordinates the program to provide essential water and sanitation facilities for Indian homes and communities on reservations, an interdepartmental activity carried out by HUD, the BIA, and the IHS. With the completion of projects authorized through 1980, more than 900 of the 1,500 Indian and Alaskan native communities were provided with community water and/or sewer systems serving about 127,000 Indian and Alaska Native homes. Half of these homes were built or renovated under Indian housing programs.

In view of the jobless and poverty rates on many reservations accompanied by a high birth rate, I asked the BIA and the IHS whether there were any family planning programs available to Indians. There is no family planning program in either agency. If asked, BIA social workers may refer Indian clients to the IHS for medical advice, but no policy or guidelines exist. The IHS will provide information on birth control methods when appropriate as a part of its medical services so that Indians wishing to regulate the size of their families may do so. There is no goal of reducing the size of families. This is a private matter for Indian families. Live births per 1,000 population in 1978 were 31.5 for Indians and 15.3 for the population at large.[19]

Department of Justice

The Department of Justice conducts several activities that are of importance to Indians.[20] The Civil Rights Division enforces the civil rights of American Indians, including prohibition of discriminatory conduct in voting, employment, public education, housing, and public accommodations and facilities as well as protecting the rights of prisoners and mental patients. Cooperation with the BIA, IHS, Administration of Native American Programs, National Congress of American Indians, the National Tribal Chairmens' Association, the National American Court Judges Association, and other Indian groups with offices in Washington results in alleged infractions being reported to the Department of Justice, which carries out appropriate investigations and actions. Close contacts also exist with U.S. attorneys, local legal aid offices, tribal councils, state officials, and other interested groups (e.g., Native American Rights Fund, All Indian Pueblo Council, National Youth Council) in states in which investigations or lawsuits are being conducted. The Office of Revenue Sharing and the Equal Employment Opportunity Commission refer cases for investigation and possible litigation. Reports of the U.S. Commission on Civil Rights are also available.

In 1973 the Office of Indian Rights (OIR) was established within the Civil Rights Division of the Justice Department in order to allow the development of expertise in Indian civil rights. However, this office has not been funded since 1980.

Since the Justice Department is the government's trial lawyer, the Indian Resources Section, in the Land and Natural Resources Division, supervises the litigation of civil suits in which the United States seeks to protect tribal assets and jurisdiction. Litigation for individual and tribal rights to property, hunting, fishing, and water is also this section's responsibility as well as supervising litigation involving alleged infringement by states of tribal rights in regard to taxation, liquor control, law enforcement, reservation boundaries, and other related matters. Approximately 540 cases were in process as of January 31, 1981.[21] The

Indian Resources Section initiates litigation only when requested to do so by the Department of Interior.

The Community Relations Service (CRS) of the Department of Justice, with the voluntary cooperation of the disputants, helps resolve problems that cause tension and conflicts. Although education, administration of justice, and economic matters are the most frequent problems, the CRS has assisted Indian groups in conflict situations involving treaty rights, hunting and fishing rights, and intratribal conflicts such as the one at Wounded Knee in the early 1970s. Training in conflict management and community relations techniques is given to tribal officials, Indian police, and education agencies.[22]

The ambivalence of Justice Department's posture is illustrated by the fact that it not only litigates for the Indians as described above, but it also has the responsibility of defending the United States in the Court of Claims against claims made by Indians. Active cases in January 1981 totaled 107.[23]

Other Federal Programs

Indian housing, financed by the Department of Housing and Urban Development, and Indian economic activity, funded by the Economic Development Administration, have virtually come to a halt under the Reagan administration. The Administration for Native Americans in the Department of Health and Human Services has a broad authorization to promote economic and social self-sufficiency for American Indians, native Hawaiians, and Alaska Natives. The Office of Indian Education Programs under the Department of Education administers grants to local educational agencies to meet the special educational needs of Indian children and adults. The Department of Labor granted over $1 billion for Native American employment and training from 1975 through 1981, and funds for Indians under the Comprehensive Employment Training Act (CETA) totaled over $177 million in 1981.[24]

In emergency situations Commodity Credit Corporation feed grains may be donated to Indian tribes for livestock feeding by the Department of Agriculture. There are many other federal programs that are available to Indians on the same basis as they are to other citizens.

Summary

The Bureau of Indian Affairs has been termed "a government in miniature." It really is more than that. It combines the tremendous variety of many local and state functions with federal functions. It has the added duties of a trustee that are normally found only in the private sector. Involved are direct service operations, technical assistance, training, the monitoring of work contracted out, and the surveillance of reimbursable work done by other Interior bureaus. The BIA also interrelates with other government services for Indian citizens. Complicating the BIA's work are racial and cultural factors, a guilt complex on the part of many citizens, and a "you owe it to us" attitude on the part of many Indians. An estimated 5,000 statutes, many treaties, and thousands of court decisions on Indian policy and procedure add to the complexity.

4

TRIBAL GOVERNMENT

The establishment of reservations resulted in placing many formerly moving bands or groups together, sometimes of the same language group (such as the Sioux or Navajo) and at other times of different groups (such as the Arapaho and Shoshone). The mixture of groups, concentrated on the land area of a reservation, was the focus of Indian–non-Indian relations. There were many leaders of former largely independent bands on the Pine Ridge Reservation in South Dakota. Other examples are the Wind River Reservation in Wyoming, where both northern Arapaho and Shoshone groups were placed, and the confederated tribes of the Warm Springs Reservation in Oregon. The removal of Indians—either because the Indians followed the game west as it disappeared from the East or because of pressure, as in the case of the Five Civilized Tribes—also resulted in Indian groups' invading the traditional areas of other groups.

Basic Concepts

Nature of Tribes

"Tribe" among the North American Indians originally meant a body of persons bound together by blood ties who were socially, politically, and religiously organized, and who lived together, occupying a definite territory and speaking a common language or dialect.

With the relegation of Indians to reservations, the word "tribe" developed a number of different meanings. Today, it can be a distinct group within an Indian village or community, the entire community, a large number of communities, several different groups or villages speaking different languages but sharing a common government, or a widely scattered number of villages with a common language but no common government.[1]

How does the Bureau of Indian Affairs or anyone else determine that a group of Indians is a tribe? For a group that is not recognized as a tribe by the federal government but wishes to be so recognized, the BIA recently established that the following criteria are necessary.

1. A statement of facts establishing that the petitioner has been identified from historical times until the present on a substantially continuous basis, as "American Indian," or "aboriginal."
2. Evidence that a substantial portion of the petitioning group inhabits a specific area or lives in a community viewed as American Indian and distinct from other populations in the area, and that its members are descendants of an Indian tribe which historically inhabited a specific area.
3. A statement of facts which establishes that the petitioner has maintained tribal political influence or other authority over its members as an autonomous entity throughout history until the present.
4. A copy of the group's present governing document or a statement describing the membership criteria and the procedures through which the group currently governs its affairs and its members.
5. A list of current members and a copy of each available list of former members, based on criteria such as descendancy from an autonomous historical tribe.
6. The membership of the petitioning group is composed principally of persons who are not members of any other North American Indian tribe.
7. The petitioner is not, nor are its members, the subject of congressional legislation which has expressly terminated or forbidden the federal relationship.[2]

The Supreme Court held in *U.S.* v. *John*[3] that even though the Mississippi Choctaw were a remnant of the Choctaw tribe and had not had a continuous governmental organization, they lived in Indian country; the federal government, rather than the state, had control over major crimes committed by Indians; and that by organizing under the Indian Reorganization Act the group had power that its members would not have had as individuals. Tribes already recognized by the federal government and receiving services are excluded from the above criteria, but serious questions are being raised about small groups—such as Alaska Native villages of just a few people and small rancherias with few residents or owners—that up until now have often been counted as "tribes."

Who Is an Indian?

Tribes or Indian groups are made up of individuals. The question, Who is an Indian? has varying answers and denotes one of the complexities of the interrelationships between tribal, local, and state governments.

Even tribal groups have differing criteria for determining their own membership. For the Cherokee in Oklahoma descent from a person on the 1906 roll (no matter how small the percentage of Indian blood may be) is all that is required. Therefore, in order to limit the fiscal impact on the federal government, the BIA has an informal agreement with the state of Oklahoma that the U.S. government will be responsible for the welfare payments of Indians with one-fourth or more Indian blood and the state will be responsible for those with less than one-fourth Indian blood. Various tribes specify one-half, one-fourth, or another degree of Indian blood for membership eligibility. The U.S. census counts anyone who declares himself or herself to be an Indian. Some federal statutes define eligibility for certain services as a minimum of 25 percent Indian blood.

Intermarriage between Indians and members of other races has resulted in much dilution of Indian blood, and there are even blond, blue-eyed members of Indian tribes. As indicated in Chapter 1, there may be 10 million to 20 million persons with some Indian blood, but a very small percentage of them identify themselves as being primarily Indian. In some cases the full bloods and mixed bloods in a given group have not gotten along very well. The Utes on the Uintah and Ouray Reservation decided to separate the mixed bloods and the full bloods. A division of assets was provided for in 1954, and the mixed bloods (one-half degree or less of Indian blood) are no longer members of the tribe.[4]

There are full-blooded Indians that are fully acculturated to the dominant society and no longer operate in a tribal group. In contrast, there are persons with but a trace of Indian blood who are in every sense culturally Indian. Tribal purity is also diminishing due to the increasing frequency of intermarriage between members of different tribes.

Indian Reservations

Indian reservations were originally areas of land with specific boundaries for Indian use. They were created through treaties, congressional acts, executive orders, and agreements. After the policy of tribal ownership in common was changed in some instances and land allotted to individual Indians, much reservation land has been sold by individual Indians

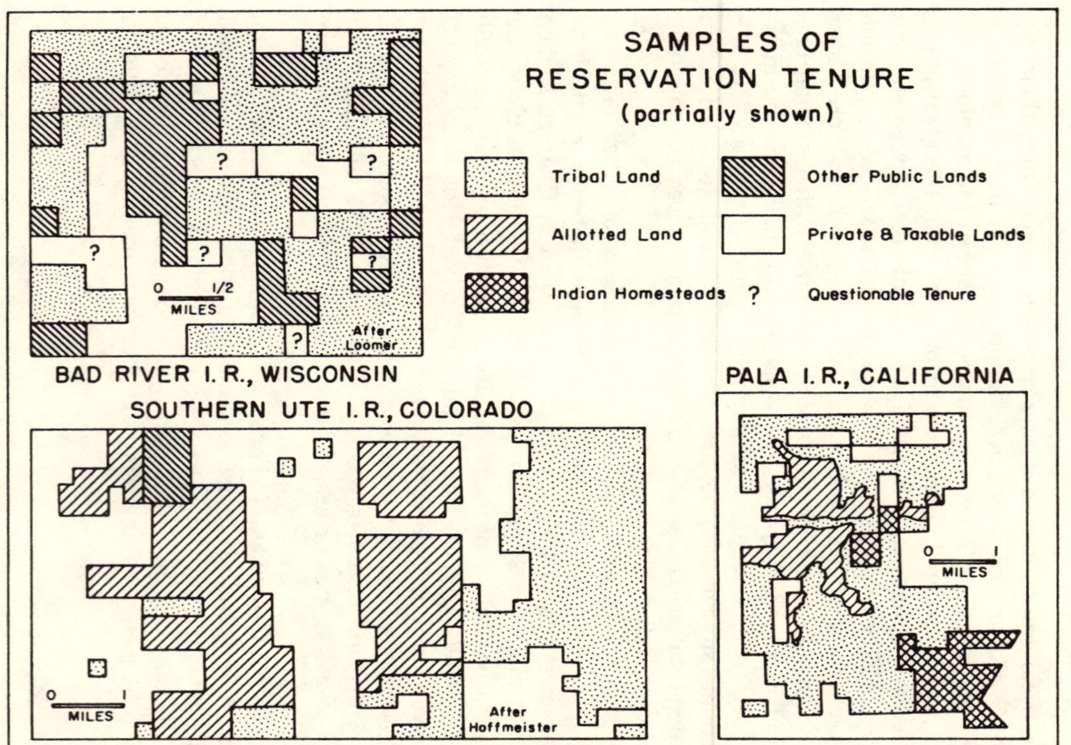

Figure 4.1. Samples of reservation tenure. (Source: Imre Sutton, *Indian Land Tenure* [New York: Clearwater Publishing Co., 1975], Figure 5, p. 85, reprinted by permission.)

who preferred cash to land, and many sales have been to non-Indians. For example, the Port Madison Reservation of the Suquamish tribe in the state of Washington has a land area of 7,276 acres, but only 37 percent of it has been retained by fifty Indians. The rest of the land within the exterior boundaries of the original reservation is owned by 3,000 non-Indians who live within the boundaries.[5] That portion of the Navajo Reservation that lies in Arizona and Utah is almost entirely tribal trust land, while much of the reservation in New Mexico is checkerboarded with non-Indian holdings. The major existing reservations are shown in Figure 1.4, and the land ownership patterns shown in Figure 4.1 indicate the situation on many reservations.

As is obvious from the movement of Indians to all geographical parts of the United States there is no requirement that Indians must stay on a reservation. They are as free to move about as any other citizens of the state wherein they reside, and they may also move as freely as other citizens throughout the United States.

Tribal Government Structures and Authorities

Of the 499 federally recognized Indian entities, 280 have written constitutions or organic documents. Only 4 of the 19 Pueblo groups (small tribes primarily in the Rio Grande Valley of New Mexico) have written documents; the other 15 have traditional governments. Tribal governments have authority over tribal members, other Indian residents, and for some types of civil cases, non-Indians. The area of tribal government jurisdiction is generally the land that lies within the exterior boundary of a reservation.

There are a variety of tribal government structures at present. Most of the larger groups have governments patterned on guidelines furnished by the BIA after 1934, particularly those tribes whose traditional governing apparatus was no longer pertinent (e.g., small bands) or whose aboriginal forms had been stamped out or atrophied as the result of the takeover of government functions after 1870 by the Indian agent and his staff. Current constitutions and bylaws are based on non-Indian ideas rather than on Indian tradition, which, in some cases in which several tribes or groups were thrown together, might not have been particularly pertinent in any event.

In addition to all the powers vested in any Indian tribe or tribal council by existing law, Section 16 of the Indian Reorganization Act (IRA) provided that constitutions and bylaws would vest the tribes with the authority to employ legal counsel; prevent the sale or encumbrance of tribal land or other assets without the consent of the tribes; and negotiate with federal, state, and local governments. Other provisions frequently found in constitutions give tribal governments the authority to determine tribal membership; assign tribal land to individuals; manage economic affairs; appropriate money for salaries or other public purposes; levy taxes, license fees, or community labor in lieu thereof; control the conduct of members of the reservation by enactment of ordinances, employment of police, and operation of a court system; regulate the conduct of trade; establish rules for domestic relations; and enact ordinances for the general welfare.

Corporate charters under the IRA establish authority for tribal economic activity through corporations with perpetual succession. These charters generally provide that supervision over powers exercised under the charter may be terminated upon request by the tribe and approval of the secretary of the Interior. For example, the tribal charter of the Saginaw Chippewa Indians of lower Michigan provided that

> transactions involving land leases or timber sales, certificates of interest in corporate property, the borrowing of money, the making of contracts calling for money payments, and other actions required approval of the Secretary of the Interior during an interim period of 5 years. Thereafter, the tribe could request the Secretary to relinquish his control over any or all of the actions, the Secretary having authority to grant and request or require the tribe to vote on the question.[6]

The Saginaw Tribal Council made such a request in the form of a resolution, and the secretary notified the council on July 18, 1949, that he saw "no reason why this Department should continue to exercise supervision" over the items in question. However, transfer of complete responsibility, including that for tribal trust land, requires legislation. The assumption of responsibility by tribes under corporate procedures has been limited (only three tribes had done so up to 1970) as most tribes have not sought to carry on business under their charters.[7]

Although the IRA did not require it, the secretary of Interior has continued to review and approve tribal actions under the provisions of the constitutions which were adopted by the tribes and approved by the secretary.[8] This policy in part may be a carry-over from the practice prior to 1934 when many tribes had constitutions subject to the approval of the secretary of Interior and based on his general supervisory powers. The tribes are now encouraged by the BIA to remove the secretarial review and approval provisions except where required by law. The earlier constitutions were "very simple in style and subject matter" according to William Zimmerman,[9] but after 1934 the constitutions were different. They were drafted for the most part by Interior lawyers, who worked closely with the tribes, and aimed at specifying in detail the operation of a tribal government.

In January 1982, in various parts of the Supreme Court's opinion in a tribal taxing authority case in which the Court held that the Jicarilla Apache tribe could impose an oil and gas severance tax on non-Indian lessees of tribal land, the Court emphasized that the secretary of Interior had approved the constitution of the Jicarilla tribe pursuant to the IRA and that he had approved the tribal severance tax ordinance in question. The Court stated that this approval authority is a constraint on tribal power and helps minimize concern over possible unfair use of such power or actions that would be inconsistent with national policies. Another constraint is the plenary power of Congress to limit tribal powers.[10] This view of the Court raises questions about the current attitude of the Interior Department and committee staffs on Capitol Hill that the secretary of Interior has no authority or responsibility over tribal constitutions after adoption or responsibility for approving tribal ordinances.

Today tribal organizations fall into three categories: (1) officially approved Indian organizations pursuant to federal statutory authority—224 groups (lower 48 states: IRA 132 and Oklahoma Indian Welfare Act 22; Alaska: Alaska Native Act 70, of which 53 are also incorporated under state law); (2) officially approved Indian organizations outside of specific federal statutory authority—56 (lower 48 states: 55; Alaska: 1); and (3) traditional Indian organizations recognized without formal federal approval of organizational structure—219 (lower 48 states: 71; Alaska: 148, of which 73 villages are also incorporated under state law). Combining the above three categories results in a total of 499 Indian entities eligible for BIA services. In the lower 48 states and Alaska, a total of 280 Indian entities have formally approved organic documents as defined in categories one and two above.[11]

The Navajo, the largest tribe in the United States, rejected the IRA and cannot now adopt a constitution under its provisions. This tribe is classified in category two above and has no written constitution as such. The Navajo pass ordinances and resolutions, and the present three volumes of such enactments constitute their governing documents. The evolving governing structure contains elements of traditional Navajo society modeled on the federal authority structure. "From a family centered, locally oriented, loosely structured, non-authoritarian society, a collectivistic, tribe-centered, authoritarian nationalistic modern state is being created."[12] According to Mary Shepardson the traditional system slows up the rate of change, but the Navajo Tribal Council has achieved a consensus of modernists and traditionalists that will result in the institutionalization of the new system.[13]

Four groups are involved in the present Navajo government: the tribal lawyer, elected officers, elected delegates, and hired personnel.

Although Shepardson wrote in 1963, her description of the job of the tribe's chairman is still generally accurate. The chairman must speak Navajo and English; he must be at ease at a sing, in a hogan, in a modern U.S. home, and on television. He is expected to have business and organizational ability, be able to deal effectively with federal and state officials, work out arrangements with corporations (especially coal and oil companies), and obtain concessions from the non-Indian society. If he moves too fast the traditionalists will be upset; if he modernizes too slowly the aggressive younger group will be disappointed. "His election base is the whole Reservation; his field of activity is the whole country." Shepardson continues: "Population increase and new, complicated economic problems cannot be handled with the old informal structures; the new system is needed because it is geared to new problems."[14] One of the strengths of the Navajo is their ability to adapt and at the same time retain much of their tradition and a feeling of being Navajo. Thus, they change without losing their identity.

Law and Order—The Judicial System

Several recent court decisions have shaken both Indians and non-Indians. The so-called Boldt decision on fishing rights stunned the Pacific Northwest non-Indian community by alloting 50 percent of the fish catch to the Indians.[15] The Oliphant decision jolted the recently developing concept of tribal government criminal jurisdiction over non-Indians by limiting tribal jurisdiction to Indians.[16]

From early times until around 1870 the general policy was to attempt to have tribes manage their own internal affairs, including law and order. "Traditional methods of trial and punishment included restitution, community scorn, banishment, and death."[17] The sovereignty of tribes over major offenses committed by Indians in Indian country was greatly modified by the Major Crimes Act of 1885 (23 Stat. 362, 385), which placed such offenses under federal rather than state or tribal jurisdiction. The seven original major crimes of murder, manslaughter, rape, assault with intent to kill, arson, burglary, and larceny have been added to from time to time, and the current list is now found in 18 USC 1153. These offenses by Indians in Indian country are prosecuted by federal district attorneys in federal courts.

As the BIA became involved in the administration of tribal affairs it had to face the problems of trial and punishment, as well as of policing for law and order. In 1884 courts were established for Indian offenses, and these still operate for twenty-nine tribes or groupings; the current regulations continue the provision that the jurisdiction of these courts is limited to Indians.[18] The purpose of the regulations is to provide machinery for law enforcement where there is no adequate tribal law or custom or for which "no adequate substitute has been provided under Federal or State law."[19] The regulations do not apply where state laws are operative, and for tribes that have a constitution, the regulations apply only until a law and order code has been adopted by the tribe and approved by the secretary of Interior.

Investigation, Arrest, and Prosecution

Two aspects of the law and order system are (1) policing, arrest, and prosecution and (2) the trial of and assessment of penalties for offenders.

The U.S. Commission on Civil Rights reported the following testimony of Michael Hawkins, the U.S. district attorney for Arizona.

> The single most dramatic thing . . . I saw [upon taking office as a U.S. attorney] was significant duplication and overlap of the law enforcement services being offered either by tribal police agencies, the Bureau of Indian Affairs Law Enforcement Services, and the FBI. I found instances, for example, where three separate reports were being prepared by three separate agencies, witnesses being interviewed three and four times by different agencies—no sense, no standards, no guidelines as to the referral of those reports, nothing beyond informal understandings between individuals about investigative jurisdictions between the agencies. I felt a compelling need, at least on my part, to deal with that situation.[20]

The district attorney continued:

> Beyond the cost to taxpayers of such duplication of responsibility, this overlap posed significant practical problems for federal law enforcement. Witnesses to crimes were often interviewed by two or three separate agencies, sometimes producing such inherently conflicting statements that subsequent criminal prosecutions were rendered enormously difficult, if not impossible.

Therefore, the district attorney worked out guidelines for the Navajo in cooperation with the tribe, the BIA, and the FBI, and these guidelines were expanded to other Indian groups in the state. The result has been the elimination of overlap, and only single investigations are carried out.

The House Committee on the Judiciary noted this situation in hearings on the authorization bill for the Department of Justice appropriation for FY 1982 and heard testimony from former District Attorney Michael Hawkins as well as from the Civil Rights Commission and the FBI. It was obvious that the FBI cannot be readily available to all places on all Indian reservations. In 1980 the FBI estimated it spent the equivalent of thirty-five full-time agents' time to police 50 million acres, and the FBI man was generally the last to arrive on the scene. The BIA has trained criminal investigators who conduct investigations of crimes on most reservations that are not under state jurisdiction. In a 1975 task force report on Indian matters the Department of Justice pointed out that most U.S. attorneys—who are the only ones who can prosecute a federal crime—will not accept BIA or tribal investigative reports, but insist that the FBI conduct an independent investigation. Further, most U.S. attorneys also require that criminal cases be presented to a grand jury before an arrest warrant is issued. Long delays ensue, and the offender typically remains at large and often goes unpunished. Further, the FBI testified to the committee that many U.S. attorneys considered the prosecution of Indian cases undesirable work and that no one had been assigned to become proficient in the prosecution of Indian crimes.

The situation needs attention. The 1975 Justice Department task force reported a crime rate for Native Americans that was 50 percent higher than for rural America as a whole: "violent crimes eight times greater, murder three times greater, and assault nine times greater."[21] The greatest single cause of most crimes on reservations is alcohol. In a 1977 BIA survey all reservations that reported indicated that over 90 percent of their court cases were alcohol related. "Alcoholism is partly a result of the depressed economic situation on most reservations." Juvenile and family relations matters, often because of the influence of alcohol in destabilizing family life, is "another important Indian court activity."[22]

The Question of Jurisdiction

The BIA courts for Indian offenses were and are limited to jurisdiction over Indians, which has been the general administrative policy. These courts also have limited authority—in most cases the maximum penalty is six months at hard labor or restitution and a five-dollar fine in the case of property damage.

The courts established under the IRA constitutions are very similar except that they are under tribal rather than BIA supervision. Under the 1968 Indian Civil Rights Act tribal courts are limited to a maximum fine of $500 and maximum imprisonment of six months. The federal government continues to have jurisdiction over major crimes. Thus, until recently there have been severe limitations on the authority of tribal courts: They could deal only with Indians; they were limited in the penalties that could be prescribed; and they had no jurisdiction over major offenses.

However, many Indian leaders believed that Indian governments, as "sovereign" entities, should have jurisdiction over both Indians and non-Indians within the exterior boundaries of a reservation. The Interior Department and congressional committees have recently been expressing this same view. This desire of the Indians came about in part because of poor law enforcement and a lack of speedy justice by the state and federal governments when cases fell into their jurisdictions.[23]

An illustration of the problem is a case involving Oliphant, one of the 3,000 non-Indian residents of the Suquamish Port Madison Reservation, who was arrested on August 19, 1973, by tribal police during the annual Chief Seattle Day celebration and charged with assaulting an officer and resisting arrest. The tribe had known that thousands of people would be present for the three days of the celebration and had requested that the local county provide police assistance. The county provided only one deputy for one eight-hour period. The tribe had also requested help from the BIA's Western Washington Agency, but since (under PL 280) the state had jurisdiction, the BIA had told the tribe it would have to provide its own law enforcement.[24] When Oliphant was arrested, at approximately 4:30 a.m., the only law enforcement officers available were tribal deputies.

Oliphant challenged the tribal court's jurisdiction, but the tribe was upheld by the U.S. district court which stated: "Without the exercise of jurisdiction by the Tribe and its courts, there could have been no law enforcement whatsoever on the Reservation during this major gathering which clearly created a potentially dangerous situation with regard to law enforcement."[25]

The Ninth Circuit Court of Appeals affirmed the stand of the district court, saying that the "power to preserve order on the reservation . . . is a sine qua non of the sovereignty that the Suquamish originally possessed" that had not been modified by a treaty or a statute.[26] This statement pleased the advocates of Indian sovereignty and deeply worried the non-Indian residents of many reservations in many states.[27]

Thus, the appeal of this case to the Supreme Court was a time of high drama for Indians and non-Indians alike. There were broad implications that everyone recognized. The states of Washington and South Dakota appeared before the court as amici curiae, presenting briefs that held that Indian tribes did not have jurisdiction to try and punish non-Indians. The attorneys general of Montana, Nebraska, New Mexico, North Dakota, Oregon, and Wyoming joined in the briefs. Arguing for the Indians' view and that of Interior, the solicitor general of the United States, as amicus curiae, stated that tribes did have jurisdiction to try and punish non-Indians. National Indian organizations also filed advisory briefs.

The Supreme Court reversed the court of appeals decision, holding that Indian tribal courts do not have inherent criminal jurisdiction to try and punish non-Indians.[28] The Supreme Court cited the history of the assumption that Indian courts do not have jurisdiction over non-Indians. The Oliphant decision put the brakes on the trend in the 1970s in the executive and legislative branches to widen the scope of "tribal sovereignty." It seemed also to reverse previous judicial trends in this century, such as the *United States* v. *Winans* decision that "a treaty was not a grant of rights to the Indians, but a grant of rights from them . . . a reservation of those not granted." As the Civil Rights Commission Report notes: "The Treaty of Point Elliott, between the United States and the Suquamish Tribes, is silent on the matter of criminal jurisdiction over non-Indians and thus, under Winans, would presumably be a reservation by the tribe of such jurisdiction."[29]

In 1980 and 1981 the Supreme Court ruled that states have the authority to impose taxes on Indian reservations under certain circumstances. In the 1980 Colville decision[30] the Court held that the tribe had authority to tax cigarette (smoke shop) purchases by non-Indians. However, the decision also stated that the state could also apply taxes to the same sales, which, of course, eliminated the competitive sales advantage previously enjoyed by the tribal shops. Other cases limited state taxing power on reservations, and further cases on the subject are pending.

Tribal jurisdiction over non-Indians is still being defined in various court cases. In the Colville decision, it was indicated that tribal powers are not necessarily lost because of dependency on the federal government. The Court applied the test of whether the power in question conflicts with an important federal interest.[31] In early 1982 the Supreme Court held that the Jicarilla Apache tribe had the sovereign power to impose an oil and gas severance tax on non-Indian lessees of tribal lands.[32]

As indicated earlier, the Oliphant decision applies to criminal actions. In civil cases tribal sovereignty is not completely clear as the two cases of Martinez[33] and Dry Creek illustrate.[34] In the Dry Creek case non-Indians owned a ranch on private land within the exterior boundaries of the Wind River Reservation in Wyoming; the ranch was three miles from the nearest highway, and access was by a private road that crossed several allotments of Indian land. The Indian owners did not want the road used for commercial purposes, and since the ranch had not obtained a right-of-way, the tribal governments closed the road. The ranch owners claimed violation of their civil rights and sought dollar damages. The Tenth Circuit Court found "an *implied* congressional waiver" of tribal sovereign immunity, which opened the door to suits for damages against the tribes. The tribes asked for a review by the Supreme Court, but the Court decided not to review.[35] The Martinez case concerned a provision by the Santa Clara Pueblo in New Mexico that children of male members married to non-Indians were eligible for tribal membership but the children of female members married to non-Indians were not. Mrs. Martinez sued the pueblo, and the U.S. Supreme Court ruled that since the Indian Civil Rights Act did not provide an express waiver of sovereign immunity, suits against the tribe are barred. So the Martinez and Dry Creek cases point in different directions.

Cases continue to come up concerning jurisdiction in water rights issues. According to Wilkinson the western states are planning to quantify rights—including Indian rights. The issues involved generally are resolved in the courts, and whether this resolution will be in federal courts, as favored by the Indians, or in state courts, as favored by local non-Indian groups, is of considerable significance. Recent suits brought in federal courts in Montana and Arizona to adjudicate water rights "were dismissed in favor of state court actions."[36]

In *Montana* v. *United States*[37] the Supreme Court denied the Crow tribe ownership of the Big Horn riverbed within the reservation, and the decision restricted the tribe's regulation of non-Indian hunting and fishing to Indian lands within the Crow Reservation. This decision, like the Oliphant decision, went against the theory that a treaty is a grant of rights from Indians and that rights not granted are reserved. The Court stated that the United States had not intended to convey the riverbed to the tribe.[38] This decision also amplified the Oliphant decision of 1978, indicating that the principles involved in that decision not only restrict tribal criminal jurisdiction over nonmembers, but also generally restrict tribal civil jurisdiction over nonmembers with certain exceptions.[39]

In 1980 and 1981 the courts also gave conflicting decisions on the application of state civil law to reservations.[40] The taxation of resident non-Indians poses a difficult question, since non-Indians cannot become tribal members. One report concluded: "Clearly, the solution to jurisdictional disputes between States and tribes in the area of taxation, as in many other areas involving the exercise of governmental powers, lies in the direction of negotiated intergovernmental agreements."[41] This method is much superior, the report stated, to "unsatisfactory" and "resource-consuming" litigation.[42]

Civil Rights and Child Welfare Acts

The main provisions of the Indian Civil Rights Act of 1968[43] largely parallel the first ten amendments to the U.S. Constitution.[44] However, there were modifications such as not providing a prohibition against the establishment of religion, not protecting the right to bear arms, and specifying recourse to federal courts in criminal matters for writs of habeas corpus only. To what extent tribes are controlled by the act's provisions in the civil area has been addressed by the Supreme Court, and, as indicated earlier, the Court decided that the act does not subject tribes to the jurisdiction of federal courts in some civil actions.[45]

The Indian Child Welfare Act[46] clarifies the jurisdiction of state and Indian agencies concerned with children. It places responsibility for children living on reservations with the tribal courts, and it also seeks to promote "the stability and security of Indian tribes and families by establishing minimum federal standards for any removal of children from the family and for placement, when needed, in homes reflecting the unique values of Indian culture."[47] The responsibility for Indian children not living on the reservation may be transferred from state to tribal courts under certain conditions.

Tribal Courts

Not all reservations have tribal courts. The Dry Creek Rancheria in California adopted a governing document in 1973 that did not refer to police or court functions, and the secretary of the Interior approved those articles of association with the understanding that PL 280 (state jurisdiction) was applicable to the Dry Creek Rancheria. The revised constitution of the Minnesota Chippewa tribes contains no reference to a tribal court system, nor do the constitutions of the Hoopa Valley tribe in California, the Seminole tribe in Florida, the Iowa tribe in Kansas, the Crow tribe in Montana, or the Kickapoo tribe in Oklahoma.

On the other hand, other reservations do have a tribal court system. Probably the most sophisticated is that of the Navajo tribe, and other examples are the courts of the Jicarilla Apache, Mescalero Apache, Menominee, Miccosukee, Zuni, and Oglala Sioux tribes. In 1977 there were sixteen traditional courts and thirty-two BIA-operated courts to deal with Indian offenses, seventy-one tribal courts, and fifteen hunting and fishing courts. Most tribal courts are based on BIA standard models of the 1930s.

Historically, the view has been that tribal courts have no jurisdiction over non-Indians, and many tribal constitutions and court documents limit tribal jurisdiction to tribal members. In 1974 the Interior solicitor reversed the department's position on this matter, and more tribes are beginning to assert authority over non-Indians. This increase in tribal interest in tribal courts was a part of the separatist-sovereignty emphasis of the 1970s, as well as an attempt to get better and faster decisions, especially in cases involving non-Indians. The dissatisfaction with the FBI–district attorney–federal court handling of major crimes and with inadequate state performance under PL 280 led to increasing talk of widening tribal court jurisdiction to cover non-Indians and major crimes. As we have seen, however, the Oliphant case closed the door for the present on Indian court jurisdiction over non-Indian criminal offenses.

Major points, repeatedly made in *Indian Courts and the Future*,[48] the report on the National American Indian Court Judges Association (NAICJA) study, are the need to strengthen tribal courts as an expression of tribal sovereignty, defend against state and federal encroachment, and provide for traditional Indian customs and values in court operation. Regarding the last point on tradition and values, only two examples are cited in the report: utilizing the traditional seating arrangement of a circle in the courtroom and having tribal power symbols placed in the courtroom. All basic court procedures recommended are heavily based on the U.S. court system.

Both Samuel Brakel and NAICJA largely agree on the weaknesses of tribal courts: susceptibility to political influence, summary justice without due process, inadequate tribal laws, dearth of civil cases, need for qualified personnel, lack of dispositional alternatives (e.g., in cases affecting minors, jail or return to the family are frequently the only options available), lack of planning, unnecessarily narrow jurisdiction.[49] NAICJA and Brakel do not agree on the strengths of tribal courts. NAICJA lists their strengths as follows: deference by federal courts (indicating backing for tribal jurisdiction); quick access to a fair forum; growing support by federal agencies, tribal leaders, and organizations; ability to bridge the gap between the law and Indian culture; and a dedicated judiciary. The deference, growing support, and dedicated judiciary probably are not subject to argument. But there does not seem to be much evidence that tribal courts do bridge the gap between the law and Indian culture. Both Brakel and NAICJA point out that many Indians are antagonistic to courts, whatever their source. Tribal codes are largely based on formerly non-Indian concepts, and Brakel's analysis is that present tribal courts are not an expression of tribal culture but a costly way to try to establish a separate court system. NAICJA points out that tribal codes frequently provide that "when an area is not covered by provisions of the tribal code, state law can be applied."[50] This procedure is more frequently resorted to than the judges are willing to admit. "Judges as a whole felt that use of tradition is a thing of the past."[51]

Brakel suggests an alternative to the effort to improve the separate systems for tribes.

> Efforts to improve the tribal courts with robes, money, new courtrooms, and more training programs are only band-aid measures, as are efforts to improve reservation conditions with more welfare money, food stamps, motels, resorts, oil and gas leases and Washington, D.C., lawyers. The alternative of integrating the tribal judicial system with state and county institutions has many advantages. By definition, it would eliminate the Kafkaesque confusion among tribal, state, and federal courts and other

> agencies. At the same time, the Indian people would be no less free to be "Indian," "rural," "traditional" or "bound to the land or community" or to choose whatever life-style and values they may want. By the same token, the many Indians who want to embark on ("acculturated") professional careers would probably have a better chance to succeed and a better setting in which to use their professional skills. Today, Indians who want professional careers often fail at both realizing their ambitions and maintaining a satisfactory contact with the reservation.[52]

NAICJA agrees that the question of jurisdiction is confusing. "Crimes going unpunished because no one knows who has jurisdiction or because the tribe lacks authority to exert jurisdiction contributes to a lack of respect by those under the tribal courts authority." In order to improve the situation NAICJA does not recommend moving to state jurisdiction, but improving the tribal courts. "Our Indian courts are necessary if tribal governments are to exercise the sovereign prerogatives of tribes as recognized by Congress and the Federal courts."[53] The training of tribal judges is a key effort of the NAICJA program, which has helped persuade the BIA and the Justice Department to put more emphasis on and money into such training.

It is clear that many Indians are not within the jurisdiction of a tribal court system. As indicated earlier, the Major Crimes Act, the Indian Civil Rights Act, and court decisions such as the Oliphant decision severely limit the juridical sovereignty of tribes. Additionally, it is obvious from a review of tribal constitutions that they are based on the concepts of the major society and that the tribal courts that do exist "are white American creations, and quite recent ones at that."[54]

Problems Resulting from Lack of Clarity on Jurisdiction

The lack of tribal jurisdiction over non-Indians and the lack of state jurisdiction over Indians in many instances create a quagmire. In testimony before the Civil Rights Commission and hearings of the American Indian Lawyer Training Program, the difficulties were specified.[55] First, how does a police officer know whether an offender is Indian or non-Indian? Second, how does the officer know whether he or she is on trust land or land under jurisdiction of the state? Third, if the nearest state or federal official is from thirty minutes to three hours away, and the offender is non-Indian and committed the offense on trust land, what should the tribal officer do? Fourth, even if there are arrangements for cross-deputization of local and state officers and Indian police, and for acceptance by the FBI and U.S. district attorneys of tribal police investigations, what is the value of those efforts if a district attorney will not prosecute? The two reports are replete with the difficulties and the lack of effective protection and justice under the present situation.

Self-Determination Act

Title 1 of PL 93-638,[56] referred to as the Indian Self-Determination Act, gives the tribes the option of operating programs of the BIA and IHS under contract with the government. It also provides for grants to the tribes to increase tribal capabilities for such contracting. The secretaries of Interior and Health and Human Services are "directed, upon the request of any Indian tribe, to enter into a contract or contracts with any tribal organization of any such tribe to plan, conduct, and administer programs, or portions thereof" that are authorized for the BIA under the Snyder Act (42 Stat. 208) and an act that transferred Indian health functions to Health and Human Services in 1954.[57]

The two secretaries may initially refuse if they find that (1) service to Indian beneficiaries will not be satisfactory, (2) adequate protection of trust resources is not assured, or (3) the proposed project or function cannot be maintained or completed by the proposed contract. Whenever a secretary declines to enter into a contract he or she shall state the objections in writing to the tribe within sixty days, (2) help the tribe overcome the objections, and (3) give the tribe the opportunity to appeal through a hearing on the objections raised. The two secretaries may require that a tribe requesting a contract obtain liability insurance with the proviso that the insurance carrier cannot waive the tribe's immunity to suit beyond the coverage of the policy.

A total of 370 tribes contracted for the operation of $200 million worth of BIA programs in fiscal year 1980. It was estimated that the number of tribes involved would remain about the same in 1981 and 1982, but that the dollar volume would increase by $10 million in 1981.[58] The contracted services involve almost all of the activities supervised by the BIA, and the Indian Health Service also uses self-determination contracts.

Title 2 of PL 638, referred to as Indian Education Assistance Act modified the Johnson O'Malley Act, which provided contracting authority, to ensure that funds for the education of Indian children were used for Indian education by the states. Such funds could be used by the state only after review and approval of a school board of which the majority of the members were Indian or by a local committee made up of Indian parents. This title also authorized funds for state school construction for Indians, including land and buildings.

Economic Viability

Tribally Developed Income Versus Outside Income

One of the distinguishing characteristics of government is the power to tax and to be largely self-supporting. The federal government is self-supporting in this sense. State and local governments raise most of their own revenues through taxes—although they are subsidized to some extent by the federal government—and they decide on their own tax rates and determine priorities of expenditures. When there are subsidies from the federal government, except for revenue sharing, those subsidies are for specific purposes, and the flexibility of local governments is strictly limited. Of course, subsidies can be refused. For the most part federal and state governments are basically self-determining; local governments are creatures of the state government and are self-determining only to the degree authorized by the state.

Many tribal governments receive a major portion of their income from taxpayers who are not subject to the tribe's jurisdiction. Even though the goal of tribal governments is to be self-sufficient,[59] funds to support the education of Indian children, tribal police, judges, law and order facilities, and many other programs come primarily from the federal government for most reservations. For many tribes local-government types of services are performed by employees on the federal payroll. In those instances in which the tribes have taken over some of these local-government-type functions from the BIA or the IHS, the tribes receive the same amount of money as was formerly spent by those two agencies plus an additional amount for overhead. This allocation of funds is accomplished through a contract arrangement. Frequently tribes also receive governmental services from the state in which they reside.

For tribes that have a major economic dependence on the larger society there is very little self-determination in the decision of how much money is to be available for tribal expenditures. Influence, yes, but the final decision on the amount and the purposes for which the money is to be spent rests with the executive and congressional branches of the federal government and with the state governments, not the tribe. A non-Indian local community, even though its self-determination is limited, can decide its priority needs and raise or lower its own taxes to meet them within the authority granted it by the state.

When money is made available to tribes from the larger society the amount of tribal influence in determining the use of the funds and the direction of the process for such use depends on the willingness of the larger society to allow tribal discretion. If this is self-determination, it is a "dependent self-determination."

State governments serve many reservation Indians whose land is not taxable by the state through public schools, institutions of higher learning, hospitals, prisons, welfare, highway traffic control, and many other ways.

Tribal Income and Expenditure: Availability of Information

Tribal governments with approved constitutions generally have the power to tax. This power is generally clear in regard to the tribe's own members. It is often not so clear in connection with non-Indians and non-Indian owned properties.

Many tribes are sensitive about publishing their income and expenditure figures. The BIA has long had a policy of considering tribal income data as a private tribal matter and of believing that it is up to the tribe how much it discloses. However, the BIA has also advised tribes that complete disclosure of all sources and amounts of tribal income, as well as the amounts and nature of expenditures, is the only way tribal members can have the basic data necessary to enable them to indicate to their leaders realistic policy direction and priorities desired. These data are also necessary if tribal members are to be sufficiently informed to demand accountability on the part of their government officials. All people in non-Indian communities can find out where every penny comes from and how it is spent by their local and state governments. This is public information.

It is difficult to determine what percentage of most tribes' expenditure is financed by a tribe's own resources as compared with the amount of subsidy from the federal government and other sources. Some tribes such as the Eastern Cherokee are willing to assemble and publish this information, but they do not have the staffs that would enable them to publish it on a regular basis or a strong demand to do so. Other tribes will answer members' questions on finance, but that is not the same thing as having a printed budget available.

A questionnaire was sent to 100 of the largest tribes, and among other questions, it asked the following:

1. Does your tribe have a budget listing income by source and amount; also listing expenditures by program and amount (including dollar cost of services provided or funded by federal agencies); and a balance sheet indicating total tribal assets and liabilities?
2. If so, is this budget information made available to tribal members? If it is public information, would you please send me a copy?[60]

Only eight tribes responded, and only one sent the budget as requested in the last part of the second question.

The Cheyenne and Arapaho tribes of Oklahoma sent a copy of the budget for FY 1981, which totaled $3,250,000 in expenditures. The sources for the funding included the IHS, HHS, BIA, HUD, and the state of Oklahoma. The tribe employed 124 employees.[61] The Chickasaw nation in Oklahoma published an article in the *Chickasaw Times*[62] on the growth of that nation's assets from $300,000 in 1963 to almost $5 million in 1981 but provided no details on annual income and expenses. The Colorado River Indian tribes indicated that tribal policy prohibits distribution and publication of budget data to outside sources.[63] The Lower Brule Sioux tribe indicated that "tribal budgets are approved by tribal council action and are public information. Copies are expensive to make."[64] The Mississippi band of Choctaw Indians reported that it did not have a single, consolidated balance sheet but that it would have one in 1982 as the tribe intended to have an audit conducted in accordance with the new provisions of the Office of Management and Budget (OMB) Circular A-102.[65]

The Muscogee (Creek) nation of Oklahoma reported that it had a budget that listed income by source and amount and listed expenditures by program and amount; it also develops a balance sheet indicating total assets and liabilities. "This budget is available upon request to all members. However, this does not make the budget . . . public information."[66] The Navajo reported an annual budget of $35 million in tribal revenues and approximately $100 million in federal funds. A tribal audit by the firm of Peat, Marwick and Mitchell shows all revenues, expenditures, and a profit and loss statement of the tribal government and tribal enterprises on an annual basis. Copies of the budget are provided to the tribal council, tribal departments, and the BIA, and the budget is available for public inspection. Cost prohibits making copies available to tribal members or the general public.[67]

The Passamaquoddy tribe does not have a consolidated budget but does have a balance sheet of tribal assets and liabilities. Budget information is made available to tribal members upon request.[68] The Zuni did not provide information directly, but in 1981 that tribe had over sixty federal programs operating on the reservation ranging from schools to elderly centers to environmental projects.[69]

These answers indicate the variable nature of the availability of income and expense data for tribal governments. The lack of larger response may have been in part due to tribes not wanting to publicize a tribal policy of limiting the availability of budget information; it might also have been partly due to a lack of staff time to respond.

Since large sums of public money are appropriated for Indian programs, Congress has begun to take note of the desirability of determining the ability of tribes to raise revenues to support themselves. For example, the American Indian Policy Review Commission, congressionally appointed and with key congressional members, recommended in 1977 that "Congress direct the Bureau of Indian Affairs to undertake a needs assessment of each tribal government to determine tribal capability to finance the basic operations of tribal government."[70] No action has been taken to date on this recommendation. The Maine Indian Claims Settlement Act of 1980 directed that a comparability study of federal and state funding for Indian tribes be made.[71] This report was to be submitted to House and Senate committees by October 30, 1982, which was done.

Without hard data on each tribe's income, the BIA and Congress operate somewhat in the dark when requesting, appropriating, and allocating funds. Obviously, if one tribe has resources and considerable tribal income it does not need the same per capita assistance as a tribe without such resources.

Even though many tribes have the power to tax, not many use taxes to support their governments. The AIPRC report points out that this procedure does not mean that tribes do not obtain revenues from their members. When tribes use the income from tribal enterprises, which are held in common by members of the tribe, for governmental expenses the tribal members are paying an indirect tax.[72]

Income from Products Grown on Indian Lands

Tribes with resources can convert those resources into tribal income, but many of the 499 Indian entities listed by the BIA are too small in terms of both members and acerage to be economically viable. There are over 200 reservations with over 50 million acres in twenty-six states, and "about 129 reservations have Indian populations of at least 200 and land of at least 1,000 acres."[73]

The gross value of products grown on Indian lands in 1975 and 1981 is shown in Table 4.1. The values were achieved on approximately 43.4 million acres operated by Indians and approximately 49.3 million acres operated by non-Indians. Since there are only approximately 50 million acres of Indian-owned land the figures are the result of multiple use of a given acre, such as timber and grazing or crops and grazing of stubble. The table indicates that 62 percent in 1975 and 61 percent in 1981 of the values were developed by non-Indian operators. If timber is not considered, 73 percent of the agricultural value was produced by non-Indians according to the AIPRC.[74]

Table 4.1
Gross Value of Products Grown on Indian Land--1975 and 1981
($ in Thousands)

Land Use	Indian Operated 1975	Indian Operated 1981	Non-Indian Operated 1975	Non-Indian Operated 1981
Cultivatable Row Crops	$16,324	$14,409	$95,182	$117,886
Small Grains	26,411	30,276	114,929	106,545
Forage, Hay, Pasture	21,962	37,034	65,310	78,920
Horticulture	5,154	4,251	37,613	16,202
Outdoor Recreation & Wildlife	6,381	3,773	7,027	3,845
Native Hay	668	562	887	1,281
Stumpage	108,537	123,759	108,537	123,759
Log Value	204,816	211,981	211,980	228,759
Grazing	52,170	89,456	79,840	126,736
Idle	64	-	64	-
Total	$442,487	$515,501	$721,369	$803,933

The above values may be understated due to incomplete reporting. For example, BIA foresters think the stumpage and log value gross for all Indian land is approximately $1 billion rather than the sum of the totals indicated above.

Source: BIA Land Use and Production Record, Report no. 50-1 for calendar year 1975, issued 1977, p. 5; BIA Inventory and Production Record, Report no. 55-38x for fiscal year 1981, processed June 1, 1982, p. 4.

Both Alan Sorkin and the AIPRC noted the relatively low productivity of Indian operators as compared with non-Indian operators. "Even casual observers have been startled by the stark contrast in economic conditions between reservation lands and adjoining non-reservation lands and communities."[75] Indian farmers have a lower productivity than non-Indian farmers because of poor management, such as not getting hay crops in on time, which is in part due to a nonagricultural background and lack of training.[76] The AIPRC places part of the problem on the doorstep of a dependency syndrome developed by past policy: "Indicators show that dependency, not productivity, continues to rise."[77] Lack of capital, the small size of holdings, and divided ownership are other negative factors.[78] Of course, non-Indians would not be able to farm or otherwise utilize Indian land unless the Indians were willing to lease such lands to them.

Table 4.2
Income from Surface and Subsurface Leases, Fiscal Year 1980
($ in Thousands)

Surface Leases and Permits	
Agricultural Acres	$ 41,532
Business Acres	14,245
Other Acres	2,033
Total	$ 57,810
Subsurface Leases and Permits	
Oil and Gas	$ 169,011
Other than Oil and Gas	31,550
Total	$ 200,561

Source: "Annual Report of Indian Lands and Income from Surface and Subsurface Leases," U.S. Department of the Interior, Bureau of Indian Affairs, Office of Trust Responsibilities, September 30, 1980. The report has no explanatory text, but discussion with the Office of Trust Responsibilities indicated that oil and gas royalties were included in the oil and gas figures but that the value of products grown on Indian land was not included in the agricultural acres figure. The reporting may be incomplete.

Income from Surface and Subsurface Leasing

Tribes and individual Indians receive income from surface and subsurface leasing as indicated in Table 4.2. The reservations and tribes that receive between $500,000 and $1,000,000 in surface lease income are Winnebago (Nebraska), Ft. Berthold (North Dakota), Pine Ridge (South Dakota), Otoe and Ponca (Oklahoma). Reservations and tribes receiving over $1,000,000 in surface lease income are Kiowa, Comanche and Apache ($4,101,923), Wichita-Caddo-Delaware, and Cheyenne Arapaho (Oklahoma); Blackfeet, Crow, and Ft. Peck (Montana); Colorado River ($3,633,284), Ak-chin (Maricopa), and Salt River (Arizona); Ft. Hall, Coeur d'Alene, and Nez Percé (Idaho); Umatilla (Oregon); and Yakima (Washington).

Reservations and tribes with an oil and gas lease and royalty income of over $1,000,000 are Ft. Berthold, North Dakota ($1,308,000); Southern Ute, Colorado ($2,310,000); Ute Mountain, New Mexico and Colorado ($1,277,000); Kiowa, Comanche, Apache, and Fort Sill Apache, Oklahoma

Table 4.3
Interest Income, Trust Fund Receipts, and Other Payments, Fiscal Year 1981 ($ in Thousands)

Interest and Investment Income	
Interest on Trust Funds in Treasury and in U. S. Government Securities	$ 17,959
Interest on Investments in Banks	108,301
Tribal Trust Fund Receipts	
Claims Commission and Court of Claims Awards	119,059
Rent of Land	19,463
Royalties	177,397
Timber	61,001
Minerals	2,639
Fees	5,172
Sale of Real Property	1,289
Fines, Penalties, and Forfeitures	45
Miscellaneous	14,515
Settlement of Maine Land Claims	81,500
Final Payment Alaska Claim Settlement	30,000
Total	$ 638,340

Source: Telephone conversation with Peggy Daniels, BIA Division of Program Development and Implementation, June 11, 1982.

($4,486,000); Cheyenne Arapaho, Oklahoma ($6,532,000); Blackfeet, Montana ($2,427,000); Ft. Peck, Montana ($2,850,000); Wind River, Wyoming ($17,382,000); Five Civilized Tribes consolidated, Oklahoma ($4,725,000); Osage, Oklahoma ($65,234,000); Navajo, Arizona, New Mexico, and Utah ($25,394,000); and Uintah and Ouray, Utah ($12,341,000).[79] Besides oil and gas tribes lease subsurface rights for coal and uranium.

Only the tribes know how much money from mineral royalty income they have in private bank accounts. The BIA figures are from tribal funds that are deposited in the Treasury or invested by the BIA for the tribes in insured bank accounts. Lease income is obtained from lease documents processed by the BIA or supplied to it. Tribal trust fund receipts, interest on tribal funds, and payments for the Alaskan and Maine land claims settlements are indicated in Table 4.3 for fiscal year 1981.

Other Income Sources

Development of business, industry, and tourism to create jobs has been a goal of the BIA since 1955 and of other agencies such as the Economic Development Administration (EDA) and the Office of Minority Business Enterprise. Many such activities have been started, and frequently non-Indian corporations have supplied management and working capital; the EDA, BIA, or tribe has supplied physical capital; and it has been hoped that the labor would come from the reservation. In 1968 Sorkin found that of 137 enterprises started, 27 had ceased operating.[80]

There are successes. The Devils Lake Sioux Manufacturing Corporation is making money; its 1980 annual report indicated net earnings of $1,370,000. The tribe owns 51 percent and the Brunswick Corporation, 49 percent—having started out in 1974 with 30 percent tribal ownership and 70 percent Brunswick. Camouflage is the company's major product. Fairchild had an electronics plant at Shiprock, New Mexico, which employed 1,200 Navajo at one time, but the American Indian Movement (AIM) took over the plant and caused havoc. Fairchild would not continue to operate the plant without Navajo tribal assurance that such disorder would not occur again, and the plant remains closed. At an electronics plant in Hollywood, Florida, on the Seminole Reservation, the majority of the employees were Indian at the beginning, but soon they dropped out, and employment became largely non-Indian. The Indians are primarily interested in the lease income from the building and land; not many of the tribal members are interested in permanent work at the plant. The White Swan Furniture Company at Yakima, Washington, is a going enterprise, but a boat manufacturing company at Yakima has ceased operation. The Chahta Enterprise, wholly owned by the Mississippi Choctaw and with a board of directors appointed by tribal council, purchases raw materials from Packard Electric and sells completed "wiring harness" for automobiles back to Packard. The Mescalero Apache own and operate Sierra Blanco, "a highly successful" ski enterprise.[81]

All told, the BIA estimates that 260 enterprises have been started, but since the early 1970s and with the drive for self-determination the BIA stopped gathering statistics, so there is a dearth of information. How many enterprises are in the black and how many have ceased operation is not known in Washington.[82]

However, a study funded by the Ford Foundation and the BIA and made by Checchi and Company resulted in a 1977 report on twelve federally financed tourism projects on Indian reservations.[83] These twelve resorts and motels represented 94 percent of all money invested in resorts and motels and 71 percent of the total funds invested in all federally financed tourism projects. In 1977 all twelve were losing money.[84]

Barriers to Indian industrial development are inadequate transportation facilities, poor location with reference to markets, poor education and work habits of the manpower available, and a dearth of facts about resources and facilities that could be used by potential industrial firms to base a decision on.[85] The lack of adequate capital for economically feasible projects was one of the many factors studied by Checchi in the twelve tourism projects. The main advantages of a reservation location to an industry are low labor costs and available natural resources.[86] According to the AIPRC, "on some of the largest reservations productive income generated by the tribe or its members only makes up 10 percent of the total distributed income."[87]

No group is completely self-sufficient economically. Even the United States is dependent on foreign trade for key resources such as oil and tin for the economy to operate at a maximum level. Most tribes recognize that they are part of a larger economic environment.

Policy Implications of Present Trends and Conflicts

Lack of Representation for Non-Indians

The Oliphant case had not arisen when Monroe Price wrote that for resident non-Indians the 1968 Civil Rights Act

> could prove a potent weapon for non-Indians asserting a right to participate in the political affairs of the tribe through the right to vote, the right to hold office and the right to serve on juries. To the extent the tribe maintains its existence on a political plane which does not include non-Indians as subject to its comprehensive governance, these efforts may be long and successfully rebuffed. But to the extent that non-Indians are integrated as subjects of the tribal government, then rights to participate will be enhanced.[88]

If the Oliphant decision had gone the other way it would have added pressure for resident non-Indian participation in tribal government affairs. The growing practice of tribal court jurisdiction in civil actions for both Indians and non-Indians will keep the question of "justice without representation" alive on Indian reservations. Most governments have jurisdiction over a given territory and all persons in that territory. On Indian reservations, non-Indians do not have the right to vote. Therefore, insofar as they are subject to tribal jurisdiction they are governed without representation. There will continue to be pressure in such situations either for state and local jurisdictions in which all citizens, including

Indian citizens, are represented or for all residents on a reservation to be able to participate equally in their governance.

Economic Viability

Tribes have the objective of becoming self-sufficient. This goal may be possible for those tribes that have adequate resources for their resident population given effective management, but for others that are small in number and resource poor or overpopulated in relation to the resource base the solution may rest in cooperation with surrounding communities.

Role of Tribal Organizations

The AIPRC report put a key question.

> Simply put, the question is whether tribes are going to be permanent, on-going political institutions exercising the basic power of local government or whether they are to be transient bodies relegated to mere "service delivery vehicles" for federal assistance programs; mere "federal instrumentalities" for the control of the social behavior of their own tribal membership pending their ultimate assimilation into the dominant society which surrounds them. This is the fundamental question for the future of Indian tribes and the fundamental question which the Congress must resolve in the formulation of the future course of Federal-Indian policy.[89]

William Schaab believes that the concept of tribal self-government as a "primordial right" or "residual sovereignty," rather than being based on congressional statutes, is an "outdated court-created" doctrine.

> Although the factual basis for the doctrine was originally sound, history has changed the facts and the doctrine should now be discarded. Judicial power should be withheld from cases involving Indian tribes or individual Indians only because intervention would violate a federal statute or some clearly defined congressional policy. To withhold judicial remedies only because Indian tribes at the beginning of the 19th Century were treated as separate "nations" is to refuse justice without reason.[90]

He also contends that the IRA was not intended to "recognize or confirm self-government by the Indian tribes on the basis of a primordial right" and continues:

> Congress realized that the Act was necessary because Indian government had "disintegrated" under prior federal policies and the Indians needed an expression of Congress' confidence in their ability to govern themselves. In the Act Congress sought to create a new system of tribal government. Upon acceptance of the Act, the tribe could exercise limited rights of self-government under a tribal constitution approved by the Secretary and obtain "the devices of modern business organization" by receiving from

> the Secretary a tribal corporate charter. Those charters became the foundation of its government; primordial rights were thereby extinguished.[91]

The AIPRC may have been considering the implications of the IRA and the fact that it could be read as Schaab interpreted it when it incorporated recommendation 22 into its report:

> Section 16 of the Indian Reorganization Act . . . which authorizes tribes to organize under the provisions of that Act be amended: (1) to specifically reflect the fact that tribes have an inherent right to form their own political organizations in the form which they desire; and (2) to provide that notwithstanding any provisions in existing tribal constitutions which vest the Secretary with authority to review and disapprove ordinances enacted by the tribal government shall only extend to those matters directly related to the trust responsibility over the use and disposition of trust assets. However, those tribes who wish to retain such authority on an interim basis shall be authorized to do so.[92]

In discussing the ability of tribes to operate their own governments Price points to the fact that many reservations are "either too weak internally or too poor to exercise their right."[93]

In *Indian Tribes as Governments* a comparison is made between local non-Indian governments (city councils) and tribal governments:

> Undoubtedly the most basic difference lies in the fact that the tribe, historically, legally and socially, comprises a self-governing unit which is outside of the federalist system. The source of an Indian tribe's authority to govern itself flows from its status as a sovereign entity (i.e., as a sovereign, a tribe possesses "inherent" powers of self-government which pre-date the United States government). . . . By contrast, any other local governmental unit in this country exists only because it has received its power . . . from the state.[94]

Thus, we see that there are varying views and interpretations of the federal-Indian relationship and the nature of tribal governments. These views and others will be debated as the Indian policy of the future is hammered out.

Nineteenth-century Indians. (Above) Blackfoot chief Charles Rivas, known as Crow Chief, was famous as a warrior. He wears the Lincoln Medal, given to those chiefs who made and kept the peace on the western frontiers. (Below) A Salish woman wearing a hand-woven shawl and carrying a delicately beaded pouch.

Reservation beauty. (Above) Aerial view of the western portion of the Warm Springs Reservation in Oregon. Mt. Jefferson is in the background. (Below) High alpine lake and timber on the Warm Springs Reservation.

Taos Pueblo, New Mexico. (Top) Adobe "beehive" ovens for baking bread. The Sangre de Cristo Mountains are in the background. (Center) Many members of the Taos community live in separate houses. (Bottom) The Taos Pueblo, now many centuries old, is kept in good condition. Racks for drying food are in the foreground. (Photos courtesy of Wallace H. Campbell)

Indian dwellings, then and now. (Above) Assiniboine Indians, Gray Breath and Strong, both age 86, at home on Fort Belknap, Montana, in the nineteenth century. (Below) Native village, Bethel Agency, Pilot Station, Alaska, 1973.

Natural resources. (Above) Indian logger bucking logs on Umatilla Reservation, Oregon, 1968. (Below) Swinomish Indians haul up a trap net full of salmon at Skagit Bay, Washington, 1980.

Indian agriculture. (Above) Wheat field at the Colorado River Agency, Arizona, 1973. (Below) Grape vineyards on the Yakima Reservation, Washington, 1961.

(Above) Onion harvest at the Salt River Agency, Arizona, 1973. (Below) The Kickapoo tribe of Oklahoma has established a hydroponic farming project to raise tomatoes and other vegetables, 1980.

Agricultural technology. (Above) Hop field on the Yakima Reservation, Washington, with trellises to support the growing vines. (Below) Trailer trucks collect boxes of lettuce as they are filled by pickers. (Right, top) Small plane dusting crops with insecticide, Colorado River Agency, Arizona. (Right, center) Machine harvesting lentils on the Coeur d'Alene Reservation, Idaho, 1982. (Right, bottom) Machines harvesting cotton, Colorado River Agency, Arizona.

Water conservation and use. (Above) Irrigation of new lettuce, Salt River Agency, Arizona. (Below) Irrigation pond, Pima Agency, Arizona. (Right, top) Watering lettuce, Colorado River Agency, Arizona. (Right, center) Watering large areas from a central source, Pine Ridge, South Dakota. (Right, bottom) Conserving water for use during prolonged dry spells in the summer can make the difference between ranching and going broke. With assistance from the Department of Agriculture through the Agricultural Stabilization and Conservation program, costs to operate such a pond are comparatively small. Nearly all ranchers participate in the program.

Water works. (Above) Test drilling for an irrigation well, Salt River Agency, Arizona. (Below) Trenching a head ditch, Colorado River Agency, Arizona. (Right, above) Laying drainage pipe, Salt River Agency, Arizona. (Right, below) Surveying for land leveling, Lone Butte, Arizona.

Indian businesses. (Above) Indian Western Wear and Hat Factory, Anadarko, Oklahoma. (Below) The Miccosukee Restaurant on the Tamiami Trail, Homestead, Florida.

Indian education. (Left, above) Minoka Hall and (right, above) Blue Eagle Hall, Haskell Institute, Lawrence, Kansas, 1962. (Below) Adult education class, Twin Lakes, New Mexico, on the Navajo Reservation, 1961. The instructor interprets the film "Defensive Driving" to a class.

Bureau of Indian Affairs and tribal activities. (Above) Grand opening of a tribal building attracts officials of local, state, and federal governments. (Below) Visits to tribal offices by Bureau of Indian Affairs officials results in a better communication process, necessary for cooperative effort in many BIA programs.

(Above) Tribal employees and officials receive training in the rules and regulations of Public Law 93-638, the Indian Self-Determination Act. (Below) Tribal police forces receive training through BIA courses. Trainees and BIA personnel participate.

Tribal councils. (Above) Meeting of the Seminole General Council, Oklahoma, 1967. (Below) Peter MacDonald, chairman of the Navajo Tribal Council (left), and Louis R. Bruce, Commissioner of Indian Affairs, at Window Rock, Arizona, 1971.

Part Two

INTERRELATIONSHIPS AND INVOLVEMENT

5

MAINE INDIAN CLAIMS: THE RESOLUTION OF A POLICY ISSUE

Introduction

Part One indicates the history of and the main participants in Indian policy creation and execution, and it also includes considerable discussion of the interaction among the people and groups involved. Part Two concentrates on interrelationships. This chapter presents a specific policy issue as a case study that illustrates in more detail some interactions and their policy results. Chapter 6 analyzes the actors, pressures, and processes demonstrated by this case, other examples throughout the book, and additional supporting incidents.

The president and Congress tend to avoid sensitive and controversial areas unless a crisis forces them to act. Indian affairs demonstrates this tendency vividly in policy areas such as Indian treaty fishing rights, aboriginal land claims, quantifying Indian water rights, firming up Indian boundaries, legislative definition of an Indian, resolution of the Indian land heirship tangle, legislative clarification of the trust responsibility, and executive and legislative clarification of the nature of tribal governments and relationships of such governments to the local, state, and federal governments. The Maine case not only indicates the complex relationships in the formation of major policy but also points up the importance of Indian policy to large segments of the American public.

History and Background

In 1777, Colonel John Allen, representing the revolutionary government, negotiated a treaty with the Maine Indians to obtain their assistance in the Revolutionary War in return for the protection of their lands by the United States and the provision of supplies in times of need. This treaty was never ratified, and the federal government did not protect the Indians following the war. In 1791, the Passamaquoddy tribe and the Commonwealth of Massachusetts (which had jurisdiction over what is now the state of Maine) entered into an agreement in which the tribe ceded all but 23,000 acres. Subsequent sales and leases by the state of Maine reduced the acreage to about 17,000 acres. The Penobscot nation, through treaties in 1796 and 1818 and a sale in 1833, ceded most of its aboriginal territory.

A Senate report in 1980 indicated that the validity of these agreements with the tribes was not seriously questioned until 1972.[1] Thus, for nearly 200 years the Indians, the state, and the federal government all believed that the state had responsibility for the Maine Indians and that the federal government was not involved.

Thomas N. Tureen, an attorney, convinced the Passamaquoddy that the lack of approval by the federal government of the treaties and agreements with the state (Massachusetts and later Maine) was a violation of the Trade and Intercourse Act of 1790, which, as amended, is now found in 25 USC 177 (in recent court cases it has been referred to as the Nonintercourse Act).[2] This act required the approval of the United States for any transfer of lands from Indian ownership.

In 1972 the Passamaquoddy tribe asked the United States to sue the state of Maine on the basis that the treaties and agreements had never been approved by the federal government. The secretary of the Interior at the time did not agree and did not sue. He argued that the Trade and Intercourse Act did not apply to nonrecognized tribes and that there was no trust relationship between the United States and the Maine tribes. The tribe went to court to try to force the federal government to sue the state of Maine. Since the Indians were claiming about two-thirds of the state of Maine this issue was considered critical by the state and its citizens as well as by the Indians. Maine was allowed to intervene in the case. The issues were (1) whether the Nonintercourse Act applied to the Passamaquoddy tribe; (2) whether the act established a trust relationship between the United States and the tribe; and (3) whether the United States could deny the tribe's request for litigation on the sole ground that there was no trust relationship. The district court ruled in the tribe's favor on all points, holding that the language of the Nonintercourse Act protected the lands of "any . . . tribe of Indians" and that the Passamaquoddy Indians constituted a tribe.[3]

So too thought the circuit court to which the case was appealed. However, the decision was narrowly defined, affirming "that the United States never sufficiently manifested withdrawal of its protection so as to sever any trust relationship. In so ruling, we do not foreclose later consideration of whether Congress or the Tribe should be deemed in some manner to have acquiesced in, or Congress to have ratified, the Tribe's land transactions with Maine."[4] The state of Maine had maintained that (1) the Nonintercourse Act "was never intended to apply to the original thirteen colonies after they became states," (2) that "the Indians transferred the lands in question before the Revolution and thus before 1790," and (3) that "in ratifying the Articles of Separation, by which Maine was separated from Massachusetts and admitted to the Union in 1820, Congress implicitly approved all treaties concluded by Massachusetts up to that time."[5]

The court action brought about by the Passamaquoddy tribe forced the federal government to act. The president, the Congress, the state, and the tribes were all interested in a more speedy and less costly solution than the judicial route. Peter Taft, who had been appointed to the Justice Department under President Gerald Ford as an assistant attorney general, Interior Solicitor Greg Austin, and Tim Vollmann of Austin's staff met with members of the White House staff on November 4, 1976. Taft indicated that it looked as if the Maine Indians had a claim, and it was agreed that an effort should be made to settle the claim by negotiation in order to avoid the festering, delay, and cost of a judicial settlement.

In March 1977 President Carter appointed William Gunter, a retired Georgia Supreme Court justice, to study the case and make recommendations. Gunter and his staff delved thoroughly into the issue. On July 15, 1977, Justice Gunter recommended to the president:

> I have given consideration to the legal merits and demerits of these pending claims. However, my recommendation is not based entirely on my personal assessment in that area. History, economics, social science, justness, and practicality are additional elements that have had some weight in the formulation of my recommendation.
>
> My recommendation to you is that you recommend to the Congress that it resolve this problem as follows:
>
> (1) Appropriate 25 million dollars for the use and benefit of the two tribes, this appropriated amount to be administered by Interior. One half of this amount shall be appropriated in each of the next two fiscal years.
>
> (2) Require the State of Maine to put together and convey to the United States, as trustee for the two tribes, a tract of land consisting of 100,000 acres within the claims area. As stated before, the State reportedly has in its public ownership in the claims area in excess of 400,000 acres.
>
> (3) Assure the two tribes that normal Bureau of Indian Affairs benefits will be accorded to them by the United States in the future.
>
> (4) Request the State of Maine to continue to appropriate in the future on an annual basis state benefits for the tribes at the equivalent level of the average annual appropriation over the current and preceding four years.

(5) Require the Secretary of Interior to use his best efforts to acquire long-term options on an additional 400,000 acres of land in the claims area. These options would be exercised at the election of the tribes, the option-price paid would be fair market value per acre, and tribal funds would be paid for the exercise of each option.

(6) Upon receiving the consent of the State of Maine that it will accomplish what is set forth in numbered paragraphs (2) and (4) above, the Congress should then, upon obtaining tribal consent to accept the benefits herein prescribed, by statutory enactment extinguish all aboriginal title, if any, to all lands in Maine and also extinguish all other claims that these two tribes may now have against any party arising out of an alleged violation of the Indian Nonintercourse Act of 1790 as amended.

(7) If tribal consent cannot be obtained to what is herein proposed, then the Congress should immediately extinguish all aboriginal title, if any, to all lands within the claims area except that held in the public ownership by the State of Maine. The tribes' cases could then proceed through the courts to a conclusion against the state-owned land. If the tribes win their cases, they recover the state-owned land; but if they lose their cases, they recover nothing. However, in the meantime, the adverse economic consequences will have been eliminated and Interior and Justice will have been relieved from pursuing causes of action against private property owners to divest them of title to land that has heretofore been considered valid title.

(8) If the consent of the State of Maine cannot be obtained for what is herein proposed, then the Congress should appropriate 25 million dollars for the use and benefit of the tribes (see paragraph numbered (1)), should then immediately extinguish all aboriginal title, in any, and all claims arising under an alleged violation of the 1790 Act as amended, to all lands within the claims area except those lands within the public ownership of the State. The tribes' cases could then proceed through the courts against the state-owned land. If the tribes win their cases they recover the land; but if they lose their cases they recover nothing against the state of Maine. However, in the meantime, they will have received 25 million dollars from the United States for their consent to eliminate economic stagnation in the claims area, and their consent to relieve Interior and Justice from pursuing causes of action against private property owners to divest them of land titles that have heretofore been considered valid.

It is my hope that the Congress can resolve this problem through the implementation of numbered paragraphs (1) through (6) above. Paragraphs (7) and (8) are mere alternatives to be utilized in the event consensual agreement cannot be obtained.[6]

These recommendations required negotiation, and the president immediately appointed a negotiating team for the government consisting of Eliot Cutler, associate director of the Office of Management and Budget for Energy, Natural Resources and Science; Leo Krulitz, solicitor of the Department of the Interior; and A. Stephens Clay, Judge Gunter's law partner. Negotiations between this work group and the tribes produced an agreement between the tribes and the administration in

February 1978. In essence it proposed extinguishment of all tribal claims for parcels of land under 50,000 acres for a monetary payment of $25 million, which would have cleared title to an estimated 9.2 million acres of the 12.5 million acres claimed. This agreement left the big landowners, about fourteen in number, and the state of Maine subject to suit and to having to defend themselves in court. After several months, Attorney General Griffin Bell turned down this agreement saying he believed all owners should be treated alike.

Meanwhile, other people seeking solutions to the Maine land problem had been active. In 1977 Senator William S. Cohen of Maine introduced a bill to extinguish the claim of aboriginal rights asserted by the Penobscot and Passamaquoddy Indians. The purposes were to remove the cloud over real estate in Maine and also to authorize court action to review whether or not a wrong had been done or damages were due. In his remarks in the *Congressional Record* Senator Cohen made the following points, among others:

1. Maine had abided by its treaties with the tribes, and the tribes had never questioned their validity, substance, or adequacy until five years before.

2. There is no equitable way of forcing the return of land that had been "settled, developed and improved in good faith by Maine people for two centuries."

3. One solution would be for the federal government "to guarantee" state and local bonds and land transactions; however, the OMB and Congress would not "be eager to undertake a contingent liability of undefined proportions." Such a solution would also set a precedent for other states with land claims.

4. Another solution was "that if the claim by the two tribes can remain viable for over 180 years, then it follows that Congress retains the power to ratify and confirm the very treaties which the tribes now claim are null and void." Such action, of course, would have resolved the issue.

Senator Cohen concluded: "Surely if the passage of time cannot bar the Indian tribes' complaint, then it follows that it cannot bar congressional review and ratification of the treaties if Congress finds they are properly negotiated at the time and were free from fraud and unfairness.[7]

Congressman Lloyd Meeds, vice-chairman of the American Indian Policy Review Commission and chairman of the House Subcommittee on Indian Affairs, recommended that Congress "adopt legislation that extinguishes for all time all tribal or Indian claims to interests in real property, possessory or otherwise, grounded on aboriginal possession alone. Indian lands held under treaty, statute, Executive order or deed would not be affected."[8] No compensation would be due under the Fifth Amendment for such extinguishment.

This recommendation by Meeds, made in May 1977, was stimulated by the Maine land claims. He emphasized that claims based on aboriginal possession cannot be asserted against the United States: Indian title is not good against the sovereign state, the nonintercourse acts are not applicable to the United States; and all pre-1946 claims not brought before the Indian Claims Commission prior to 1951 were barred by section twelve of the Claims Commission Act.[9]

Meeds pointed out that entities such as states do not have the same protection as the United States against "ancient and stale Indian claims based on aboriginal possession." Thus, the Maine Indians sought the aid of the United States in suing the state of Maine for violation of the nonintercourse acts. Meeds recommended also "the enactment of a statute of limitations that all such claims not yet reduced to judgment shall be forever barred." As to morality, Meeds stated:

> Neither the Passamaquoddys whose possessory rights may have been interfered with, nor the people of the State of Maine or Massachusetts who may have dealt with them in the absence of a Federal treaty, are now alive. There is nothing unfair about denying the descendents of the Passamaquoddys a windfall and preventing the imposition of a bizarre and unjust burden on the descendents of the people of the States of Maine and Massachusetts.
>
> It seems to me that this is the correct solution because history clearly shows that the tribes for almost 200 years acquiesced in their land transactions with Maine and that the Congress had ratified Maine's and Massachusett's actions.[10]

In March 1978 the American Land Title Association (ALTA) issued a memorandum stating that Congress had the authority to one, approve the transfer of lands made by the tribe as of the date of the transfer; two, extinguish Indian title as of the date of the transfers; and three, extinguish any claims for trespass. ALTA indicated that Congress might compensate the Indians for the extinguishment of claims.[11]

In opposition to proposals such as those made by Cohen, Meeds, and ALTA "Indian advocates have contended that such action would constitute a taking of property without just compensation—a clear transgression of the fifth amendment." Large claims would be filed as a result. ALTA, however, maintained that Congress could extinguish Indian aboriginal title without liability and cited *Tee-Hit-Ton Indians* v. *United States*.[12]

How this policy issue and the proposed ALTA-type legislation to settle other aboriginal land claims affected other states was still being debated in Congress when this book went to press. The ALTA bill was not favored by either the House or Senate committees in 1978 and was never subject to hearings.

Negotiations

The Gunter recommendations had an effect on subsequent negotiations. Not only was the pressure for a negotiated settlement the result of the desire to avoid a costly judicial process over a long period of time and the economic stagnation that would be involved pending the outcome, but there was also the threat of Gunter's last two options (seven and eight), which closely paralleled some of the suggestions of Cohen, Meeds, and ALTA. Since these options were regarded as undesirable by the Indians and the state, they were undoubtedly a factor in encouraging serious negotiations.

Since the federal agencies were not coordinated and had been unable to come up with any proposal to which both the state and the tribes could agree, the Indians and the state took action. The result was a state act to implement the settlement of the Indian claims, which was approved by the governor on April 3, 1980.[13] This state act was contingent on the enactment by the federal government of legislation to extinguish the Indians claims and to provide the necessary funds to do so, as well as provision for the "ratifying and approving this Act without modification" by the federal government.

State and Indian representatives brought this state legislation to Washington and presented it to the White House, the secretary of the Interior, the OMB, and committees on Capitol Hill. The first formal meeting took place in late June 1980 in Washington. There were differences between the Senate committee staff and other participants. The people representing the federal government did not appreciate the "take it or leave it" attitude of the state and the Indians, and it was reported that the meeting ended on a bitter note. Those involved from time to time in this and other meetings were Tim Woodcock and Peter Taylor from the staff of the Senate Select Committee on Indian Affairs; Thomas N. Tureen and Suzanne Harjo from the Native American Rights Fund; Barbara Cohen of the Justice Department; Maine Attorney General Richard Cohen; James St. Clair, special counsel for Maine; John Paterson from the Maine attorney general's office; Dave Flanagan from the governor's office; John Hull, legislative counsel for the state legislature of Maine; Bonny Post, chairperson of Indian Affairs Committee of the state legislature; Reid Chambers for the Houlton band of Maliseet; and Tim Vollmann of the Interior Department's solicitor's office. Also involved in sessions from time to time were Senators William Cohen, George

Mitchell, and John Melcher, officials of the OMB, and members of the House Committee on Interior and Insular Affairs.

A July 10, 1980, meeting in Portland, Maine, had representatives from Interior, Justice, the state of Maine, the Maine legislature, the Senate Select Committee on Indian Affairs, legal counsel to the private landowners, and special counsel to the state of Maine. According to Peter Taylor, the July 10 meeting "may well have been the most important. We spent an entire day reviewing the bill, exchanging views. Out of that meeting everyone realized agreement was possible and that everyone genuinely wanted a settlement. From that point on we all pulled in harness and worked diligently toward solutions."[14]

The general procedure during the ten or so meetings through September 10, 1980, was to discuss the issues and agree on adjustments. Tim Vollmann assumed the redrafting responsibility all the way through these sessions and clearly was a key person.

The issues that were the most difficult to resolve were (1) the extent to which federal support would supplant the support the state would normally give the tribes as a result of their status as municipalities under the new state law—the exchange of correspondence on this issue was made a part of the record; (2) the benefits, if any, to the Houlton band of Maliseet—the bill presented to Congress would have extinguished any claim those Indians might have but would not have provided trust status for the land involved; (this issue was not resolved until the final drafting sessions); and (3) the date upon which Indian claims would be extinguished—the date of the act or the date Congress appropriated money to implement the act (the latter date was finally put in the bill).

Analysis

Settlement of the Maine land claims involved interactions among Indian tribes, attorneys, outside interest groups, courts, the state, Maine land owners, Interior, Justice, the OMB, the president, an outside consultant (Gunter) and Congress. The BIA was not an active participant.

At the signing of the Maine Indian Claims Settlement Act of 1980 on October 10 President Carter stated:

> It's a reaffirmation that our system of government works. A hundred and ninety years after the Passamaquoddy and Penobscot Indians and Maine settlers fought side by side to protect Maine's borders, to help defend all thirteen colonies in the Revolutionary War, the people of Maine have again shown themselves to be an example to us all, by working together, by acting with patience and fairness and understanding. This should be a proud day for . . . the tribes who placed their trust in the system that has

> not always treated them fairly, the leaders of the state of Maine who came openly to the bargaining table, the landowners who helped make the settlement a reality by offering land for sale that they might not otherwise have wanted to sell, the members of Congress who realize the necessity of acting and all the citizens of Maine who have worked together to resolve this problem of land title.[15]

However, it took a great deal of pushing, crisis creating, compromise, and hard work to achieve this result. As at the Constitutional Convention in Philadelphia, nobody was completely happy. Many people involved in the Maine claims case undoubtedly thought they should have done better for themselves.

The Indians and their attorneys, assisted by the courts, created an action-forcing situation. The federal government had to sue the state or change the law, and there were proponents of both courses. Evidently, it would have been legal to follow the suggestions of Cohen, Meeds, and ALTA, and their approach did have the apparent advantage of a speedy removal of the cloud on land title, which would eliminate that barrier to free economic activity. Depending on the wording of the legislation, it could also have provided for compensation to be determined through the courts. It is, of course, impossible to predict what might have been the end result of this process in terms of costs and benefits to the state and the Indians. This approach, however, might have turned out to be poor public relations, as it had the potential for leaving bitter feelings between two groups of Maine citizens. Undoubtedly Justice Gunter considered the social, economic, and political aspects of the case before drawing up his recommendations. Writing in 1979, before the settlement, Vollmann, in support of negotiation rather than unilateral action, stated that if the ALTA or Meeds concept were to approach enactment

> the affected tribes may well seek to unite with the national Indian leadership and its allies, and take all political steps necessary to defeat it. Indeed, Indian leaders are likely to view such a battle as a struggle to the death, characterizing the legislation as a perverse culmination of 200 ill-starred years of federal Indian policy, as a proclamation of a new rule that courts of law are accessible to all but Indian land claimants, and as a classic example of the principle that "might makes right." Such an ugly confrontation is unnecessary.[16]

Had not the president or the secretary of the Interior Department taken the lead in seeking a consensus, a long and costly court process or unilateral action by Congress might have resulted. However, President Carter seized the initiative by appointing Justice Gunter and followed up Gunter's recommendations by appointing a team to represent the federal government in negotiations with the Indians and the state. This action, in effect, forced the Indians and the state to negotiate.

Nobody likes to recede from a preannounced position, but the state and the Indians did so, as did the federal government in agreeing to a modification of Gunter's recommendations. In the background was the possibility of resorting to Gunter's last two options. The concepts involved in these options had strong supporters (Meeds, Cohen, and ALTA, among others), and the Indians and the state knew this. The Indians and the state were aware that if they appeared to be unreasonable in the negotiation process they would greatly strengthen the hand of the proponents of either unilateral action to extinguish alleged aboriginal rights or the payment of an indemnity without any return of land. The state also had the economic pressure of needing to clear land titles and thus wanted a speedy resolution. The negotiating team for the federal government knew that the president wanted a consensus solution that would not be too costly to the federal treasury. If a solution were too expensive, Congress probably would not go along with it.

All of these factors, plus the generally pro-Indian attitude of a large segment of the U.S. citizenry, played a part in forcing the consensus. Further, if the negotiators had not been skillful, the whole effort could have come to naught. But the environment made it possible for the negotiators of all three parties to succeed in developing a workable compromise.

Had the president opted to support abrogation of aboriginal rights or "approval after the fact" of the land transfers between the tribes and the state, he might have succeeded in getting Congress to take this approach. Had the courts put a different interpretation on the Nonintercourse Act, ruling that it did not apply to non–federally recognized Indians or to the original thirteen states, no action-forcing situation would have been created, since this interpretation would have affirmed the belief of the state of Maine and the Interior Department. So the courts also played an important part in determining this particular policy outcome. It will be remembered from Chapter 1 that under the Articles of Confederation Indian matters within each state were the responsibility of the state. Thus, it is easy to see how the federal government and the states along the eastern seaboard arrived at policies for Indians that were different from policies in the West where the states were established after the adoption of the U.S. Constitution with its specific Indian provisions.

The Maine Indian Claims Settlement Act of 1980 resolved the Maine case, but it did not resolve at one stroke the old aboriginal land claim issues arising in other states as a result of the Trade and Intercourse Act. Meeds had sought this result. The 1980 act did set a precedent that may influence the resolution of other cases.[17]

6

THE INDIAN POLICY MILIEU

The Bureau of Indian Affairs is at the center of Indian policy creation and execution. Under the U.S. constitutional system many other parts of the government and nongovernment actors are involved, but the institutional memory, expertise, and continuity are lodged in the BIA as the central federal agency concerned with Indian matters. If Indian legislation is not originally developed in the BIA or in cooperation with its professionals, such legislation inevitably is referred there by a congressional subcommittee and the Office of Management and Budget for the comments of BIA experts on the subject matter of the bill. The same situation is true for the IHS and Indian health concerns, and the execution of adopted legislation is carried out mainly by BIA, IHS, and other agency personnel in the field as detailed in Chapters 2 and 3. Although the foregoing is generally true, some major policy issues may be influenced only in a minor way by the BIA as is indicated in the Maine claims example. Even in these exceptional cases, however, the job of carrying out the policy generally falls on BIA staff. The same kinds of societal forces are at work in the Indian policy area as in other fields.[1]

Indians: Individuals, Tribes, and Interest Groups

Individual Indians and tribes as clients interact with service programs all of the time, and this interaction affects both the Indian and the agency. The government employee learns what is and is not acceptable in the nature of a service or in the way in which it is provided. The Indian client becomes aware of the necessary information required for a particularly desired action and of the limits of personnel time or funds available. Changes in policy may result from this interaction. The agency may propose a regulation or a legislative change on the basis of the experiences of its field personnel. Clients may band together to influence action by their agency, other agencies, or Congress. Both the agency and its clients may also strive to increase resources available through increased funds or personnel—e.g., for improved education or health services.

The Navajo tribe has a Washington, D.C., office, and officials of many tribes frequently visit the state and national capitals to influence programs and policies. The Washington, D.C., visits include those to executive departments, the OMB, the White House, (on occasion), congressional committees and their staffs, and individual members of Congress. The BIA and IHS receive some of this attention.

Indians have discovered that in unity there is strength. Thus the National Congress of American Indians has stated "that a prime purpose is to help achieve unity among tribes to address issues and concerns common to all so that Indians can speak with one voice on national issues."[2]

Indian interest groups can be classified in different ways—by purpose, by size, by whether all Indian or both Indian and non-Indian, by source of funding, and by general effectiveness. Indian interest groups deserve to be the subject of a special study, and in order to obtain specific data about these groups I sent a letter to approximately sixty nonprofit groups or organizations.

General Indian interest groups such as the National Tribal Chairmen's Association (NTCA), the National Congress of American Indians (NCAI), and the Association of American Indian Affairs (AAIA) are concerned with many aspects of Indian policy. Both the NTCA and NCAI maintain Washington, D.C., offices. Specialized Indian interest groups concentrate on a limited or single subject-matter area. Examples are the Council of Energy Resource Tribes (CERT), the Native American Rights Fund (NARF), and the Association of American Indian Physicians. Regional Indian interest groups are often very influential within their jurisdictions. The Alaska Federation of Natives, the Affiliated Tribes of Northwest Indians, and the All Indian Pueblo Council are primarily area oriented.

The various organizations differ widely in their dependence on public funding. Dependence on federal funding might compromise independence, but officials dealing with the organizations do not find that the NCAI, NTCA, or CERT, which are primarily dependent on federal funding, are any less vitriolic, critical, or reluctant to lobby vigorously against a BIA or administration stand than the AAIA, which is privately funded. The influences of these organizations, of course, are subtle and difficult to determine. More important, perhaps, is the degree of grass roots support by Indians themselves, which is indicated by their financial contributions. Government contract funding to carry out certain services or functions with some of these organizations may in part result from the congressional policy of turning the execution of programs over to Indians insofar as possible. Such contracts may not always be based on an evaluation and a determination that a particular Indian organization is the most effective mechanism to achieve a given result.

The BIA, IHS, and other agencies sometimes use such groups as the NCAI and NTCA in the consultation process. The current emphasis on self-determination and participation and involvement of Indians in Indian policy formation and execution requires some mechanism or methods for accomplishment. Presenting an administrative proposal to the NCAI or NTCA for evaluation and comment may help achieve this end. However, consultation is generally through direct contact with individual tribes.

Examples of Influence

After the administration's institution of block grants that combined several BIA activities for the 1982 budget submission, Indian and congressional resistence reversed the action in the committee. In the Martinez case the Supreme Court held in 1978 that except for habeas corpus, the Indian Civil Rights Act of 1968 does not provide access to federal courts for individuals who feel their civil rights have been violated by actions of their tribal government. Rather, the Court determined that such matters are to be resolved through the use of tribal forums. The BIA decided that even though it had no authority to review alleged infringement of civil rights, it did have the responsibility to see that tribes lived up to the terms of their approved constitutions. If the obligations of tribal officials under these constitutions were breached it was a violation of the political government-to-government relationship between the tribe and the federal government. A memorandum issued on June 12, 1980, by the acting assistant secretary of Indian affairs, provided for progressively severe sanctions for such violations—from refusal of the federal government to approve a specific act of tribal government to withdrawal of recognition of all tribal officials or cutoff of BIA funding to the tribe. The NCAI, the Pueblo, Red Lake, Mescalero, Penobscot, Puyallup, and many others opposed the policy. As a result of this pressure the June 12 memorandum was withdrawn on January 17, 1981.

The Ak-Chin Indian community in Arizona went directly to Congress in initiating the process that resulted in the Ak-Chin Indian Community Water Rights Settlement Act in 1978.[3] When the Interior Department was asked to testify, the solicitor's office and the Bureau of Reclamation represented the department; the BIA was left out. However, the BIA receives the funding and is contracting with the tribe for construction.

Until recently the House Committee on Interior had a subcommittee on Indian affairs. The later chairmen and members of this former subcommittee were pulled back and forth between the militants and responsible leadership and between Indian, state, and private sector interests. Since the national Indian constituency is not large enough to yield much in the way of political rewards for a congressman in the forms of national recognition and promotion to key leadership posts in the House, an assignment to a subcommittee on Indian affairs was not particularly attractive. When the lack of possible leadership reward was combined with sometimes savage attacks by segments of the Indian community, even when Congress had done its best, few people were interested in an Indian committee assignment. As a result, there is now no subcommittee on Indian affairs in the House as no one could be talked into taking the chairmanship. Indian affairs are handled by the full committee, and they do not receive much attention from the elected members. One result is an increased influence on the part of the committee staff in Indian matters.

As an example of the effect of conflicting Indian attitudes, the three attorneys who secured a handsome settlement for the Sioux in a Black Hills case against almost impossible odds have been attacked by the traditional Sioux. The elected Sioux leaders cannot put up a vigorous defense without seeming to favor the loss of the Black Hills, which is a very emotional issue. Use of the court-awarded funds is blocked for the present by this controversy.

An example of the operation of the subsystem is provided by the restoration of trust status to Menominee Indian land and the reinstitution of BIA-subsidized services to Menominee tribal members. These changes were achieved by the active leadership of a group of Menominee known as the Determination of Rights and Unity of Menominee Shareholders (DRUMS). DRUMS, with the help of OEO legal services and the Native American Rights Fund, drafted the proposed legislation to restore BIA trust control of resources and provision of services. This legislation was successfully lobbied through Congress with the help of the BIA. Menominee testimony and careful follow-up with key legislators helped achieve the desired result.

Still other examples of Indian interest group influence on Indian policy and execution are found throughout this book.

State and Local Governments

The Constitution provides for a division of responsibilities between the federal and state governments, but a clear-cut delineation of the responsibilities for and services to Indian citizens by the state and federal governments has been difficult because of the constitutional provisions regarding Indians, the location of many governmental functions at the state level for most citizens, and constantly changing circumstances.

In the Indian policy formation and execution process the states have played an important role as is illustrated throughout this book. Chapter 5 indicates the influence of the state of Maine in the claims settlement process, for example, and the state of Alaska participated vigorously in the process leading to the Alaska Claims Settlement Act of December 18, 1971.

State and local governments provide an estimated 80 to 85 percent of the government services received by Indians.[4] The heavy involvement of states in services to their Indian citizens is not very well known by either the special groups interested in Indian matters or by the general public. Indians, the BIA, and Indian interest groups play down the state services and emphasize the federal relationship. Even the states tend to emphasize the federal relationship because their tax burden is relieved when the federal government assumes responsibility.

The American Indian Policy Review Commission (*Final*) *Report* places little emphasis on state services except to say that such services should be severely limited. Members and staff of the Senate Select Committee on Indian Affairs have been a part of the Indian subsystem and have pushed for a separate Indian status and a direct federal relationship with Indian tribes. However, the committee has recommended that state and county governments sit down with tribal governments in an attempt to resolve their jurisdictional conflicts.[5]

Since many reservations are small and a limited number of people live on them, their economic viability often depends on cooperation with the surrounding non-Indian society and government. Some of the larger reservations have also found that cooperation with non-Indian neighbors is profitable. On the Yakima Reservation in the state of Washington there are approximately 5,000 Indians, 8,000 Chicanos, and 21,000 Anglos. These varied residents work together in the cultivation of apples, sugar beets, and hops. The tribe has invested in a sugar plant in Toppenish and has cooperative activities with the towns of Toppenish and Yakima. The public schools serving the reservation area, in Toppenish and Wapato, have worked cooperatively with the Yakima tribe in offering an Indian cultural education program. Both Indians and non-Indians can take the course for credit.[6] Good relationships among tribal, local, and state governments facilitate economic, social, and political progress for the areas concerned.

State governments serve Indians mainly through the same divisions of government that serve other citizens as is illustrated in the educational area. However, some states have established Indian commissions or offices to assist the regular state government departments in working with Indian citizens. This seems to be the general practice for most states that have federal reservations as the problems of mixed civil and criminal jurisdiction, child custody, hunting and fishing rights, tax jurisdiction, and similar matters provide a major challenge to tribal and state governments as well as to the BIA and other agencies on the federal level.

Twenty states have Indian commissions or the equivalent. The purposes of these Indian commissions vary with the several states, but most have the general objectives of gathering information on Indian needs and the adequacy of serving them; working with Indian, local, state, and federal governments to help coordinate actions to provide adequate services; acting as a liaison between Indians and the state when regular state services do seem not to fit or serve a particular need; working with tribes when requested to help develop effective relationships between state service agencies and Indian citizens; and advising and recommending policies and legislation on Indian matters to the governor, legislature, and the state's congressional delegation.

Specific instances and examples of commission activity are cited in *The States and Their Indian Citizens*, which was published in 1972,[7] and many of these same arrangements were in effect in 1982. Some of the same problems exist and, in some cases, have been intensified—as in the Pacific Northwest. Some problems have peaked and seem to have been resolved; for example, the land claim cases of Alaska and Maine.[8]

The Impact of Specialists

The BIA illustrates the characteristics of large organizations: specialization, continuity, and incremental policymaking. The specialists are the primary reason for the influence of the BIA on Indian policy. They are experts in their subject-matter fields, know the history and results of past policy and action, and have a desire to achieve the maximum favorable results in their area of expertise.

The BIA's specialists are like all specialists—they want their specialty to have the highest priority, and they want maximum freedom to carry out their functions. When responsibility for Indian health was still under the BIA, the medical doctors continually sought autonomy from generalists such as agency superintendents and area directors. Eventually this responsibility was transferred to the Public Health Service, where the medical personnel found an environment molded by the medical profession.

Indian education officials in the BIA have historically sought to have the freedom to deal directly with school personnel on the reservations and have resisted the coordinating roles of the commissioner, area directors, and Indian agency superintendents. As indicated in Chapters 2 and 3, the educationists, with the help of committee staffs on Capitol Hill, have succeeded in achieving independence from the commissioner, area directors, and agency superintendents for educational matters such as curriculum and direct supervision of school teachers, but not for necessary support and facility maintenance activities. The separation of education from other BIA activities on the area and agency levels has sometimes resulted in a stalemate. In one instance a school superintendent would not ask the area contracting officer to negotiate a contract with the tribe, even though the school superintendent had promised the tribe the contract. The BIA agency superintendent and area director had no authority to resolve the situation as they had no control over the school superintendent.

When the area offices were formed the personnel of already existing consolidated field headquarters for functions such as irrigation, forestry, and roads resisted the combination of their functions with the area functions of other specialists under the supervision of an area director.

These inclinations on the part of BIA specialists are not entirely the result of pure cussedness, but largely stem from the fact that the mission of each specialty is different. To best achieve the goal of a specialty the professionals desire maximum freedom and certainly no interference from nonspecialist generalists such as an agency superintendent or an area director. When the overall goal of the bureau requires that specialist activities be coordinated the specialists are unhappy. For example, a BIA road through an Indian soil conservation watershed control project can raise havoc unless the soil conservation and road engineers get together and make such modifications as may be necessary to achieve the maximum benefits of both programs. If these specialists do not get together as a matter of course, the agency superintendent can require that they do so.

The Subsystem

An important aspect of policy formation and execution in Indian affairs is the interrelationship of the BIA, Indian congressional committees, and Indian interest groups. This triangular relationship develops and oversees most policy. Figure 6.1 indicates this relationship by the triangle joining the assistant secretary/Bureau of Indian Affairs, Indian committees of Congress, and Indian interest groups. J. Leiper Freeman referred to this relationship as a subsystem and used the Indian policy

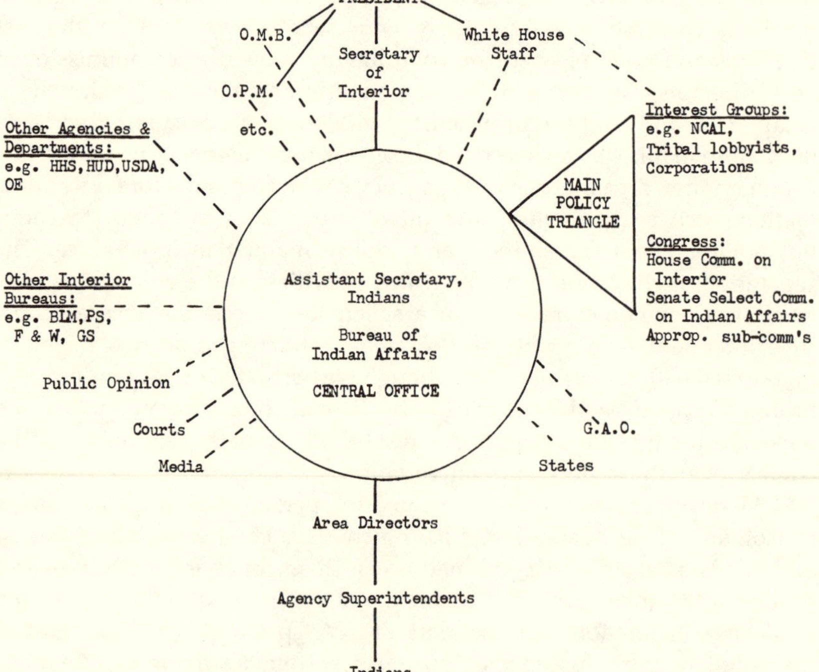

Figure 6.1. Relationships of the assistant secretary, Indians, and the Bureau of Indian Affairs with other groups.

area during the time of Roosevelt, Ickes, and Collier as an example in his book, *The Political Process: Executive Bureau—Legislative Committee Relations*.[9] Other people have referred to the relationship as the "iron triangle."

The participants in this subsystem have a vested interest in this Indian subgovernmental process as it provides their power base. They get to know each other well, and except for a very few major issues, they determine Indian policy and its method of execution. The subsystem, however, is only a part of the total environment as is indicated in Figure 6.1.

Economic Pressures

Relationships between Indian tribes and the BIA on the one side and the private sector and the states on the other side may be tense as a result of the volatile economic impacts of court decisions. For example, there will be major challenges in the Pacific Northwest and the Great Lake areas as treaty provisions are implemented. Placing the maintenance of the fish run ahead of other activities such as lumbering and irrigated farming without regard for the relative economic benefits is almost certain to lead to court, legislative, and administrative actions of importance to many non-Indians as well as Indians.

In 1975 the Department of Interior filed suit on behalf of Papago Indian water rights. The defendants were the city of Tucson, the state of Arizona, six mining companies, a farming enterprise, and 1,600 other private water users in the basin. These defendants got together with Arizona Congressman Morris Udall, who was chairman of the House Interior and Insular Affairs Committee; the Indians were assisted by a private consulting firm. The consultants produced a bill, HR 5118, which was reported out of committee on January 29, 1982. The bill's solution to the problem was to have the federal government furnish more water so that all of the users could continue unabated water consumption and the Indians could still be provided with their water rights. (The court suit had been aimed at the defendants' reducing water use so that the Indians' share would be available to them without the provision of additional water.)

Garrey E. Carruthers, assistant secretary of the Interior for land and water resources, testified before the Senate Select Committee on Indian affairs in opposition to the House bill and the Senate version.[10] He stated that although the bills settled the liabilities of all the nonfederal parties responsible for the water problem, they did so at an estimated federal cost of between $100 million and $200 million, not including liabilities or costs of the delivery of water from the Central Arizona Project to the Tucson-Papago area. The assistant secretary further stated that the final act should provide for the defendants' sharing in the costs of providing the Papago Indians with water rather than placing the costs on the general taxpayer. President Reagan vetoed the final bill on June 1, 1982.

However, Morris Udall came back with a package that the president was forced to sign. The act, "To Authorize the Secretary of the Interior to Construct, Operate, and Maintain Modifications of the Existing Buffalo Bill Dam and Reservoir, Shoshone Project, Pick-Sloan Missouri River Basin Project, Wyoming, and for Other Purposes," had three titles: (1) Construction of Buffalo Bill Dam Modifications, (2) Reclamation Reform Act of 1982, and (3) Southern Arizona Water Rights Settlement Act (Papago Reform). Interior wanted titles 1 and 2, so had to agree to title 3, which provided a compromise solution to water around Tucson. The act, PL 97-293, became law on October 12, 1982.

Other Bureaus and Departments

Other Interior Deparment bureaus have their own basic missions—as do other departments and agencies. Many of them have Indian programs and services or carry out such services on a reimbursable basis. However, their missions sometimes conflict with the BIA's Indian-oriented missions: for example, (1) the Bureau of Reclamation's water claims for non-Indian farmers versus BIA claims for Indian water rights, (2) the authorization by the Federal Power Commission of a dam that would flood portions of an Indian reservation, or (3) the Corps of Engineers' plans for a flood control dam that either interrupts water flow for Indian irrigation or floods Indian land. Sometimes different departments and agencies have parallel goals such as fire suppression on forest land. The Forest Service (USDA), the states (Washington, Oregon, Idaho), the Bureau of Land Management (Interior), and the BIA all administer forests in the Pacific Northwest. These agencies have pooled their fire suppression efforts under a coordinated command, with each agency providing its proportion of support.

Attempts to achieve interagency coordination are sometimes difficult. Both the BIA and the Children's Bureau in the Department of Health and Human Services (HHS) are authorized to fund Indian child welfare services, and in September 1980 the secretary of the Interior initiated correspondence to coordinate the efforts of the two groups. The BIA proposed that the Children's Bureau transfer Indian child welfare funds to the BIA to simplify administration. This suggestion was turned down in December 1980 by the HHS, which claimed that its statute prohibited this approach. The BIA and the Children's Bureau must try to coordinate their efforts.

Interactions among Interior agencies, the OMB, and Congress are illustrated by the Navajo Indian Irrigation Project (NIIP), which was authorized in 1962 for a total of 110,000 acres. About half the total acreage had been served as of 1982. However, Congress had questioned the size of the full project when considering the 1979 budget. There had been a long-simmering disagreement between the Bureau of Reclamation (which was doing the construction work with funds appropriated to the BIA) and the BIA concerning the ultimate acreage and Indian water entitlement. The OMB reduced funds for 1982 and eliminated funds entirely for 1983 to force Interior to resolve this issue. The Interior Office of Policy, Budget, and Administration and the OMB favor the smaller Bureau of Reclamation numbers rather than the BIA and Navajo figures. To complicate matters, the Navajo Agricultural Products Industry (NAPI), the tribal entity farming NIIP land, has had serious management problems.

Influence of Able Leadership

The initiative and originality of developing the legal theory of the applicability of the Nonintercourse Act to the Passamaquoddy tribe by attorney Thomas Tureen have had tremendous impact, not only in Maine but up and down the East Coast. The positive leadership of President Carter and the quality of the settlement proposal by Judge Gunter helped divert the Maine land claim case from a possibly long, costly, and bruising judicial process or a unilateral congressional action. Either of those courses of action would have left a bad taste in many quarters. Strong leaders such as Emil Notti and Willie Hensley in the Alaska Federation of Natives; the forceful land freeze by Interior Secretary Stewart Udall, which prevented strong oil interests and Alaskan state officials from proceeding with development of oil; and the able negotiations of Alaska Congressman Nick Begich certainly had impacts on the Alaska claims settlement.

Charles Rovin's establishment of the Tribal Work Experience Program to replace the normal welfare payment system (see Chapter 3), when he was in charge of BIA Social Services, indicates the kind of innovative leadership that moves to correct the cause of a problem as well as to build human dignity rather than lessen it. The leadership of William Benjamin, as head of the Navajo-Hopi Resettlement Office, resulted in an outstanding job of working with the courts, the Hopi and Navajo tribes, and the Phoenix and Navajo Area Offices in moving to resolve the long and bitter dispute between the Navajo and the Hopi. The battle is not over, however.

Political Executives and Civil Servants

The political appointee–civil service linkage in the BIA is important in respect to the quality of leadership. The commissioner of Indian affairs and the assistant secretary for Indians in the Interior Department are presidential appointees confirmed by the senate. One of the characteristics of political appointments is short tenure.[11] An exception was John Collier who served as commissioner of Indian affairs for thirteen years (1933–1945). Since 1969, when Louis R. Bruce was appointed commissioner, there have been at least fifteen different people occupying the assistant secretary and commissioner slots, some officially confirmed and others on an acting basis. The sequence is as follows: Louis Bruce for two and one-half years to January 20, 1973; Marvin L. Franklin as an assistant to the secretary in charge of the BIA, January to December 1973; Morris Thompson, commissioner for three years to November 1976; Raymond V. Butler, acting commissioner to December 1976; Ben

Reifel, commissioner, December 1976 to January 1977; Raymond V. Butler, acting commissioner, January to September 15, 1977; Forrest Gerard, assistant secretary for Indians, September 15, 1977, to January 1, 1980, followed by Sidney Mills, Thomas Fredericks, and James Canon as acting assistant secretary to May 15, 1981. Finally, another commissioner was appointed, William E. Hallett, and he served from November 19, 1979, to January 19, 1981; acting commissioners following Hallett were Martin Seneca and Theodore Krenzke to May 15, 1981; Kenneth L. Smith was appointed assistant secretary for Indians on May 15, 1981. Under Smith the BIA has been operated by two different people: Kenneth Payton was acting deputy assistant secretary to December 13, 1981, and John W. Fritz has been deputy assistant secretary (operations) and serving as head of the BIA since that time.

In contrast, Dr. Emery A. Johnson was director of the Indian Health Service from 1969 to 1981, a period of twelve years. This stability resulted in a completely different organizational climate than that experienced by the BIA during the same period of time.

When one looks back over the history of the bureau John Collier stands out as one of the most prominent commissioners, and one of the factors was his extended tenure. He was on the job long enough to follow through on a program and have an impact. Collier was able to correct actions that did not yield results and to emphasize programs that worked. With a reasonable length of tenure a commissioner or an assistant secretary would have to suffer the consequences of unwise or mistaken initiatives and would be able to follow through effectively on basically sound initiatives. These factors do not apply to short tenures. Added to the high turnover in BIA leadership is the frequent turnover in tribal leadership in many tribes. This situation places an even greater premium on BIA continuity for productive effort over a period of time.

Short-term political appointees have little chance of getting to know either their fellow political appointees—with whom they must work in external BIA relations—or their key career civil service staff on whom the work of the agency depends. There is no time for a political appointee and his or her senior career staff to really get acquainted, evaluate each other's competence in carrying out their respective responsibilities, and develop the trust in one another that is so essential for effective organizational effort. This problem has certainly been demonstrated in the BIA.

One of the pressures on new political appointees is to show results fast, and often the quickest and easiest way to give an impression of action is to reorganize. Every ten years or so some reorganization may be beneficial, or sooner if an agency has a major change in overall responsibility. But frequent reorganizations, one every time a new political head arrives to supervise the BIA, have had the effect of slowing things down, disrupting work processes, and breaking up the informal systems and relationships that often are the best way of achieving expeditious action. Moving the boxes and people around too frequently also has a negative impact on morale and productivity. To a large extent reasonable continuity and accountability go together.

Because of the problem of a high rate of turnover of politically appointed officials, one of the issues in public administration under our constitutional system is to what level should such appointments extend. For responsibility to the electorate, the president, and Congress there is little question but what department heads should be appointed by the president with the advice and consent of the Senate. Deputy and assistant secretaries who supervise several bureaus are generally considered to be appropriate political appointees to help the elected administration carry out its policies. The bureau level raises a great deal more debate. Bureaus should be responsive to major policies of elected officials, but do their chiefs have to be politically appointed to achieve this result?

This issue was debated by the Hoover Commission, which recommended in 1949 that the commissioner of the Bureau of Indian Affairs be a "professional, permanent administrator." It further recommended that the secretary of Interior, being a political appointee and politically responsible for the department, appoint the commissioner.[12] Since the 1970s the trend has been to increase the number of political appointees at ever-lower grades or in added superstructure. Events in the area of Indian affairs have illustrated this trend, too.

Inadvertent Results of Policy Formation Process

Sometimes people use the constitutional system in a peculiar way. The Watergate crisis and the antagonism of some congressmen toward environmentalists may have been primary factors in returning land to the small Havasupai tribe in the Grand Canyon in Arizona. The BIA and Interior were opposed to returning up to 251,000 acres of Forest Service and Park Service land to the tribe. Senator Barry Goldwater and Representatives Sam Steiger and John Rhodes (House minority leader)—all of Arizona—favored the transfer. John Whitaker, Interior undersecretary, thought the transfer might bolster Nixon's stock at a time when Republicans seemed to be wavering in their opposition to impeachment during the Watergate crisis. So Whitaker sold the OMB on changing the administration's policy. Nixon announced his support of the transfer on May 3, 1974, at a political rally in Phoenix.

As the transfer was debated in the House, Representative Thomas S. Foley of Washington noted that the 700-member Havasupai tribe had accepted a Claims Commission award of $1,240,000 for the taking of their land and that "if we now undertake to transfer the lands in question to the Havasupai Tribe, I will absolutely predict that other tribes will ask for lands in addition to whatever claims have been paid to them." The environmentalists opposed the proposed bill. "Republican Representative Sam Steiger of Arizona, a gleeful environmentalist-baiter," persuaded "a good many Republican members of Congress" to support the transfer "for the bizarre reason that environmentalists—'green bigots,' Steiger used to call them—so vehemently opposed it." The bill was passed. "The Havasupai restoration was, on the whole, an inadvertent act, motivated by two reasons which border on the base: impeachment politics and anti-environmentalist animus."[13]

Balancing of Special Interests

For issues such as gun control, abortion, clean air, and smoking there are interest groups on all sides of each question. The executive departments, regulatory agencies, and the committees on Capitol Hill are continuously bombarded from several directions, and research is supplied by the special interests concerned to support their various viewpoints. These counterbalancing pressures do not exist to the same degree in Indian Affairs. Indian affairs policy might be divided into two areas for analysis: (1) resource concerns and (2) governmental and social service relationships and services.

In the resource field there are often counterbalancing pressures. In connection with the Navajo Indian Irrigation Project it was noted earlier that the OMB and the program staff of the secretary of the Interior favored less acreage and less water for the Indians and the BIA and the Indians favored more acreage and more water. Sportsmen and environmentalists, as well as the U.S. Forest Service, opposed the return of 48,000 acres of land and Blue Lake to the Taos Pueblo in 1970. Commercial fishermen oppose court interpretations of Indian treaty fishing rights; states, cities, and private water users, and often the Bureau of Reclamation, oppose claimed Indian treaty water rights. One of the most recent water battles was over the allocation of Central Arizona Project water between Indian and non-Indian uses. Counties are concerned about additional land being placed under federal trust, which lessens the tax base. There are forces at work in the resource area that tend to bring about a balance in the development of resource policy.

However, in the governmental and social services area conflicts of interest do not exist to the same extent. Jurisdiction on Indian reservations is an exception as that issue has strong advocates on both sides. The philosophy of self-determination, the statements about the sovereignty of Indian tribes and the loose use of the concept of "federal trust responsibility" seem to have no organized opposition. These phrases find their way into congressional legislation, presidential statements, and budget justifications apparently without question. The only opposing group seems to be the Interstate Congress for Equal Rights and Responsibilities, and it has not had much impact. Along with these philosophical underpinnings go considerable federal funds. Since the 1940s and 1950s no serious challenge to the efficacy of federal Indian programs has been raised, except in regard to education. No effective public interest groups, parts of the executive branch, or committees on Capitol Hill challenge the programs. In 1977 the American Indian Policy Review Commission supported the current programs and assumptions. There apparently is no ongoing evaluation as to whether current policy is creating an Indian dependency on government largess or whether it is increasing self-sufficiency. Without challenge from some source this lack of evaluation may continue and result in a policy imbalance and a decrease in the possibility of obtaining desired results.

The Agency View

The Bureau of Indian Affairs, like other agencies, has an institutional culture. Harold Seidman says an agency's culture reflects "institutional history, ideology, values, symbols, folklore, professional biases, behavior patterns, heros and enemies."[14] For competent Indian tribes and groups the federal government's termination of the trust relationship for Indian resources and other special services was the "agency line" in the 1950s. To oppose this view was "to make waves." In the 1970s the agency dogma included self-determination, continued trust responsibility, contract with tribes, Indian preference for both jobs and contracts, a continued federal-tribal government-to-government relationship, and tribal sovereignty. To question these verities required a brave soul. The subtle influence of the "agency view" on the views of employees has been noted by scholars such as Seidman. If an employee has a question about agency policy and knows his or her boss would not appreciate the question's being raised, the employee frequently squelches the doubt and, in time, may unquestioningly follow the agency line. Assistant Commissioner John Provinse and D'Arcy McNickle, who were on the BIA staff in the 1950s, had doubts about the results of the termination policy. They were not warmly applauded by the commissioner or the rest of his staff (see Chapter 7 for a discussion of Provinse and a conference of anthropologists in 1954).

Employees of the BIA in 1983 who have questions about current policies and trends are not encouraged to voice them. The agency line tends to be pervasive. It generally conforms with the thinking of Indian leaders, Indian interest groups, and committee staff members on Capitol Hill. It is almost incestuous. It tends to mold political appointees who may come in with different ideas so that they soon become proponents of the agency view.

Because of the "brainwashing" aspects of the agency view it is essential to have competing interest groups or institutions if program policy is to have a chance to relate to the broader societal reality.

Part Three

THE FUTURE

7

POLICY ISSUES

There are certain key policy issues discussed in Parts One and Two that are still in a state of flux and about which there are divergent views and proposals for resolution. My formulation and summary of these issues are discussed in this chapter. I make no recommendations but do present some optional policy alternatives.

The March of Events

Events overtake policy. The issues of land claims, treaty fishing and water rights, self-determination, the federal trust responsibility, reservation poverty, and reservation oil revenues appear in the headlines and flash across television screens. Old policy is reshaped in attempting to work out solutions. Constant change—on and off the reservation, in technology and the economy, in society and government—requires continuous adjustment. Culture does not stand still. The rate of change seems to constantly accelerate and society must meet the challenge of our collision with tomorrow described by Alvin Toffler.[1]

Those portions of the Indian community that are more or less isolated from society's main currents—e.g., those Indians on reservations or in small rural groups found in many states—have a double challenge. These Indians face the task of trying to bridge the gap between their current condition and the circumstances of the larger society by which they are surrounded. In addition, they have to try to keep up with ever-increasing changes in the larger society itself. Many members of the larger society find this second task alone difficult.

A gradual diffusion of Indian citizens (or citizens with some Indian blood) has been occurring. Census figures indicate the movement of many Indians to urban centers. This diffusion began with Indian-white contact but was accelerated by World War I and World War II. Many Indians fought in World War I or worked in defense plants, and the

Indians who underwent these experiences changed. They became, in part at least, familiar with many aspects of non-Indian culture. World War II provided another stimulus, and since many reservation economies could not support their populations this off-reservation trend continued. The relocation policy of the 1950s provided financing for Indians to learn a skill and also provided living expenses until a job was obtained. This policy perhaps accelerated the diffusion of Indians during the period following World War II. On the other hand, during the Depression of the 1930s the policy had been reservation based as jobs were scarce, and federal spending and policy in the 1970s again tended to provide opportunities on the reservation and probably slowed the trend. Some people even suspect the trend may have been reversed.

Two major factors will tend to support the continuance of movement from Indian enclaves to the larger society: (1) the ever-increasing impact of education and (2) the burgeoning reservation overpopulation in many instances in relation to the jobs and resources available. Ever-higher percentages of reservation Indian children are graduating from elementary and high school, and accelerating numbers are attending college. Many Indians have been tempted by jobs and improved opportunities for their children in urban centers. Education and training programs provided by the BIA, other federal agencies, or the states have made it possible for more and more Indians to qualify for jobs in the non-Indian society as well as to take over leadership positions in both the private and the government sectors on the reservation. The high unemployment rate on many reservations and the accompanying poverty tend to stimulate many to try to find a better life. When Indians obtain the requisite skills many of them enter the broader American society and succeed.

Also, there is an inward flow of influences from the white culture to the reservation such as piped water, electricity, radio, television, automobiles, state public schools, frequently state law and order, washing machines, small business, and some manufacturing. Over the years the BIA has also been a major cause of cultural change in tribal government, education, land and resource management, social services, health, and many other areas on the reservation.

Some people may believe that Indian culture is threatened. Although many Indian values and beliefs continue, Indian culture is constantly changing as circumstances change, just as all cultures do. The horse was borrowed from the Spanish; it was unknown to Indians before the white man introduced it. Both Navajo sheep and "traditional" Navajo dress were borrowed from the invaders. The horse and wagon for the most part are now being replaced by the pickup truck and the dog sled by the snowmobile. Instead of grass for a horse and fish for a dog, both obtainable in a subsistence economy, the Indian or Eskimo needs cash for gasoline. This need is forcing the Native Americans into a wage economy. The Indian would rather use a steel axe or chain saw than his original stone tools and fire. The movement from a subsistence to a wage economy is fundamental and results in a gradual change in life-style. It is in part responsible for the pressure to develop a wage economy on the reservations. Earning a salary or wages in a nine-to-five job, five days a week, is quite different from the requirements of subsistence economies. Raising cash crops for sale is different from subsistence agriculture. Traditional Indian ways have to be modified if individuals are to succeed in the new wage economy. This modification is not easy for many of the Indian individuals involved. However, the transition can be and is being made in many instances.

Wilcomb Washburn points out that Indian individuals and tribal groups can share the values of both the non-Indian and the Indian societies. He cites the interrelationships of the traditionalist-oriented and white-oriented groups on the Blackfeet Reservation in Montana, as well as the gradual absorption of "white" values and life-styles and integration with the larger community on the Hoopa Valley Reservation in northern California. In contrast, he points to the clinging to past traditions of the Hopi in Arizona, although the Hopi are divided, and some inroads of modern technology have occured. Also, he notes the general acceptance of a government over all of the Hopi villages, which at one time was thought to be improbable.[2] Scholarly studies can inform on the impact of Indian-white contact and cultural change, but there are also several excellent fictionalized accounts by keen observers of the cultural interchange that may be of interest.[3] Not all Indians like the changes that are occurring. Those aspects of their culture they do find valuable or useful are retained, as is the case with other ethnic groups in our society.

As pointed out in the chapter on tribal governments there are very few traditional governments in operation, and those that do exist are mainly in the pueblos of New Mexico. Historically, the Navajo had no general central government—individuals bands migrated from place to place in a general area. Using western forms to a large extent the Navajo have developed a fairly sophisticated central government—a necessity if modern challenges are to be met. This is a change of major magnitude.

Both Indians and non-Indians have had to face many changes in the last 300 years, and not all of these changes were foreseen very far in advance. Time does not stand still. Both Indian and non-Indian citizens will face continual change in the future. If the past is any indication of the future the reader may only dimly perceive at present, if at all, future changes in Indian policy and their impact on all citizens.

The policy of today may be unsuitable for solving the problems of tomorrow.

Indian Land

The basic legal responsibility of the Bureau of Indian Affairs is the managing of Indian land in trust. The American Indian Policy Review Commission and many BIA personnel, tribal leaders, and congressional staff members have been lumping all federal functions and services to Indians together as "trust responsibility." This tendency is not factually correct. Education, social services, and tribal assistance have been gratuitous services and of the same character as for any other citizen, except for brief periods required in some treaties that have been fulfilled and have expired. Social services are not a trust responsibility. These services are authorized by statute but are dependent upon appropriations, which can be increased or stopped without violating any statute.

The trust responsibility for land and its management is different. If this trust responsibility is not adequately performed the BIA is subject to court suit, and the responsibility includes the products of the land, such as range grass and trees, and the mineral riches lying beneath the surface. Most treaty provisions that are still applicable relate to physical resources—primarily fishing, hunting, and water rights. Managing the land and its products requires expertise and sophistication. The BIA has this expertise for most matters relating to Indian land and receives help from the Geological Survey, the Bureau of Mines, the Bureau of Reclamation, the Fish and Wildlife Service, the Park Service, and the Bureau of Land Management.

Even though the BIA has the legal responsibility the Indian owners are largely responsible for determining the use and management of trust land. This policy is laudable, and it is in large measure the result of education, training, and encouragement by BIA personnel over the years. This acceptance of responsibility should be encouraged and rewarded.

There is a real catch, however. The BIA is still legally responsible for the results. In other words, when Indians exercise the initiative not only are they availing themselves of the freedom to act, but they also have the safeguard of government recompense if mistakes are made. This is a very enviable position, and one that is desirable during the learning process. But whether this paternalism is warranted for the indefinite future is a major policy issue.

An example of the problems caused by this situation is found in a 1975 General Accounting Office (GAO) study, which stated in part:

> An estimated 13 million acres, or 30 percent of Indian rangeland are not being properly managed and are in poor condition because (1) the range has been overgrazed, (2) range improvements have not been effectively used or maintained, and (3) limited use has been made of training and education programs. These problems have existed on some reservations for years. Short-term stopgap measures have been taken to relieve the situation but the long-term problems still remain. An important factor hindering the effective management of Indian rangelands on some reservations is the conflict between tribal and individual Indian desires with respect to accepted range management practices.[4]

On the Papago Reservation the GAO found the range grazed at double its capacity, in the face of the fact that the Indian Reorganization Act directs the secretary of Interior to restrict livestock to the carrying capacity of the range, and in spite of the requirement that a trustee prudently manage a trust responsibility. Although the BIA had been telling the tribe for forty years that its rangeland was severely overgrazed, and the topsoil washing and blowing away, no controls had been imposed by the tribe or the BIA. The GAO correctly cited the foremost cause as the individual owners' desire to graze without restriction. From my own study it is obvious that this feeling was so strong that had tribal officials tried to regulate grazing they probably would not have been reelected. The BIA has made attempts to control grazing on the Papago Reservation from time to time, but the Indians have gone public, and the press has cited the dire poverty of the Papago sheep owners and the necessity of their maintaining their few sheep as a matter of survival. Public pressure invariably has backed the Indians. The BIA has been effectively muzzled and still is. The same problem exists on the Navajo Reservation, and Navajo topsoil is filling up the dams on the Colorado River as well as drastically reducing the capacity of the range. If either of these tribes decided to sue the trustee (the BIA) for mismanagement they would likely win a substantial settlement. But a suit might cost them considerably. They are aware that if a large settlement did occur and the cause was basically because of Indian pressure for misuse of the land the American public and Congress might question the validity of the continuance of the BIA's trust responsibility.

More and more frequently tribes with land resources are following the lead of the Council of Energy Resource Tribes (CERT). These tribes are employing their own consultants, dealing directly with the development companies, and then going to the BIA and the secretary of the Interior for approval of a lease or sale, as required by the federal trust. Except for the trust requirement there would seem to be no reason for federal government approval.

Many individual Indians and tribal groups are just as competent to manage their realty resources as any other individuals or groups in the

United States. Non-Indians with land or valuable mineral resources sometimes use poor judgment or poor business practices and lose them; others succeed. Tribes and individual Indians would likely perform in the same manner as non-Indians. Most would not be competent land managers; therefore, they would make their living in some other fashion. A few might become land management and development specialists and build up large and successful enterprises based on the land and its resources.

Indian spokesmen strongly proclaim that an Indian-owned land base is essential to Indian culture and life. The "Tentative Final Report" of the AIPRC of March 4, 1977, contained the following statement: "Indian opinion is overwhelming that the importance of a stable and adequate tribal land base cannot be overemphasized. Their economic security and development of tribal economics depend on it; the very survival of Indian cultures and the permanency of Indian tribes as governmental units depend on it."[5] I commented on this statement at the time as follows.

> This statement may be a statement of belief, but it is not supportable. The Indian land base, under present use, is inadequate to provide "economic security." Tribal investment for economic gain may be squandered in non-economic activities on a reservation. Investment outside of tribal lands may in some instances, prove to be more profitable. With tribal population growing at over twice the national average, population pressure will increase. There is no possibility of providing an agricultural or mineral land base for all Indians.[6]

Historically, for a hunting, fishing, and gathering economy land had to be available, but this way of life is gone in the lower forty-eight states. Owning land is not necessary for present-day economic activity. A great deal of agribusiness is conducted on rented land, and oil companies own much land but obtain a high percentage of their production from someone else's land—private, including Indian, or government owned. This land is leased, and the landowner receives a portion of the oil income.

Why, then, the Indian desire to maintain a land base in trust? First, if the land encompasses the ancestral home it is natural to wish to keep it. Many Indian tribes have moved, frequently under duress, some several times during the last 200 years. Some are no longer living on ancestral lands, and others no longer live on tribal land. Large numbers have moved to cities. In many instances the tribal estate could not possibly support the total tribal membership. If the land were not in trust a tribe could keep its land if it wanted to and had sufficient funds to meet any taxes that might be levied. The trust has nothing to do with ownership.

Second, the trust maintains a tax-free status for the land. From a purely economic point of view this status is a tremendous advantage. Since this tax-free service frequently requires subsidization by other taxpayers for needed government services that are normally supported by a real estate tax, the question sometimes is raised as to how long this special privilege should be continued.

Third, the trustee is responsible for competent management, which means obtaining maximum income for the owner consistent with the general educational objective of the BIA and prudent use of the resource. If a mistake is made that results in a loss of tribal land resource or adequate income from its development, the federal government is subject to suit. This management service also has economic value for the Indians.

Under the circumstances it is not logical to assume that federally recognized tribes will voluntarily desire to terminate the tax-free status. The part that past policy, particularly the holding of Indian land in federal trust, has played in Indians' staying in uneconomic reservation situations with little hope for real economic development in many cases needs to be seriously studied and evaluated. The American Indian Policy Review Commission stated that although "the exact parameters of the trust duty are not clearly defined, the Commission has concluded that it would not be desirable to attempt to spell out the duty in terms of statutory specificity."[7] This is another tough job set aside for the future.

The policy options for Indian land are (1) to continue Indian land in federal trust and largely permit the Indian owners to act on their own in many instances, as at present, (2) to continue Indian land in federal trust and firmly exercise the trust responsibility, or (3) to discontinue the federal trust responsibility for Indian land. The first option provides for considerable Indian freedom of action, but it also entails potentially large liabilities for the federal treasury because of failure of the trustee to carry out the trust responsibility as provided by law. The Indian owners and the general public seem generally satisfied with this option, although the general public may be unaware of the taxpayer liability involved. This option also jeopardizes the preservation of the tribal land estate and the obtaining of maximum income from that estate consistent with prudent management.

The second option provides for a firm exercise of the federal trust responsibility but would involve less freedom of decision on the part of the Indian owners. It would avoid federal liability for damage to or mismanagement of the tribal trust estate, except for the results of poor judgment or mistakes. Although this option is based on current legal requirements, it is open to question whether the Indian owners and the general public would support its execution. The third option transfers the responsibility for Indian land decisions to the Indian owners. This option was involved in the so-called termination actions of the 1950s, and the reaction to this policy in the 1960s and 1970s has already been discussed.

Sovereignty, Self-Determination, and Limited Government

The degree of independence and self-sufficiency of Indian tribes in colonial times and the early days of our republic has been greatly modified. Indians are U.S. citizens; many are well educated; and large numbers have entered the mainstream of American life, and yet there is still much talk about Indian sovereignty.

Sovereignty is defined by Webster as "a: supreme power, esp. over a body politic: DOMINION b: freedom from external control: AUTONOMY." Tribal governments are not described by this definition. Congress can legislate on any Indian matter, and such legislation is controlling. Indian tribes are dependent on the U.S. government for international negotiations and protection in the world environment. Very few tribal groups are economically self-sufficient. As indicated in Chapter 4, many tribal groups do not exercise police or judicial power, and when they do those powers are severely limited.

As quoted earlier, William Schaab, an Albuquerque attorney, considers tribal sovereignty based on primordial right as an "outdated court-created" doctrine. "Although the factual basis for the doctrine was originally sound, history has changed the facts and the doctrine should now be discarded."[8] Schaab goes on to point out that the IRA of 1934 provided for limited self-government by Indian tribes under tribal constitutions approved by the secretary of the Interior.

When a tribe does not come under the IRA and no other specific legislation for the tribe has been passed, the courts have held that the tribe's authority to legislate on internal matters is based on inherent sovereignty within the limits of federal statutes. This area could be clarified by congressional legislation.

Another factor is the intermixture of Indians and non-Indians on many reservations, such as the Yakima and Suquamish examples. The Oliphant case took place on the Suquamish reservation, and Price pointed out (as noted in Chapter 4) that if non-Indians are subject to tribal government there will be pressure for the right of such non-Indians to participate in such government. Government without representation has raised a battle cry since the time of the American Revolution.

The Navajo Reservation–trust land situation in Apache County, Arizona, presents another question of adequate representation. Apache County had a total population of 52,000 in 1980, of which 39,000 (75 percent) were Indians, primarily Navajo. The Navajo live on trust land within that portion of the Navajo Reservation in Apache County so the county cannot tax, pass zoning ordinances, or otherwise exercise jurisdiction over the reservation and its Navajo residents. However, the Navajo can vote in county elections and are eligible as county citizens to run for county office. The Navajo captured the county government in 1982 and passed ordinances and taxes that were not applicable to themselves but only to non-Indians living in other parts of Apache County. This situation has turned the concept of representative government upside down.

The Arizona state legislature was working on a bill in 1982 to create a new "all Indian" county which would virtually follow the Navajo Reservation boundary. The non-Indians favored this move, but two state legislative representatives from the Navajo Reservation opposed it. State Representative Bob Hanley, a Navajo from Window Rock, referred to the bill as "legislative scalping" and charged that it would violate the 1965 Voting Rights Act and the Constitution. Representative Dan Peaches, also a Navajo from Window Rock, said the county had one of the lowest tax rates in the state and that nonreservation residents were being treated fairly. "If they're saying that those who do not pay taxes are not entitled to hold public office, then I think that would require a change in the U.S. Constitution," Peaches continued.[9] Ambrose Shepherd, a Navajo and chairman of the Apache County Board, warned Governor Bruce Babbitt that he had better veto the bill if it passed if he (the governor) hoped to have Navajo support for his reelection in 1982. The bill did not pass the legislature, but had it become law it would have been subject to approval by the Justice Department to determine if it were discriminatory in diluting minority voting strength. There may have been some party politics involved as Governor Babbitt was a Democrat and the Republicans controlled the legislature.

Another question is, If tribal governments do not have jurisdiction over all within their geographical borders are they truly governments? In a case involving fishing rights a judge held that the Puyallup tribe did not exist and that the Puyallups' organization was "no different than the Italian-American Club or the Sons and Daughters of Norway. . . . Over the years, the defendants have blended themselves into the dominant Western-European society."[10] This finding was rejected by the Washington Supreme Court and the Supreme Court of the United States.

In addition to the "extent to which a particular Indian group is *entitled* to exercise power to define the rules of behavior for its membership," Price points to a second reason for self-government, which involves "the extent to which it is easier, wiser, more civilizing and necessary to allow Indian groups to engage in self-rule."[11] Price also says: "The history of America is filled with efforts by communities to find a piece of land and establish a societal pattern which encouraged peculiar or special behavior."[12] Examples are the Mormons, Hutterites, nudist colonies, and slave-owning groups. The relationships of these groups to the larger society and the degrees of self-government allowed them have been the subject of legislation in several states and also the subject of court cases.

In Iowa in 1906 there was a case involving the Amana Society.

> Lastly, it is argued that the organization and maintenance of such a society is obnoxious to sound public policy. Certain it is that the status of the individual members is not in accordance with prevailing ideals. Community life is thought by many to be inconsistent with the development of individuality, and to be destructive of the incentives to individual growth and higher living. But in this country all opinions are tolerated and entire freedom of action allowed, unless this interferes in some way with the rights of others.[13]

In 1972 the U.S. Supreme Court recognized the right of an Amish community to have some leeway with regard to state education laws so that they could conform to their beliefs.[14] These people owned their own land and were economically self-sufficient as a general rule. Also, their society was not dependent on the larger society for financial support in order to function.

Self-government, according to the dictionary, means "self-command, self-control; government under the control and direction of the inhabitants of a political unit rather than by an outside authority." This definition is too broad to describe most tribal and local governments. Tribal government is severely circumscribed, and local governments have only those powers authorized by the state legislatures. "Limited self-government" might more accurately describe both tribal government and local government.

The loose use of terms such as "self-determination" and "tribal sovereignty" seems to satisfy the emotional objectives of some people, but in large measure, such use may tend to obfuscate the facts of the real world. What does self-determination mean? Neither the statutes, the BIA, nor the IHS provide a definition. To Indians the term means whatever they want it to mean. What is "tribal sovereignty"? Certainly tribes are not sovereign in the dictionary sense of the word. In actual fact, this term seems to refer to the tribe's power to do what is not prohibited by federal statute. This lack of clarity in the use of terms such as "self-determination" and "sovereignty" does not mean that tribalism is not a vital factor. Indian group culture is very important; even to many Indians who have moved to the city. The point being made here is that the BIA very actively uses such undefined terms. This may be a major factor in frustrating meaningful dialogue and the development of programs leading to Indian and tribal self-sufficiency. The AIPRC report promotes both the concepts of (1) self-determination by Indians and (2) trust responsibility for Indians on the part of the federal government. These concepts appear to be somewhat contradictory, but AIPRC's rationalization of this apparent conflict is found on pages 126–136 of its *Final Report*.

The options posed under the heading "Sovereignty, Self-Determination, and Limited Government" are one, to continue the loose use of vague terms or two, to do some hard thinking about Indian goals and processes and define them in more specific terms. Option one continues confusion and allows each person or group to interpret these vague concepts in their own way. This option may frustrate real communication, but it may also avoid controversy. It is apparently acceptable partly because of its lack of clarification and partly because it points to a generally desired, but not specifically defined, goal or goals. Option two would provide more specificity and improve the ability of the various participants in the Indian policy process to understand one another. However, development of specifically defined objectives or processes related to the existing Indian environment might involve overcoming certain uncritically accepted beliefs, often-repeated slogans, and vague concepts, which are pleasing in part because they do not force one to face the prickly facts of reality. Some lines of thought pertinent to option two have been briefly explored in this section, but this type of effort might generate so much heat and disagreement that some people might conclude that it would slow down rather than speed up progress toward understanding.

Self-Sufficiency

As frequently noted earlier the goal of tribal chairmen, of the BIA, of Congress, and of Indian interest groups is Indian self-sufficiency—both economic and governmental. Income-producing activities of tribes, Indian groups, and Indian individuals are discussed in Chapters 3 and 4, as are the subsidies to Indian tribes, Indian groups—including Indian interest groups—and individual Indians. A review of this material does not give a clear picture of the degree of economic or political self-sufficiency of individual tribes or tribes collectively. Chapter 4 shows tribes for the most part do not freely publicize their income and expenditures or their budget information and that requests to tribes for this information yielded few reponses. The BIA's attitude has been that tribal financial data is a tribe's own business.

In reviewing the previous chapters a logical question arises: What is the status of tribal economic self-sufficiency? For example, how many families could the Pine Ridge Reservation support at an income above the poverty level? If cattle raising is one of the main economic enterprises, how many herds large enough to provide a decent living to the average family could be supported at Pine Ridge? What other options are there at Pine Ridge, and how many families could they support? How does the number of families that could be supported by the various options compare with the number of families residing on the Pine Ridge Reservation? Across the board, how many tribes are fully self-sufficient, 75 percent self-sufficient, 50 percent self-sufficient, or 25 percent or less self-sufficient? The Osage and Palm Springs tribes have the potential to be self-sufficient. How many more tribes do? One of the reasons for the Menominees' wanting to return to BIA services and a trust status for their land and commercial forest was the difficulty they experienced in maintaining their economic self-sufficiency as a Wisconsin county.

In a letter to Kenneth Smith, the assistant secretary of the Interior for Indians, I presented some of these types of questions and asked if there were a summary of tribal progress toward self-sufficiency and a general evaluation of government policy in achieving self-sufficiency. The assistant secretary replied: "We do not keep the kind of data base you seek on economic enterprises and developments—it is not information we would need to use in that aggregate form."[15] As for individual examples he suggested talking with Gordon Evans of the BIA (which I had already done) and contacting the tribes.

I knew when I asked the questions that answers with hard data were probably not available for an across-the-board evaluation of self-sufficiency of individual tribes or tribes collectively as I had already asked the same questions of BIA officials. Data on specific enterprises undoubtedly are available, but not much was volunteered by the tribes. If enterprises are losing money it is natural to not to want to publicize that fact. An indication of too much tribal income might jeopardize a current or hoped-for amount of federal subsidy. I was interested in the Interior Department's response to the general question to see if it would indicate any appreciation of the need for summary data from individual tribes and for tribes collectively and whether there were any programs in motion to try to obtain such data. The response seems to indicate that the Interior Department sees no need for and is not trying to obtain the basic economic data that would make it possible to answer such questions. Congress has shown some interest as it indicated in Chapter 4.

It would appear to be next to impossible to evaluate the results of Indian policy without a reservation-by-reservation analysis of their degrees of economic self-sufficiency. If a reservation were not already self-sufficient a projection of when it could achieve that status would be a logical goal-setting objective. In Texas the Alabama-Coushatta Indians and the Ysleta Tigua community in El Paso are moving toward economic self-sufficiency. Both are on state Indian reservations and are working closely with the Texas Indian Commission.

Also, it would be helpful to have an overall summary of the economic condition of tribes as a whole to provide a benchmark that would indicate if Indian policy is actually achieving any results toward economic self-sufficiency. Measurements of this kind are very difficult to obtain and may yield results that are only approximate. Such measurements certainly cannot be obtained without competent specialists and a strong follow-through by agency leaders.

A major policy issue for the future, then, continues to be to determine how to achieve economic self-sufficiency for Indians and the development and adoption of a program of systematic evaluation of progress toward self-sufficiency. If the present policy is achieving only a subsidized, dependent economy, then that is an issue the American public and Congress should know about and debate. On the other hand, if economic self-sufficiency is being achieved, the public and Congress should know this fact. Such information would help support the continuance of effective programs, and would also inform tribal leaders and other people of the status of a given tribe so that appropriate decisions could be made.

The policy options are (1) to continue current programs without a systematic effort to determine progress in tribal economic self-sufficiency or (2) to adopt a policy of developing self-sufficiency criteria and data on an organized basis for both large tribes and all tribes collectively. The BIA attempts to measure the results of individual programs by functions as is indicated in Chapter 3. In this summary of options the concern is with the balance sheet for a tribe (including all individual programs) and totals for all tribes.

The first option is the current course being followed. It is easier, raises less controversy, and leaves the participants in Indian policymaking largely in the dark as to progress. The second option would have to be approached very carefully. It would necessarily involve working with tribes in the development of standard indicators and a regular reporting of data concerning the degree of economic self-sufficiency. It would also require working with the tribes in developing programs and a policy of disciplined follow-through by tribal officials and the BIA to stimulate movement toward the goal. If progress were not made, funding could stop. This action might raise temperatures to a high level, but would tend to curtail easygoing, nonaccountable performances in many situations. It would mean hard thinking and hard work against tough odds. It might also mean facing up to the fact that on some reservations either the population base, the resource base, or the economy would have to be modified to achieve economic self-sufficiency. Whether the Department of the Interior and the BIA, the Congress, or the Indians want to face the issues involved in the second option is debatable.

Contrasting Premises: One Objective

The two basic and contrasting philosophic premises involved in BIA-Indian relations have been:

1. To regard Indians as a special category of citizens entitled to self-government and the subsidies necessary to achieve it, a continuation of the trust and federal management of trust assets, an expansion of trust responsibility to include all present services by the BIA and IHS to Indians, and direct federal-to-Indian relationships with minimum involvement of the states. This is the view stated in the report of the American Indian Policy Review Commission.[16]

2. To regard Indians as being in a state of transition toward self-sufficiency within the normal state-federal framework, in the same manner as other groups and individuals, and to remove trust and other special services when education and self-sufficiency make it possible. Lewis Meriam stated this view.[17]

Special Status for Indians

The "special status for Indians" view is presented in previous chapters. The American Indian Policy Review Commission report stated:

> The fundamental concepts which must guide future policy determinations are:
>
> 1. That Indian tribes are sovereign political bodies, having the power to determine their own membership and power to enact laws and enforce them within the boundaries of their reservations.
>
> and
>
> 2. That the relationship which exists between tribes and the United States is premised on a special trust that must govern the conduct of the stronger toward the weaker. The concept of sovereignty and the concept of trust are imperative to the continuation of the Federal-Indian

> relationship. These form the foundation upon which our entire legal relationship with the Indian tribes stands.[18]

The AIPRC report noted that the "Commission recognizes that there is substantial controversy surrounding the concept of tribal sovereignty and the exercise of governmental authority by the tribes within their reservations." It also proposed that there be no legislative action with regard to the jurisdiction or authority of tribal governments, indicating that any such effort would be "premature."[19] The commission believed the jurisdiction of Indian tribes should extend to all persons within reservation borders; otherwise, "the tribes were mere social clubs, an assembly of property owners, with no more authority than any civic association."

The commission recommended that state and county governments "sit down with tribal governments and to the extent possible resolve their jurisdictional conflicts." As the commission noted, "there are many areas in which both the States and the tribes have a commonality of interest." If resolution cannot be achieved, said the commission, legislative action by Congress would be appropriate.

Speaking for the Navajo tribe, Arizona State Representative Daniel Peaches, a Navajo from Window Rock, wrote:

> The policy of the Interior Department regarding the Indians for the 80's should be one of: (1) protecting federal trust responsibilities to the Indian people (federal treaties); (2) protect tribal resources; and (3) promote economic development on Indian reservations. All federal agencies should allocate funds directly to the Indian tribes, bypassing state governments. . . . The President's [Reagan's] policy of returning most of the federal responsibilities back to the states would be a disaster for the Indian people. There is simply no mechanism by which states and Indian tribes can have a mutual relationship."[20]

In the Indian Self-Determination and Education Assistance Act of 1975 Congress recognized the "obligation . . . to respond to the strong expression of the Indian people for self-determination by assuring maximum Indian participation in the direction of educational as well as other Federal services to Indian communities." Further, Congress declared "its commitment to the maintenance of the Federal Government's unique and continuing relationship with and responsibility to the Indian people," which is the basic direction of stated Indian policy today.

Movement Toward Normal State-Federal Relationship

The AIPRC report recognized, at least in part, the legitimacy of moving toward a normal state-federal relationship and recommended that states and tribes work out mutual problems. But the commission did this only on the basis of retaining tribal sovereignty and the supervision and services of the federal government under a trust arrangement. For many Indians the transition to being responsible to state and local governments has occurred. Optional approaches remain only for federal reservations where the land is held in trust by the federal government and the tribes have their own governments.

It will be recalled that the Meriam report of 1928 stated that it was "highly desirable that the states should as rapidly as possible assume responsibility for the administration of activities which they can effectively perform alike for whites and for Indians with a single organization." Also, in 1943 Commissioner Collier indicated that postwar planning should consider "what additional services to Indians might be assumed by State, county or municipal agencies, such as law and order, health and education."[21] House Concurrent Resolution 108 (HCR 108) in 1953 stated in part: "it is the policy of Congress, as rapidly as possible, to make the Indians within the territorial limits of the United States subject to the same laws and entitled to the same privileges and responsibilities as are applicable to other citizens of the United States."

These statements of policy are contrary to the philosophy of the AIPRC report and the Indian Self-Determination and Education Assistance Act of 1975. However, as indicated previously, many functions such as education are currently performed for reservation Indians by state governments. There has, indeed, been a great deal of movement toward state services for Indians.

Proponents of both policies (separateness and integration) have the goal of self-sufficiency for tribal groups. They also each have a desire for the government's responsiveness to Indian citizens—one through an Indian government organized under federal law and the other through state-authorized governmental procedures.

One of the problems of the separate tribal government policy is determining which groups are of sufficient size and have sufficient resources to make such an option feasible. Certainly it is not practicable for the Ramona Reservation in California, which has three residents, to have its own government. There may be a question about the Pojoaque Pueblo in New Mexico (78 people), the Chemehuevi Reservation in California (124 people), the Duckwater Reservation in Nevada (139 persons), or some of the small Alaskan villages. What criteria should guide determination of minimum feasible size and resources necessary for a viable separate tribal government?

A Middle Course

The National Association of Counties (NAC) recognizes the "unique citizenship status" of Indians and the importance of Indian contributions to our national heritage. It supports the principle of tribal self-government and pledges "cooperation with Indian tribes for the provision of constituent services within our individual jurisdictions."[22] The association has indicated that "historically inconsistent federal policies toward Indian reservations and recently expressed moves by Indian tribes on the reservations toward complete self-government have created a local government crisis in many parts of the nation." The association's statement also emphasizes that "by failing to spell out tribal jurisdictions, Congress has allowed a situation of conflict to develop in which tribal aspirations and treaty interpretations are pitted against other constitutional principles and rights." The result has been "a further deterioration of relations between Indians and non-Indians." It is clear "that Congress must decide matters of jurisdiction—civil, criminal, control of resources."

Specifically, the NAC "calls upon Congress to enact comprehensive legislation which makes clear the governmental powers granted tribes by Congress and/or treaty, balancing the unique status of the tribes with other constitutional concerns."

The congressionally appointed American Indian Policy Review Commission, which had House and Senate as well as Indian members, did consider the possibility of recommending legislation to clarify jurisdictional questions but decided not to do so. It is no wonder. The possible complexity of the effort boggles the mind unless such an attempt were based on phasing Indian government into the normal federal-state system. Tribes vary in size, resources, self-government capacity, and many other ways.

In developing clarifying legislation the NAC suggests the following considerations.

1. To what extent do tribal governments have sovereign immunity from legal action: Is it more or less than that accorded state and local governments?
2. Within "Indian country" what jurisdiction do tribal governments have over tribal members, nonmembers, and members outside of "Indian country"?
3. Who regulates hunting and fishing on reservations and off reservations for Indians and non-Indians?
4. Who has jurisdiction on the reservations over natural resource development such as water, timber, coal, oil shale, and grazing?

5. What is the extent of tribal water rights?

Further points made by the NAC are:

1. If additional land is placed under trust Congress should compensate local governments for loss of revenue.
2. Where redress of Indian rights violations requires limiting longstanding practices and assumed rights of nontribal members Congress should make appropriate redress.[23]

The NAC does not recommend the Meriam and Hoover Commission approach of the eventual melding of Indian government into the state-local system. Neither does it recommend complete separateness as implied in the AIPRC and Indian self-determination act approach. The NAC suggestions seem to strike a middle course: distinctive tribal governments with a clear legislative statement of the responsibilities of such governments, and of the responsibilities in Indian matters of the county, state, and federal governments as well. Whether such a specification of responsibilities can be developed remains to be seen.

An Earlier Example

Although current reservation and nonreservation Indian policymakers are aware of the complexity of the various options, they do not have any final answers. This is not a new phenomenon. A conference of social scientists, including anthropologists, was held in 1954 and chaired by the former assistant commissioner for Indian affairs, BIA anthropologist, John H. Provinse. The purpose was to discuss Indian policy. The group considered the then-dominant assumption that assimilation of the Indians into the dominant culture was inevitable. This prediction, the group believed, was unwarranted. The members were of the opinion that Indian group identity would continue and that attempts at forced acculturation were self-defeating. The conference predicted that Indian communities would maintain themselves as cultural islands "more or less well adjusted to or integrated into the American system." Individual Indians would continue to out-migrate and make personal adjustments in the larger society. Noted, too, was the existence of other "cultural islands" that were generally accepted by the general public "if they do not violate the public sense of basic decency and are not considered an economic burden." At the same time the conference noted that the public had a "contradictory feeling that differences should disappear in time." This opinion was particularly strong in the case of Indian policy, most likely because "assimilation is thought to solve a problem—the present economic burden of nonproductive Indian groups—which problem is not seen solvable in any other way."[24]

This conference pointed up a fundamental aspect of the Indian dilemma—how to provide freedom for organized Indian groups to decide for themselves without a substantial subsidy from the larger society. The Hutterites and the Amish do not pose this same dilemma as they are self-supporting. Indian groups desire to become self-supporting, but strenuous efforts and millions of dollars to assist them in this effort apparently have had uneven and limited success. The Indians, their desires and their abilities, are a fundamental part of the equation. Indian governmental and business efforts have often suffered from management ineptness or lack of interest, on the part of both the Indians and their non-Indian advisors. Indian labor is sometimes unreliable from the standpoint of a western-oriented, profit-making enterprise. Traditional Indian culture is not oriented toward an eight-hour, five-days-a-week schedule. This fact, together with inadequate resources upon which to build self-sufficiency, is a serious problem for many tribes in developing the freedom to choose and decide in their own economic and governmental matters. Subsidies continue, and they are accompanied by a designation of the purpose for which funds are to be used, other criteria, the requirement for reporting accountability, and submission to auditing and monitoring.

Whether a solution to the Indian dilemma is any nearer today than when the conference was held in 1954 is a matter of judgment. It seems to me that the conference stated the issues more clearly than the AIPRC or any other group or individual has stated the issues for the 1980s. Today the general assumption of federal legislation and policy is not that assimilation is inevitable, as was the case in 1954. Present policy supports pluralism and Indian self-determination. However, one of the clouds hanging over this objective is still the same as in 1954—the "economic burden of nonproductive Indian groups," that is, economic dependency. Another cloud is the increased intermixing of Indian and non-Indian populations both off and on most reservations with resulting jurisdictional problems involving or related to police, courts, social services, water resources, game, fish, and the like. A third cloud is the lack of guidelines to determine which Indian reservations have the size, resources, and a sufficient percentage of Indian residents to even have a chance of becoming self-sufficient viable Indian units, economically or governmentally.

The options that emerge from this discussion of "Contrasting Premises: One Objective" seem to be (1) continuance of a special status for

Indian citizens and Indian governments, (2) movement toward normal federal-state relationships on the part of Indians and Indian governments, and (3) a course involving some elements of both one and two but with clear legislative specification of the relationships.

Tribal and Indian Roles

Tribal leaders and Indian interest groups—as well as tribal members in the legislative and executive branches of local, state, and federal governments—will have a great deal of influence, perhaps the dominant influence, in the development of Indian policy and actions to carry out such policy. This impact of Indian leaders and interest groups will not only be a major factor on the reservations, but will also frequently prevail in school board decisions, state legislatures, and the halls of Congress. Their influence on the executive organizations charged with carrying out policy will continue to be substantial.

Indians have their own backgrounds, beliefs, and value systems—their own culture. If this culture does not provide an adequate framework for self-sufficiency in the economic, political, and social environment by which they are surrounded, there is a profound dilemma. It has already been noted that cultures are in a constant state of change and modification and that the degree of Indian blood and place of residence may be factors in the rate of change. But up until the present, different beliefs and views by many reservation Indians have not fit the non-Indian ways of economic or governmental behavior, and it may be necessary that they do fit if the Indians are going to cope with the economic and governmental practices of the dominant society.

Bureau of Indian Affairs Role

The BIA's role in the future is not clear. The shift from direct services to contracts and grants described in Chapters 2 and 3 is one factor that will have an effect. If the reduction of funds for social services and economic development programs continues, the 1970s involvement of many federal agencies in Indian programs will decrease, which may thrust more responsibility back on the BIA, the tribes, and the states in the 1980s. The BIA itself is not immune to reductions in funds. As long as the federal trust responsibility for Indian land and resources remains some agency will be required to exercise that responsibility, and likely it will continue to be the BIA. On important Indian policy issues in the recent past the BIA has sometimes had only a minor role or was shouldered aside, as in the events leading to the Alaskan and Maine settlement acts, the resolution of the Trail of Broken Treaties confrontation, and the control of policy on treaty fishing rights. The courts, the Interior secretary and attorneys, the president, the attorney general, the Indians and their pressure groups and attorneys, the states, and Congress often have the major roles in important Indian policy matters. However, then the BIA may propose alternatives, provide its expertise, and carry out the government's responsibilities that result from the final policy determinations. The options for the future are to (1) use the BIA for most Indian-related matters considered a responsibility of the federal government or (2) continue the gradual dispersion of BIA functions to other agencies, the states, and the Indians themselves.

Conclusion

Indian tribes are no longer independent groups in the same sense that they were prior to the invasion of North America by the Europeans. Indians are now citizens of the United States and of the states in which they reside. There are millions of people with some Indian blood who do not identify themselves as Indians. The Bureau of Indian Affairs serves only federally recognized Indians who are primarily located on or near federal Indian reservations. Nearly one-half of the people who identify themselves as Indians live in non-reservation situations, primarily in metropolitan areas.[25] The states also serve large numbers of Indians, including many who are on federal reservations—approximately 90 percent of all Indian children are educated in state public school systems.

Indian history reflects a constant ebb and flow in the two main policy concepts: maintenance of Indian tribes as separate groups served with special programs and integration of Indian tribal governments and members into federal-state-local relationships. Under both of these policies the objective has been Indian governmental and economic self-sufficiency. There have been sporadic efforts to look at the progress of tribes and Indians as individuals. Individual subject-matter programs such as Indian education, forest management, social services, and trust services for Indian lands and funds have had some consistency. But there is a lack of data and analyses of the Indian situation as a whole—either by individual tribe or by the tribes collectively. How do the individual, tribal, BIA, and other governmental and private sector activities affect the total tribal balance sheet? It is difficult to see the picture as a whole. Although there are little economic data available, one of the objectives of this book has been to portray the various aspects of the Indian policy environment in order to provide as much of a view of the whole as possible.

The various policy issues relating to Indian lands, sovereignty, self-determination, government, and self-sufficiency are important, as are the two main policy alternatives mentioned above. What the Indians do with their governments, their programs, and their training will have a major impact on future policy. The public attitude or view of the Indian citizen and Indian governments will control in large measure the kind and volume of Indian programs sponsored by the federal government.

It is certain that Indian policy will be of great importance to many citizens in the last two decades of the twentieth century. Many people, Indian and non-Indian, have a vital stake in Indian policies related to fishing, land claims, water rights, and energy resources, and the conflicting premises and unresolved problems and issues are in large measure due to the complex nature of Indian affairs. There are no easy answers.

Appendixes

APPENDIX A

INDIAN SERVICE POPULATION AND LABOR FORCE ESTIMATES

This appendix was published by the Bureau of Indian Affairs in January 1982, based on estimates from its field offices. Figures have been rounded and some do not add to exact totals. These statistics are the best available on the number of Indians in various locations served by the BIA and the labor force situation for each group. This information is part of the basic data required for realistic analysis and for consideration of feasible policy options. Other desirable data, not now available, are indicated in the chapter on policy issues.

LOCAL ESTIMATES OF RESIDENT INDIAN POPULATION AND LABOR FORCE STATUS: DECEMBER 1981

Coverage: The term "resident Indian" means Indians living on Federal reservations or nearby, and who are eligible for services from the Bureau of Indian Affairs. The term "near reservations" is defined in CFR 25 par. 20.1 (r). Special legislation governs eligibility in Alaska and Oklahoma. In Alaska the figures include all Alaska Natives, i.e. Aleuts, Eskimos, as well as Indians. Since very few are actually living on reservations, the term "nearby " refers to all the rest of Alaska. In Oklahoma, the area covered is composed of former reservations. Thus, in both states the Bureau's responsibility extends almost entirely to the total Indian population of those states.

The statistics compiled herein refer basically to the population of a geographic area; they do not refer to tribal membership. The latter figures are maintained by the individual tribes according to their specific rules of membership, which may include members wherever they may be living. The few cases where membership rather than residency was used are so indicated in the appropriate table.

In certain instances the figures for individual Reservations are higher than the figures shown in the 1980 census for the counties where these reservations are located. Some of the reasons for these differences may be: (1) the tribes may have included in their count members that have left the reservation on a temporary basis (students, employment, etc.); (2) as stated above the tribes may have included tribal membership in their count; (3) possible variance of tribal population counts among tribes residing in the same county; and (4) not all members were counted in the 1980 census. Consequently in this report the total Indian population in some states differs somewhat from the 1980 census.

The total of approximately 735,000 Indians covered in these tables represents over half of the total Indian population of the United States, which in the 1980 U.S. census numbers 1,418,195. The remainder consists of members of Federally recognized tribes who live off-reservation, or Indian people who are not members of any Federally recognized tribe, or those who claimed Indian ancestry.

Estimated Figures: The statistics are labeled "estimates" because they are not based to any major extent on actual surveys. The local Agency offices of the Bureau of Indian Affairs estimated the data using whatever information was available. Accuracy varies from place to place; it is relatively high at small, isolated locations where everyone's activity is common knowledge. Generally, data for the Navajo Area, the State of Oklahoma (Anadarko and Muskogee Areas), and the State of Alaska are considered the least accurate and the most difficult to estimate because of the large population scattered over large geographic areas. This is particularly true in estimating the labor force status. Because of the considerable cost, household surveys of the labor force status are not frequently conducted.

Labor Force Status: Considered in this category are all those 16 years old and over (480,961) representing about 65% of the total population. This category is divided into three major groups for the purposes of this report--unable to work, employed, and able to work but not employed.

(1) Unable to work (columns 5 and 6) the total 155,857, or 32% of those 16 years old and over, includes those who are prevented from working by attendance at school, those who have to care for children, or those who are disabled, retired, or too old. Students make up some 42% of this group. Reservations differ considerably in the proportion estimated to fall into this category.

(2) Employed (column 7) The total, 174,990, or 36% of those 16 years old and over includes full-time and part-time employees. Of those about, two-thirds earn $7,000 or more (column 8)--the $7,000 figure being based on the annual income of a worker earning minimum wage. In other words, one-third of the employed are earning less than the minimum wage for a full-time job. It could be argued that employment, excluding marginal jobs, provides a better picture of the economic health of a reservation than the total employment. As one possible index of this condition, column 9 shows the number of employed Indians earnings $7,000 or more as a percent of the 16 years old and over population.

(3) Not employed but able to work (column 10) The total, 150,114, or 31% of those 16 years old and over, includes persons actually seeking work and those not seeking work. This distinction underlies two concepts of labor force: (a) The "potential labor force" consisting of all those 16 years old and over who are able to work, whether employed or not (columns 7 and 10 totaling 325,104). Forty-six percent of the potential labor force are not employed (column 11). (b) Those not seeking work and who are omitted from the standard Labor Department definition of labor force and unemployed. By this definition the labor force consists of columns 7 and 12, totaling 255,153 and the unemployment rate is 31 percent (column 13).

Table Format: The basic data is compiled in Table 3. They are arranged by BIA area and within them by Agency or equivalent unit of organization below the area level, the reservation, and State.

Table 1 and 2 are summary tables. The former shows the totals for each State. The latter shows totals for each of the areas into which the BIA is administratively divided.

Additional Comments: In the compilation of this Labor Force Report, a conscious effort was made to present as accurately as possible the resident Indian population on and near reservations. It should be noted, however, that there are problems with statistics on Indian reservations. First of all, the collection of statistics in Indian urban areas is particularly difficult since household surveys are infrequent or non-existent. Further, in isolated rural areas, it is difficult to separate the job-seekers from those not seeking jobs because there are no jobs available to draw out this distinction. Were jobs available, the unemployment rate would be somewhere between the two measures given in this report namely 31 percent and 46 percent.

Any questions pertaining to this report should be directed to the Office of Financial Management, Bureau of Indian Affairs, Washington, D. C.

Table 1. - LOCAL ESTIMATES OF POPULATION AND LABOR FORCE STATUS; INDIANS LIVING ON AND ADJACENT TO RESERVATIONS; SUMMARY BY STATE: DECEMBER 1981

State	TOTAL	Years of Age			Labor Force Status, 16 Years Old & Over									1980 Census
					Unable to Work		Employed			Not Employed, Able to Work				
								Earn $7000+		Total		Seeking Work		
		65 & Over	Under 16	16 & Over	Students	Others	Total	Number	% of Col.4	Number	% of 7+10	Number	% of 7&12	
	(1)	(2)	(3)	(4)	(5)	(6)	(7)	(8)	(9)	(10)	(11)	(12)	(13)	
BIA Total	734,895	44,715	253,934	480,961	65,686	90,171	174,990	118,720	25%	150,114	46%	80,163	31%	1,418,195
Alaska	64,047	3,170	25,303	38,744	5,696	7,107	9,851	6,251	16%	16,090	62%	10,582	52%	64,047
Arizona	152,145	7,764	53,432	98,804	11,441	17,872	28,298	17,412	18%	41,193	59%	14,042	33%	152,857
California	19,946	1,374	6,543	13,403	907	1,876	4,534	2,958	22%	6,087	57%	3,229	42%	201,311
Colorado	2,624	81	1,063	1,561	414	153	436	371	24%	558	56%	515	54%	18,059
Florida	1,881	71	763	1,118	37	139	589	374	33%	353	37%	188	24%	19,316
Idaho	6,953	393	2,541	4,413	694	793	1,882	1,491	34%	1,043	36%	705	27%	10,521
Iowa	695	26	305	390	37	78	131	110	28%	144	52%	134	50%	5,453
Kansas	2,165	151	892	1,273	63	223	821	566	44%	166	17%	136	19%	15,371
Louisiana	550	36	198	352	27	99	207	160	45%	19	8%	13	6%	12,064
Maine	2,326	109	820	1,506	206	268	556	274	18%	476	46%	358	39%	4,087
Michigan	5,551	298	2,034	3,517	434	528	1,439	774	22%	1,116	44%	807	36%	40,038
Minnesota	16,511	1,067	6,294	10,217	1,324	2,518	3,050	2,178	21%	3,325	52%	2,691	47%	35,026
Mississippi	4,914	281	2,113	2,801	385	737	1,120	850	30%	559	33%	277	20%	6,180
Montana	27,463	1,059	9,573	17,890	2,304	3,038	6,406	4,934	28%	6,142	49%	2,708	30%	37,270
Nebraska	3,097	231	1,016	2,081	187	312	718	649	31%	864	55%	678	49%	9,197
Nevada	7,361	496	2,533	4,827	563	608	1,965	1,237	26%	1,692	46%	1,067	35%	13,304
New Mexico	106,840	6,219	35,028	81,852	9,163	7,221	37,125	30,549	37%	18,418	33%	9,904	21%	104,777
New York	10,626	733	3,560	7,066	712	1,591	2,180	1,335	19%	2,583	54%	2,180	50%	38,732
North Carolina	5,664	390	1,825	3,839	725	707	1,384	1,038	27%	1,023	42%	416	23%	64,635
North Dakota	20,044	786	8,148	26,426	1,724	2,782	3,557	2,743	23%	3,832	52%	2,698	43%	20,157
Oklahoma	156,501	14,146	48,343	108,158	19,126	28,243	46,337	25,445	23%	14,452	24%	9,055	16%	169,464
Oregon	4,777	166	1,924	2,853	340	618	1,238	906	32%	657	35%	442	26%	27,309
South Dakota	41,321	2,179	14,895	26,426	3,157	4,180	6,766	5,456	21%	12,324	65%	5,300	44%	45,101
Utah	6,649	307	2,453	4,190	594	491	1,402	1,027	24%	1,703	55%	900	39%	19,256
Washington	41,233	2,123	14,145	27,088	2,817	4,647	8,142	5,836	21%	11,482	58%	8,170	50%	60,771
Wisconsin	17,106	1,181	6,387	10,719	1,514	1,968	4,185	3,379	31%	3,052	42%	2,432	37%	29,497
Wyoming	5,705	195	1,803	3,902	1,095	1,375	671	404	10%	761	53%	532	44%	7,125
TOTAL OTHER STATES														683,300

Note:

1. The difference in Indian population between the Census Bureau figure and the BIA total, represents Indian people of federally recognized tribes but living off reservation, or Indian people who are not members of any federally recognized tribe, and all those who claimed Indian ancestry.

Table 2. - LOCAL ESTIMATES OF POPULATION AND LABOR FORCE STATUS; INDIANS LIVING ON AND ADJACENT TO RESERVATIONS; SUMMARY BY BIA AREA AND WITHIN AREA BY STATE: DECEMBER 1981

Area & State	TOTAL	YEARS OF AGE			LABOR FORCE STATUS, 16 YEARS OLD & OVER								
					UNABLE TO WORK		EMPLOYED			NOT EMPLOYED, ABLE TO WORK			
		65 & Over	Under 16	16 & Over	Stu-dents	Others	Total	Earn $7000+ Number	Earn $7000+ % of Col.4	Total Number	Total % of 7&10	Seeking Work Number	Seeking Work % of 7 + 12
	(1)	(2)	(3)	(4)	(5)	(6)	(7)	(8)	(9)	(10)	(11)	(12)	(13)
BIA TOTAL	734,895	44,715	253,934	480,961	65,686	90,171	174,990	118,720	25%	150,114	46%	80,163	31%
ABERDEEN	(64,774)	(3,199)	(24,194)	(40,580)	(5,086)	(7,304)	(11,166)	(8,897)	(22%)	(17,024)	(60%)	(8,680)	(44%)
Nebraska (Part)	3,046	225	997	2,049	184	299	703	635	31%	863	55%	677	49%
North Dakota	20,044	786	8,148	11,896	1,724	2,782	3,557	2,743	23%	3,832	52%	2,698	43%
South Dakota	41,321	2,179	14,895	26,426	3,157	4,180	6,766	5,456	21%	12,324	64%	5,300	44%
Montana (Part)	363	9	154	209	21	43	140	63	30%	5	3%	5	3%
ALBUQUERQUE	(45,425)	(2,595)	(16,681)	(28,744)	(3,974)	(3,985)	(11,902)	(7,695)	(27%)	(8,883)	(43%)	(4,488)	(27%)
Colorado	2,624	81	1,063	1,561	414	153	436	371	24%	558	56%	515	54%
New Mexico (Part)	42,801	2,514	15,618	27,183	3,560	3,832	11,466	7,324	27%	8,325	42%	3,973	26%
ANADARKO	(36,719)	(2,225)	(11,119)	(25,600)	(4,465)	(5,666)	(9,462)	(7,117)	(28%)	(6,007	(39%)	(4,510)	(32%)
Kansas	2,165	151	892	1,273	63	223	821	566	44%	166	17%	136	19%
Oklahoma	34,503	2,068	10,208	24,295	4,399	5,430	8,626	6,537	27%	5,840	40%	4,373	34%
Nebraska (Part)	51	6	19	32	3	13	15	14	L	1	L	1	L
BILLINGS	(32,805)	(1,245)	(11,222)	(21,583)	(3,378)	(4,370)	(6,937)	(5,275)	(24%)	(6,898)	(50%)	(3,235)	(32%)
Montana	27,100	1,050	9,419	17,681	2,283	2,995	6,266	4,871	27%	6,137	49%	2,703	30%
Wyoming	5,705	195	1,803	3,902	1,095	1,375	671	404	10%	761	53%	532	44%
EASTERN	(25,961)	(1,620)	(9,279)	(16,682)	(2,092)	(3,541)	(6,036)	(4,031)	(24%)	(5,013)	(45%)	(3,432)	(36%)
Florida	1,881	71	763	1,118	37	139	589	374	33%	353	37%	188	24%
Louisiana	550	36	198	352	27	99	207	160	45%	19	8%	13	6%
Maine	2,326	109	820	1,506	206	268	556	274	18%	476	46%	358	39%
Mississippi	4,914	281	2,113	2,801	385	737	1,120	850	30%	559	33%	277	20%
New York	10,626	733	3,560	7,066	712	1,591	2,180	1,335	19%	2,583	54%	2,180	50%
North Carolina	5,664	390	1,825	3,839	725	707	1,384	1,038	27%	1,023	42%	416	23%
JUNEAU	(64,047)	(2,853)	(25,303)	(38,744)	(5,696)	(7,107)	(9,851)	(6,251)	(16%)	(16,090)	(62%)	(10,582)	(52%)
Alaska	64,047	2,853	25,303	38,744	5,696	7,107	9,851	6,251	16%	16,090	62%	10,582	52%
MINNEAPOLIS	(39,863)	(2,572)	(15,020)	(24,843)	(3,309)	(5,092)	(8,805)	(6,441)	(26%)	(7,637)	(46%)	(6,064)	(41%)
Iowa	695	26	305	390	37	78	131	110	28%	144	52%	134	50%
Michigan	5,551	298	2,034	3,517	434	528	1,439	774	22%	1,116	44%	807	36%
Minnesota	16,511	1,067	6,294	10,217	1,324	2,518	3,050	2,178	21%	3,325	52%	2,691	47%
Wisconsin	17,106	1,181	6,387	10,719	1,514	1,968	4,185	3,379	31%	3,052	42%	2,432	37%
MUSKOGEE	(121,998)	(12,078)	(38,135)	(83,863)	(14,727)	(22,813)	(37,711)	(18,908)	(22%)	(8,612)	(19%)	(4,682)	(11%)
Oklahoma	121,998	12,078	38,135	83,863	14,727	22,813	37,711	18,908	22%	8,612	19%	4,682	11%

Table 2 - Continued

Area & State	TOTAL	YEARS OF AGE			LABOR FORCE STATUS, 16 YEARS OLD & OVER								
					UNABLE TO WORK		EMPLOYED			NOT EMPLOYED, ABLE TO WORK			
		65 & Over	Under 16	16 & Over	Students	Others	Total	Earn $7000+ Number	Earn $7000+ % of Col.4	Total Number	Total % of 7+10	Seeking Work Number	Seeking Work % of 7+12
	(1)	(2)	(3)	(4)	(5)	(6)	(7)	(8)	(9)	(10)	(11)	(12)	(13)
NAVAJO	(160,722)	(8,679)	(51,551)	(109,171)	(13,158)	(11,694)	(39,643)	(33,960)	(31%)	(44,676)	(53%)	(16,407)	(29%)
Arizona (Part)	92,144	4,766	30,539	61,696	7,105	8,038	13,121	10,064	16%	33,432	71%	9,716	43%
New Mexico (Part)	64,039	3,705	19,410	44,744	5,603	3,389	25,659	23,225	51%	10,093	29%	5,931	19%
Utah (Part)	4,539	208	1,602	2,731	450	267	863	671	25%	1,151	57%	760	47%
PHOENIX	(71,933)	(3,721)	(27,034)	(44,899)	(5,140)	(10,950)	(18,366)	(9,305)	(21%)	(10,443)	(36%)	(5,841)	(24%)
Arizona (Part)	60,001	2,998	22,893	37,108	4,336	9,834	15,177	7,348	20%	7,761	34%	4,326	22%
California (Part)	2,085	115	698	1,387	90	269	645	317	23%	383	37%	253	28%
Idaho (Part)	176	13	59	118	7	15	40	28	24%	55	58%	55	58%
Nevada	7,361	496	2,533	4,827	563	608	1,965	1,237	26%	1,692	46%	1,067	35%
Utah (Part)	2,310	99	851	1,459	144	224	539	356	24%	552	51%	140	21%
PORTLAND	(52,787)	(2,669)	(18,551)	(34,236)	(3,844)	(6,043)	(11,222)	(8,205)	(24%)	(13,127)	(54%)	(9,262)	(45%)
Idaho (Part)	6,777	380	2,482	4,295	687	778	1,842	1,463	34%	988	35%	650	26%
Oregon	4,777	166	1,924	2,853	340	618	1,238	906	32%	657	35%	442	26%
Washington	41,233	2,123	14,145	27,088	2,817	4,647	8,142	5,836	21%	11,482	58%	8,170	50%
SACRAMENTO	(17,861)	(1,259)	(5,845)	(12,016)	(817)	(1,607)	(3,889)	(2,641)	(22%)	(5,704)	(59%)	(2,976)	(43%)
California (Part)	17,861	1,259	5,845	12,016	817	1,607	3,889	2,641	22%	5,704	59%	2,976	43%

NOTE:

1. Figures in parentheses are non-add
2. L means Base for percentage is less than 50; no percental shown

Table 3. Local Estimates of Population and Labor Force Status;
Indians Living On and Adjacent to Reservations; Compiled by BIA Area,
and within Area by Agency, Reservation, and State: December, 1981

AREA, AGENCY, RESERVATION, & STATE	TOTAL	YEARS OF AGE			LABOR FORCE STATUS, 16 YEARS OLD & OVER								
					UNABLE TO WORK		EMPLOYED			NOT EMPLOYED, ABLE TO WORK			
		65 & Over	Under 16	16 & Over	Students	Others	Total	Earn $7000 +		Total		Seeking Work	
								Number	% of Col. 4	Number	% of 7+10	Number	% of 7+12
	(1)	(2)	(3)	(4)	(5)	(6)	(7)	(8)	(9)	(10)	(11)	(12)	(13)
BIA TOTAL	734,895	44,715	253,934	480,961	65,686	90,171	174,990	118,720	25%	150,114	46%	80,163	31%
Aberdeen (NE,ND,SD)	64,774	3,199	24,194	40,580	5,086	7,304	11,166	8,897	22%	17,024	60%	8,680	44%
Cheyenne River Agcy. & Res. (SD)	4,449	190	1,958	2,491	297	290	875	582	23%	1,029	54%	1,029	54%
Crow Creek Agcy. & Res. (SD)	2,091	70	891	1,200	113	137	312	306	25%	638	67%	170	35%
Flandreau F.O. & Res. (SD)	413	22	165	248	19	62	147	134	54%	20	12%	15	9%
Ft. Berthold Agcy. & Res. (ND)	3,194	106	1,437	1,757	240	285	454	255	14%	778	63%	666	59%
Ft. Totten Agcy. & Res. (ND)	2,916	63	1,646	1,270	120	125	450	380	30%	575	56%	450	50%
Lower Brule Agcy. & Res. (SD)	988	27	445	543	67	56	224	185	34%	196	47%	94	29%
Pine Ridge Agcy. & Res. (SD)	13,417	959	3,736	9,681	776	1,471	1,878	1,408	14%	5,556	75%	1,500	44%
Rosebud Agcy. & Res. (SD)	9,484	528	3,640	5,844	721	591	2,285	1,908	33%	2,247	50%	795	26%
Sisseton Agcy. & Res. (ND,SD)	4,054	115	1,804	2,250	454	517	566	461	20%	713	56%	293	34%
Est. ND Pt. (8%)	(324)	(9)	(144)	(180)	(36)	(41)	(45)	(37)	(20%)	(57)	(56%)	(23)	(34%)
Est. SD Pt. (92%)	(3,730)	(106)	(1660)	(2,070)	(418)	(476)	(521)	(424)	(20%)	(656)	(56%)	(270)	(34%)
Standing Rock Agcy. & Res. (ND,SD)	7,958	320	2,821	5,137	927	1,230	618	591	12%	2,362	79%	2,008	76%
Est. ND Pt. (47%)	(3,740)	(150)	(1,326)	(2,414)	(436)	(578)	(290)	(278)	(12%)	(1,110)	(79%)	(944)	(76%)
Est. SD Pt. (53%)	(4,218)	(170)	(1,495)	(2,723)	(491)	(652)	(328)	(313)	(12%)	(1,252)	(79%)	(1,064)	(76%)
Trenton F.O. (MT,ND)	1,577	39	670	907	93	186	608	276	30%	20	3%	20	3%
Est. MT. Pt. (23%)	(363)	(9)	(154)	(209)	(21)	(43)	(140)	(63)	(30%)	(5)	(3%)	(5)	(3%)
Est. ND. Pt. (77%)	(1,214)	(30)	(516)	(698)	(72)	(143)	(468)	(213)	(30%)	(15)	(3%)	(15)	(3%)

Table 3 - Continued

AREA, AGENCY, RESERVATION, & STATE	TOTAL	YEARS OF AGE			LABOR FORCE STATUS, 16 YEARS OLD & OVER								
					UNABLE TO WORK		EMPLOYED			NOT EMPLOYED, ABLE TO WORK			
		65 & Over	Under 16	16 & Over	Stu-dents	Others	Total	Earn $7000 +		Total		Seeking Work	
								Number	% of Col. 4	Number	% of 7+10	Number	% of 7+12
	(1)	(2)	(3)	(4)	(5)	(6)	(7)	(8)	(9)	(10)	(11)	(12)	(13)
Aberdeen - Continued													
Turtle Mt. Agcy. & Res. (ND)	8,656	428	3,079	5,577	820	1,610	1,850	1,580	28%	1,297	41%	600	24%
Yankton Agcy. & Res. (SD)	2,531	107	905	1,626	255	445	196	196	2%	730	79%	363	65%
Winnebago Agency	[3,046]	[225]	[997]	[2,049]	[184]	[299]	[703]	[635]	31%	[863]	[55%]	[677]	[49%]
Omaha Res. (NE)	1,469	96	439	1,030	95	129	323	303	29%	483	60%	387	54%
Santee Sioux Res. (NE)	434	39	161	273	24	59	131	131	48%	59	31%	59	31%
Winnebago Res. (NE)	1,143	90	397	746	65	111	249	201	27%	321	56%	231	48%

NOTES:

1. Figures in brackets and parentheses non-add
2. Percentages assigned to each State for Reservations extending into more than one State are based on the proportions of Indian populations in the 1980 census for the counties in which the Reservations are located.

Table 3 - Continued

AREA, AGENCY, RESERVATION, & STATE	TOTAL	YEARS OF AGE			LABOR FORCE STATUS, 16 YEARS OLD & OVER								
					UNABLE TO WORK		EMPLOYED			NOT EMPLOYED, ABLE TO WORK			
		65 & Over	Under 16	16 & Over	Students	Others	Total	Earn $7000 +		Total		Seeking Work	
								Number	% of Col. 4	Number	% of 7+10	Number	% of 7+12
	(1)	(2)	(3)	(4)	(5)	(6)	(7)	(8)	(9)	(10)	(11)	(12)	(13)
Albuquerque (CO,NM)	45,425	2,595	16,681	28,744	3,974	3,985	11,702	7,695	27%	8,883	43%	4,488	27%
Jicarilla Agcy. & Res. (NM)	2,269	62	851	1,418	284	13	619	247	17%	502	44%	30	5%
Laguna Agcy. & Res. (NM)	6,406	426	2,224	4,182	479	772	876	770	18%	2,055	70%	500	36%
Mescalero Agcy. & Res. (NM)	2,415	93	1,120	1,295	190	189	570	293	22%	346	38%	150	21%
Northern Pueblos Agcy.	[7,383]	[558]	[1,860]	[5,523]	[701]	[741]	[2,800]	[1,826]	[33%]	[1,281]	[31%]	[921]	[25%]
Nambe (NM)	370	11	115	255	31	41	139	130	50%	44	24%	10	7%
Picuris (NM)	177	17	73	104	8	22	60	39	37%	14	19%	14	19%
Pojoaque (NM)	78	5	21	57	6	5	34	22	38%	12	26%	6	15%
San Ildefonso (NM)	430	28	128	302	40	34	124	114	37%	104	46%	54	30%
San Juan (NM)	1,842	161	298	1,544	164	245	863	464	30%	272	24%	188	18%
Santa Clara (NM)	2,327	111	603	1,724	208	217	964	592	34%	335	26%	285	23%
Taos (NM)	1,860	203	497	1,363	216	148	537	433	31%	462	46%	328	38%
Tesuque (NM)	299	22	125	174	28	29	79	32	18%	38	32%	36	31%
Ramah-Navajo Agcy. & Res. (NM)	1,696	58	786	910	61	63	300	249	27%	486	62%	321	52%
South Pueblos Agcy.	[15,633]	[967]	[5,807]	[9,826]	[1,179]	[1,667]	[4,559]	[2,916]	[29%]	[2,421]	[35%]	[1,126]	[20%]
Acoma (NM)	2,940	178	1,173	1,767	162	428	720	672	38%	457	39%	232	24%
Cochiti (NM)	910	58	305	605	34	96	310	293	48%	165	35%	37	11%
Isleta (NM)	3,110	277	1,199	1,911	365	593	864	487	25%	89	9%	49	5%
Jemez (NM)	1,889	106	494	1,395	150	55	283	257	18%	907	76%	260	48%
Sandia (NM)	295	24	76	219	17	27	135	60	27%	40	23	19	12%
San Felipe (NM)	2,072	88	861	1,221	158	204	723	397	32%	136	16%	70	8%
Santa Ana (NM)	501	58	134	367	52	22	253	149	0%	40	14%	40	14%
Santo Domingo (NM)	3,332	149	1,359	1,973	178	218	1,107	486	24%	470	23%	388	20%
Zia (NM)	584	29	216	368	63	24	164	115	31%	117	42%	31	16%

Table 3 - Continued

AREA, AGENCY, RESERVATION, & STATE	TOTAL	YEARS OF AGE			LABOR FORCE STATUS, 16 YEARS OLD & OVER								
					UNABLE TO WORK		EMPLOYED			NOT EMPLOYED, ABLE TO WORK			
								Earn $7000 +		Total		Seeking Work	
		65 & Over	Under 16	16 & Over	Stu- dents	Others	Total	Number	% of Col. 4	Number	% of 7+10	Number	% of 7+12
	(1)	(2)	(3)	(4)	(5)	(6)	(7)	(8)	(9)	(10)	(11)	(12)	(13)
Albuquerque (CO,NM,UT) - Continued													
Southern Ute Agcy. & Res. (CO)	1,096	51	309	787	304	65	183	160	20%	235	56%	235	56%
Ute Mt. Agcy. & Res. (CO)	1,528	30	754	774	110	88	253	211	27%	323	56%	280	52%
Zuni Agcy. & Res. (NM)	6,999	350	2,970	4,029	666	387	1,742	1,023	25%	1,234	41%	925	35%

NOTES:

1. Figures in brackets non-add.

Table 3 - Continued

AREA, AGENCY, RESERVATION, & STATE	TOTAL	YEARS OF AGE			LABOR FORCE STATUS, 16 YEARS OLD & OVER								
					UNABLE TO WORK		EMPLOYED			NOT EMPLOYED, ABLE TO WORK			
		65 & Over	Under 16	16 & Over	Students	Others	Total	Earn $7000 +		Total		Seeking Work	
								Number	% of Col. 4	Number	% of 7+10	Number	% of 7+12
	(1)	(2)	(3)	(4)	(5)	(6)	(7)	(8)	(9)	(10)	(11)	(12)	(13)
ANADARKO (KS,NE,OK)	36,719	2,225	11,119	25,600	4,465	5,666	9,462	7,117	28%	6,007	39%	4,510	32%
Anadarko Agency	[10,536]	[578]	[3,874]	[6662]	[850]	[1,567]	[2,439]	[1,603]	[24%]	[1,806]	[42%]	[1,622]	[40%]
Apache Tribe (OK)	517	18	228	289	38	50	91	53	18%	110	55%	71	44%
Caddo Tribe (OK)	1,215	73	307	908	167	244	353	240	26%	144	29%	115	25%
Comanche Tribe (OK)	3,597	211	1,436	2,161	288	405	814	457	21%	654	45%	631	44%
Delaware Tribe (OK)	522	20	218	304	43	41	137	114	37%	83	38%	58	30%
Ft. Sill Apache Tribe (OK)	70	10	15	55	9	12	20	14	L	14	L	9	L
Kiowa Tribe (OK)	4,005	212	1,420	2,585	252	709	877	595	23%	747	46%	698	44%
Wichita Tribe (OK)	610	34	250	360	53	106	147	130	36%	54	27%	40	L
Concho Agency (OK)	5,153	78	1,576	3,577	387	134	887	682	19%	2,169	71%	1,084	55%
Horton Agency	[2,216]	[157]	[911]	[1,305]	[66]	[236]	[836]	[580]	[44%]	[167]	[17%]	[137]	[14%]
Iowa Reservation (KS,NE)	280	34	103	177	17	73	81	75	42%	6	L	4	L
Est. KS Pt. (82%)	(229)	(28)	(84)	(145)	(14)	(60)	(66)	(61)	(42%)	(5)	(L)	(3)	(L)
Est. NE Pt. (12%)	(51)	(6)	(19)	(32)	(3)	(13)	(15)	(14)	(L)	(1)	(L)	(1)	(L)
Kickapoo Reservation (KS)	598	33	240	358	28	32	260	209	58%	38	L	30	L
Prairie Potawatomi Res. (KS)	1,302	87	549	753	18	126	488	289	38%	121	20%	101	17%
Sac & Fox Reservation (KS)	36	3	19	17	3	5	7	7	L	2	L	2	L
Pawnee Agency	[7,178]	[400]	[2,858]	[4,320]	[576]	[455]	[1,792]	[1,379]	[32%]	[1,497]	[45%]	[1,335]	[43%]
Kaw Tribe (OK)	617	37	246	371	46	59	158	119	32%	108	41%	78	33%
Otoe-Missouria Tribe (OK)	1,165	71	460	705	40	63	320	220	31%	282	47%	260	45%
Pawnee Tribe (OK)	2,066	125	824	1,242	335	138	384	280	22%	385	50%	362	48%
Ponca Tribe (OK)	2,065	123	826	1,239	59	93	627	517	42%	460	42%	423	40%
Tonkawa Tribe (OK)	1,265	44	502	763	96	102	303	243	32%	262	46%	212	41%

Table 3 - Continued

AREA, AGENCY, RESERVATION, & STATE	TOTAL	YEARS OF AGE			LABOR FORCE STATUS, 16 YEARS OLD & OVER								
					UNABLE TO WORK		EMPLOYED			NOT EMPLOYED, ABLE TO WORK			
		65 & Over	Under 16	16 & Over	Stu-dents	Others	Total	Earn $7000 +		Total		Seeking Work	
								Number	% of Col. 4	Number	% of 7+10	Number	% of 7+12
	(1)	(2)	(3)	(4)	(5)	(6)	(7)	(8)	(9)	(10)	(11)	(12)	(13)
ANADARKO (KS,NE,OK) Cont'd.													
Shawnee Agency	[11,636]	[1,012]	[1,900]	[9,736]	[2,586]	[3,274]	[3,508]	[2,873]	[29%]	[368]	[99%]	[332]	[9%]
Absentee-Shawnee Tribe (OK)	1,365	127	336	1,029	199	365	415	362	35%	50	11%	44	L
Citizen Potawatomi Tribe (OK)	6,354	477	590	5,764	1,747	1,798	2,018	1,614	28%	201	9%	191	9%
Iowa Tribe (OK)	203	23	23	180	44	51	74	58	32%	11	L	7	L
Mexican Kickapoo Tribe (OK)	715	69	117	598	113	223	238	198	33%	24	L	19	L
Sac & Fox Tribe (OK)	1,352	138	362	990	110	384	444	370	37%	52	10%	47	L
Other Tribes *	1,647	178	472	1,175	373	453	319	271	23%	30	L	24	L

NOTES:

1. Figures in brackets and parentheses non-add.

2. L means base for percentage if less than 50; no percentage shown.

3. The Indians of other tribes(*) include the Five Civilized Tribes residing in areas under the jurisdiction of the Shawnee Agency.

Table 3 - Continued

AREA, AGENCY, RESERVATION, & STATE	TOTAL	YEARS OF AGE			LABOR FORCE STATUS, 16 YEARS OLD & OVER								
					UNABLE TO WORK		EMPLOYED			NOT EMPLOYED, ABLE TO WORK			
		65 & Over	Under 16	16 & Over	Students	Others	Total	Earn $7000 +		Total		Seeking Work	
								Number	% of Col. 4	Number	% of 7+10	Number	% of 7+12
	(1)	(2)	(3)	(4)	(5)	(6)	(7)	(8)	(9)	(10)	(11)	(12)	(13)
BILLINGS (MT,WY)	32,805	1,245	11,222	21,583	3,378	4,370	6,937	5,275	24%	6,898	50%	3,235	32%
Blackfeet Agcy. & Res. (MT)	6,632	334	1,972	4,660	802	458	1,586	1,117	24%	1,814	53%	440*	22%
Crow Agcy. & Res. (MT)	4,969	167	1,736	3,233	476	823	1,001	665	21%	933	48%	793	44%
Flathead Agcy. & Res. (MT)	3,300	14	1,510	1,790	109	367	687	473	26%	627	48%	211	23%
Fort Belknap Agcy. & Res. (MT)	2,097	105	648	1,449	243	70	338	321	22%	798	70%	319	49%
Fort Peck Agcy. & Res. (MT)	5,095	236	1,692	3,403	371	872	1,437	1,209	35%	723	33%	200	12%
No. Cheyenne Agcy. & Res. (MT)	3,110	122	1,103	2,007	88	201	957	873	43%	761	44%	500	34%
Rocky Boys Agcy. & Res. (MT)	1,897	72	758	1,139	194	204	260	213	19%	481	65%	240	48%
Wind River Agcy. & Res. (WY)	5,705	195	1,803	3,902	1,095	1,375	671	404	10%	761	53%	532	44%

NOTES:

1. Blackfeet figures include tribal enrollment count and are somewhat larger (by about 16%) than those shown in the 1980 census for the counties in which the tribal members reside.

2. Asterisked numbers indicate Central Office estimates of incomplete or missing data.

Table 3 - Continued

AREA, AGENCY, RESERVATION, & STATE	TOTAL	YEARS OF AGE			LABOR FORCE STATUS, 16 YEARS OLD & OVER								
					UNABLE TO WORK		EMPLOYED			NOT EMPLOYED, ABLE TO WORK			
		65 & Over	Under 16	16 & Over	Stu- dents	Others	Total	Earn $7000 +		Total		Seeking Work	
								Number	% of Col. 4	Number	% of 7+10	Number	% of 7+12
	(1)	(2)	(3)	(4)	(5)	(6)	(7)	(8)	(9)	(10)	(11)	(12)	(13)
EASTERN (FL,LA,ME,MS,NY,NC)	25,961	1,620	9,279	16,682	2,092	3,541	6,036	4,031	24%	5,013	45%	3,432	36%
Miccosukee Agency & Res. (FL)	457	13	181	276	17	40	185	65	24%	34	16%	30	14%
Seminole Agency (FL)	[1,424]	[58]	[582]	[842]	[20]	[99]	[404]	[309]	[37%]	[319]	[44%]	[158]	[28%]
Choctaw Agency	[5,464]	[317]	[2,311]	[3,153]	[412]	[836]	[1,327]	[1,010]	[32%]	[578]	[30%]	[290]	[18%]
Chitimacha Reservation (LA)	278	12	104	174	15	42	111	94	54%	6	5%	6	5%
Choctaw Reservation (MS)	4,914	281	2,113	2,801	385	737	1,120	850	30%	559	33%	277	20%
Coushatta Reservation (LA)	272	24	94	178	12	57	96	66	37%	13	12%	7	7%
Eastern Area	[2,326]	[109]	[820]	[1,506]	[206]	[268]	[556]	[274]	18%	[476]	[46%]	[358]	[39%]
Houlton Band of Maliseet Indians (ME)	239	6	100	139	10	41	48	19	14%	40	45%	40	45%
Indian Township Passamaquoddy (ME)	367	12	144	223	25	51	60	34	5%	87	59%	37	38%
Pleasant Point Passamaquoddy (ME)	691	29	216	475	63	45	120	86	18%	247	67%	197	62%
Penobscot Reservation (ME)	1,029	62	360	669	108	131	328	135	20%	102	24%	84	20%
New York Liaison Office	[10,626]	[733]	[3,560]	[7,066]	[712]	[1,591]	[2,180]	[1,335]	[19%]	[2,583]	[54%]	[2,180]	[50%]
Oneida Tribe (NY)	145*	11*	49*	96*	11*	24*	38*	19*	20%	23*	38%	11*	22%
Onondaga Reservation (NY)	850*	61*	289*	561*	69*	139*	222*	108*	19%	131*	37%	65*	23%
St. Regis Mohawk Res. (NY)	2,799	225	605	2,194	282	329	559	434	20%	1,024	65%	1,024	65%
Seneca Nation-Allegany and Cattaraugus Reservation (NY)	5,418	325	2,136	3,282	237	875	981	577	18%	1,189	55%	969	50%
Tonawanda Reservation (NY)	600*	46*	210*	390*	48*	96*	155*	76*	20%	91*	37%	45*	22%
Tuscarora Reservation (NY)	725*	57*	246*	479*	58*	119*	190*	93*	19%	112*	37%	56*	23%
Cayuga Reservation (NY)	89	8	25	64	7	9	35	28*	44%	13	L	10*	L

Table 3 - Continued

AREA, AGENCY, RESERVATION, & STATE	TOTAL	YEARS OF AGE			LABOR FORCE STATUS, 16 YEARS OLD & OVER								
					UNABLE TO WORK		EMPLOYED			NOT EMPLOYED, ABLE TO WORK			
								Earn $7000 +		Total		Seeking Work	
		65 & Over	Under 16	16 & Over	Stu-dents	Others	Total	Number	% of Col. 4	Number	% of 7+10	Number	% of 7+12
	(1)	(2)	(3)	(4)	(5)	(6)	(7)	(8)	(9)	(10)	(11)	(12)	(13)
EASTERN - Cont'd.													
Cherokee Agency & Res. (NC)	5,664	390	1,825	3,839	725	707	1,384	1,038	27%	1,023	42%	416	23%

NOTES:

1. Figures in brackets are non-add.

2. L means base for percentage is less than 50; no percentage shown.

3. Asterisked numbers indicate Bureau Central Office & New York State estimates of incomplete data.

4. The count for the Seminole Agency includes the Reservations of Big Cypress, Brighton, and Hollywood. The individual reservation characteristics were not provided for the report.

Table 3 - Continued

AREA, AGENCY, RESERVATION, & STATE	TOTAL	YEARS OF AGE			LABOR FORCE STATUS, 16 YEARS OLD & OVER								
					UNABLE TO WORK		EMPLOYED			NOT EMPLOYED, ABLE TO WORK			
		65 & Over	Under 16	16 & Over	Students	Others	Total	Earn $7000 +		Total		Seeking Work	
								Number	% of Col. 4	Number	% of 7+10	Number	% of 7+12
	(1)	(2)	(3)	(4)	(5)	(6)	(7)	(8)	(9)	(10)	(11)	(12)	(13)
JUNEAU (AK)	64,047	2,853	25,303	38,744	5,696	7,107	9,851	6,251	16%	16,090	62%	10,582	52%
Anchorage Agency	[20,666]	[915]	[8,170]	[12,496]	[1,831]	[2,299]	[3,176]	[2,017]	[16%]	[5,190]	[62%]	[3,414]	[52%]
Ahtna Area	641	25	253	388	58	70	98	62	"	162	"	106	"
Aleut Area	1,889	85	755	1,134	167	210	287	183	"	470	"	310	"
Bristol Bay Area	4,003	174	1,581	2,422	356	444	616	391	"	1,006	"	663	"
Chugah Area	1,332	59	526	806	119	147	205	131	"	335	"	220	"
Cook Inlet Area	10,324	462	4,077	6,247	910	1,154	1,589	1,009	"	2,594	"	1,706	"
Kodiak Area	2,477	110	978	1,499	221	274	381	241	"	623	"	409	"
Bethel Agency	11,957	535	4,723	7,234	1,064	1,327	1,840	1,168	"	3,003	"	1,975	"
Fairbanks Agency	[10,452]	[467]	[4,128]	[6,324]	[931]	[1,158]	[1,608]	[1,020]	["]	[2,627]	["]	[1,728]	["]
Barrow	3,938	176	1,555	2,383	351	436	606	384	"	990	"	651	"
Tanana Chiefs Conference	6,514	291	2,573	3,941	580	722	1,002	636	"	1,637	"	1,077	"
Nome Agency	[8,864]	[395]	[3,501]	[5,363]	[789]	[983]	[1,364]	[865]	["]	[2,227]	["]	[1,464]	["]
Kawerak	4,438	198	1,753	2,685	395	492	683	433	"	1,115	"	733	"
Mauneluk	4,426	197	1,748	2,678	394	491	681	432	"	1,112	"	731	"
Southeast Agency	[12,108]	[541]	[4,781]	[7,327]	[1,081]	[1,340]	[1,863]	[1,181]	["]	[3,043]	["]	[2,001]	["]
Tlingit and Haida	9,191	411	3,630	5,561	819	1,019	1,414	897	"	2,309	"	1,519	"
Sitka	1,941	87	766	1,175	174	214	299	189	"	488	"	321	"
Metlakatla Reservation	976	43	385	591	88	107	150	95	"	246	"	161	"

NOTES:

1. Figures in brackets are non-add.

2. L means base for percentage is less than 50; no percentage shown.

3. Population for each area was derived from the 1980 Distribution of the Native population and the percentage applied to the population in the 1980 census (64,047).

Table 3 - Continued

AREA, AGENCY, RESERVATION, & STATE	TOTAL	YEARS OF AGE			LABOR FORCE STATUS, 16 YEARS OLD & OVER								
					UNABLE TO WORK		EMPLOYED			NOT EMPLOYED, ABLE TO WORK			
		65 & Over	Under 16	16 & Over	Stu-dents	Others	Total	Earn $7000 +		Total		Seeking Work	
								Number	% of Col. 4	Number	% of 7+10	Number	% of 7+12
	(1)	(2)	(3)	(4)	(5)	(6)	(7)	(8)	(9)	(10)	(11)	(12)	(13)
MINNEAPOLIS (IA,MI,MN,WI)	39,863	2,572	15,020	24,843	3,309	5,092	8,805	6,441	26%	7,637	46%	6,064	41%
Field Offices	[4,631]	[362]	[1,886]	[2,745]	[386]	[398]	[1,350]	[1,024]	[37%]	[611]	[31%]	[420]	[24%]
Lower Sioux Community (MN)	209	13	62	147	9	10	68	37	25%	60	47%	45	40%
Menominee Res. (WI)	3,384	300	1,379	2,005	335	297	1,042	816	41%	331	24%	213	17%
Prairie Island Ind. Com. (MN)	118	6	38	80	0	0	46	36	45%	34	42%	12	21%
Sac & Fox Community (IA)	695	26	305	390	37	78	131	110	28%	144	52%	134	50%
Shakopee Sioux Com. (MN)	98	3	61	37	0	2	30	15	L	5	L	2	L
Upper Sioux Com. (MN)	127	14	41	86	5	11	33	10	12%	37	53%	14	L
Great Lakes Agency (WI)	[13,722]	[881]	[5,008]	[8,714]	[1,179]	[1,671]	[3,143]	[2,563]	[29%]	[2,721]	[46%]	[2,219]	[41%]
Bad River Res.	1,316	70	499	817	152	207	248	222	27%	210	46%	210	46%
Forest County Potawatomi Com.	390	16	162	228	38	82	38	26	11%	70	65%	54	59%
Lac Courte Oreilles Res.	1,811	81	654	1,157	223	172	296	222	19%	466	61%	185	38%
Lac Du Flambeau Res.	1,485	77	584	901	136	210	320	298	33%	235	42%	176	35%
Mole Lake Res.	280	6	117	163	21	29	41	23	14%	72	64%	72	64%
Oneida Res.	3,384	345	1,161	2,223	326	499	1,189	927	42%	209	15%	209	15%
Red Cliff Res.	1,349	68	476	873	118	167	253	217	25%	335	57%	320	56%
St. Croix Res.	1,041	72	283	758	17	143	222	196	26%	376	63%	376	63%
Stockbridge-Munsee Res.	948	73	346	602	64	67	235	183	30%	236	50%	230	49%
Wisconsin-Winnebago Res.	1,718	73	726	992	84	95	301	249	25%	512	63%	387	56%
Michigan Agency (MI)	[5,551]	[298]	[2,034]	[3,517]	[434]	[528]	[1,439]	[774]	[22%]	[1,116]	44%	[807]	36%
Bay Mills Res.	466	11	224	242	48	23	123	81	33%	48	28%	36	23%
Hannahville Res.	344	5	131	213	44	35	87	56	26%	47	35%	39	31%
Grand Traverse Band	834	78	168	666	10	40	294	160	24%	322	52%	130	31%
Isabella Res.	768	24	307	461	71	35	132	82	18%	223	63%	207	72%
Keewenaw Bay Res.	893	71	384	509	164	32	140	59	12%	173	55%	138	15%
Sault Ste. Marie Tribe	2,246	108	820	1,426	97	363	663	336	24%	303	31%	257	28%

Table 3 - Continued

AREA, AGENCY, RESERVATION, & STATE	TOTAL	YEARS OF AGE			LABOR FORCE STATUS, 16 YEARS OLD & OVER								
					UNABLE TO WORK		EMPLOYED			NOT EMPLOYED, ABLE TO WORK			
		65 & Over	Under 16	16 & Over	Stu-dents	Others	Total	Earn $7000 +		Total		Seeking Work	
								Number	% of Col. 4	Number	% of 7+10	Number	% of 7+12
	(1)	(2)	(3)	(4)	(5)	(6)	(7)	(8)	(9)	(10)	(11)	(12)	(13)
Minneapolis - Continued													
Minnesota Agency (MN)	[11,560]	[846]	[4,216]	[7,344]	[970]	[1,910]	[1,926]	[1,333]	18%	[2,538]	57%	[2,318]	55%
Fond Du Lac Res.	1,431	76	519	912	154	142	369	185	20%	247	40%	203	35%
Grand Portage Res.	310	29	103	207	4	72	86	71	34%	45	34%	45	34%
Leech Lake Res.	4,034	302	1,426	2,608	394	880	610	450	17%	724	54%	724	54%
Mille Lacs Res.	897	71	371	526	15	95	205	138	26%	211	51%	99	33%
Net Lake Res.	940	49	260	680	68	225	163	75	11%	224	58%	160	49%
White Earth Res.	3,948	319	1,537	2,411	335	496	493	414	17%	1,087	69%	1,087	69%
Red Lake Agcy. & Res. (MN)	4,399	185	1,876	2,523	340	585	947	747	30%	651	41%	300	24%

NOTES:

1. Figures in brackets non-add.

2. L means base for percentage is less than 50; no percentage shown.

Table 3 - Continued

AREA, AGENCY, RESERVATION, & STATE	TOTAL	YEARS OF AGE			LABOR FORCE STATUS, 16 YEARS OLD & OVER								
					UNABLE TO WORK		EMPLOYED			NOT EMPLOYED, ABLE TO WORK			
		65 & Over	Under 16	16 & Over	Stu- dents	Others	Total	Earn $7000 +		Total		Seeking Work	
								Number	% of Col. 4	Number	% of 7+10	Number	% of 7+12
	(1)	(2)	(3)	(4)	(5)	(6)	(7)	(8)	(9)	(10)	(11)	(12)	(13)
MUSKOGEE (OK)	121,998	12,078	38,135	83,863	14,727	22,813	37,711	18,908	22%	8,612	19%	4,682	11%
Ardmore Agcy. (Chickasaw Tribe)	8,507	960	2,198	6,309	1,325	2,110	2,140	1,555	25%	734	25%	685	24%
Miami Agcy.	[3,829]	[281]	[1,197]	[2,632]	[317]	[442]	[1,704]	[1,454]	[55%]	[169]	[9%]	[152]	[8%]
Eastern Shawnee Tribe	335	18	111	224	29	41	140	121	54%	14	9%	13	8%
Miami Tribe	350	23	123	227	32	52	130	120	53%	13	9%	12	8%
Modoc Tribe	150	8	59	91	10	10	65	57	63%	6	8%	5	7%
Ottawa Tribe	336	43	105	231	28	59	131	115	50%	13	19%	11	8%
Peoria Tribe	355	43	92	263	35	57	155	131	50%	16	9%	14	8%
Quapaw Tribe	1,193	56	357	836	83	84	609	551	66%	60	9%	54	8%
Seneca-Cayuga Tribe	670	45	174	496	66	78	320	240	48%	32	9%	29	8%
Wyandotte Tribe	440	45	176	264	34	61	154	119	45%	15	9%	14	8%
Okmulgee Agcy. (Creek Tribe)	37,679	1,959	13,188	24,491	3,629	6,178	11,894	7,195	29%	2,790	19%	748	6%
Osage Agcy. & Tribe	5,612	568	1,686	3,926	471	1,385	1,708	1,675	43%	362	17%	92	5%
Tahlequah Agcy. (Cherokee Tribe)	42,992	4,815	13,671	29,321	6,427	6,392	13,169	3,291	11%	3,333	20%	2,095	14%
Talihina Agcy. (Choctaw Tribe)	19,660	3,123	5,116	14,544	2,278	5,576	5,653	2,656	18%	1,037	15%	871	13%
Wewoka Agcy. (Seminole Tribe)	3,719	372	1,079	2,640	280	730	1,443	1,082	41%	187	11%	39	3%

NOTES:

1. Figures in brackets are non-add.

Table 3 - Continued

AREA, AGENCY, RESERVATION, & STATE	TOTAL	YEARS OF AGE			LABOR FORCE STATUS, 16 YEARS OLD & OVER								
					UNABLE TO WORK		EMPLOYED			NOT EMPLOYED, ABLE TO WORK			
		65 & Over	Under 16	16 & Over	Students	Others	Total	Earn $7000 +		Total		Seeking Work	
								Number	% of Col. 4	Number	% of 7+10	Number	% of 7+12
	(1)	(2)	(3)	(4)	(5)	(6)	(7)	(8)	(9)	(10)	(11)	(12)	(13)
NAVAJO (AZ,NM,UT)	160,722	8,679	51,551	109,171	13,158	11,694	39,643	33,960	31%	44,676	53%	16,407	29%
Chinle Agency (AZ)	21,921	994	6,415	15506	2,656	4,515	2,851	2,621	17%	5,484	66%	3,565	56%
Eastern Navajo Agcy. (NM)	35,407	2,232	9,253	26,154	2,628	1,036	19,828	18,058	76%	2,662	12%	1,400	7%
Ft. Defiance Agcy. (AZ)	42,007	2,594	12,775	29,232	1,484	2,871	4,833	4,411	15%	20,044	80%	223	4%
Shiprock Agcy. (NM,UT)	[31,591]	[1,619]	[11,162]	[20,429]	[3,269]	[2,586]	[6,408]	[5,678]	[29%]	[8,166]	[56%]	[4,979]	[44%]
Est. NM Pt. (91%)	28,632	1,473	10,157	18,590	2,975	2,353	5,831	5,167	28%	7,431	56%	4,531	44%
Est. UT Pt. (9%)	2,959	146	1,005	1,839	294	233	577	511	28%	735	56%	448	44%
Western Navajo Agcy. (AZ,UT)	[29,796]	[1,240]	[11,946]	[17,850]	[3,121]	[686]	[5,723]	[3,192]	[18%]	[8,320]	[59%]	[6,240]	[52%]
Est. AZ Pt. (95%)	28,216	1,178	11,349	16,958	2,965	652	5,437	3,032	18%	7,904	59%	5,928	52%
Est. UT Pt. (5%)	1,580	62	597	892	156	34	286	160	18%	416	59%	312	52%

NOTE:

1. **Figures in the brackets are non-add.**
2. **Percentages assigned to each State for reservations extending into more than one State are based on the proportions of Indian populations in the 1980 census for the counties in which the reservation is located.**

Table 3 - Continued

AREA, AGENCY, RESERVATION, & STATE	TOTAL	YEARS OF AGE			LABOR FORCE STATUS, 16 YEARS OLD & OVER								
					UNABLE TO WORK		EMPLOYED			NOT EMPLOYED, ABLE TO WORK			
		65 & Over	Under 16	16 & Over	Students	Others	Total	Earn $7000 +		Total		Seeking Work	
								Number	% of Col. 4	Number	% of 7+10	Number	% of 7+12
	(1)	(2)	(3)	(4)	(5)	(6)	(7)	(8)	(9)	(10)	(11)	(12)	(13)
PHOENIX (AZ,CA,ID,NV,UT)	71,933	3,721	27,034	44,899	5,140	10,950	18,366	9,305	21%	10,443	36%	5,841	24%
Colorado River Agency	[2,745]	[143]	[1,058]	[1,687]	[242]	[273]	[725]	[464]	[27%]	[447]	[38%]	[317]	[30%]
Chemeheuvi Res. (CA)	124	4	43	81	4	13	39	33	41%	25	39%	17	30%
Colorado River Res. (AZ,CA)	2,084	92	829	1,255	188	180	566	367	29%	321	36%	240	30%
Est. AZ Pt. (96%)	(2,000)	(88)	(796)	(1,204)	(180)	(173)	(543)	(352)	(29%)	(308)	(36%)	(230)	(30%)
Est. CA Pt. (4%)	(84)	(4)	(33)	(51)	(8)	(7)	(23)	(15)	(29%)	(13)	(36%)	(10)	(30%)
Fort Mojave Res. (AZ,CA)	537	47	186	351	50	80	120	64	18%	101	46%	60	33%
Est. AZ Pt. (62%)	(333)	(29)	(115)	(218)	(31)	(50)	(74)	(40)	(18%)	(63)	(46%)	(37)	(33%)
Est. CA Pt. (38%)	(204)	(18)	(71)	(133)	(19)	(30)	(46)	(24)	(18%)	(38)	(46%)	(23)	(33%)
Eastern Nevada Agency	[2,474]	[179]	[907]	[1,567]	[158]	[291]	[583]	[408]	[26%]	[535]	[48%]	[475]	[45%]
Battle Mt. Colony & City (NV)	196	18	58	138	54	37	43	26	19%	4	8%	4	8%
Duck Valley Res. (ID, NV)	1,103	84	368	735	41	94	253	176	24%	347	58%	347	58%
Est. ID Pt. (16%)	(176)	(13)	(59)	(118)	(7)	(15)	(40)	(28)	(24%)	(55)	(58%)	(55)	(58%)
Est. NV Pt. (84%	(927)	(71)	(309)	(617)	(34)	(79)	(213)	(148)	(24%)	(292)	(58%)	(292)	(58%)
Duckwater Res. (NV)	139	16	49	90	6	6	44	25	28%	34	44%	13	23%
Elko Colony & City (NV)	468	24	203	265	33	55	127	98	37%	50	28%	35	22%
Ely Colony & City (NV)	234	11	90	144	15	26	61	46	32%	42	41%	42	41%
Goshute Res. (NV,VT)	211	11	109	102	6	37	24	17	17%	35	59%	20	45%
Est. Nevada Pt. (83%)	(175)	(9)	(90)	(85)	(5)	(31)	(20)	(14)	(17%)	(29)	(59%)	(17)	(45%)
Est. Utah Pt. (17%)	(36)	(2)	(19)	(17)	(1)	(6)	(4)	(3)	(17%)	(6)	(59%)	(3)	(45%)
South Fork (NV)	123	15	30	93	3	36	31	20	21%	23	43%	14	31%
Fort Apache Agcy. & Res. (AZ)	8,010	281	3,110	4,900	301	1,317	2,200	1,200	24%	1,082	33%	600	21%
Fort McDowell F. O. & Res. (AZ)	383	23	202	181	33	27	70	32	18%	51	42%	51	42%
Fort Yuma Agency	[2,335]	[117]	[707]	[1,628]	[63]	[252]	[854]	[366]	[22%]	[459]	[35%]	[318]	[27%]
Cocopah Res. (AZ)	835	37	220	615	15	34	349	152	25%	217	38%	153	30%
Quechan Res. (CA)	1,500	80	487	1,013	48	218	505	214	21%	242	32%	165	25%
Hopi Agency	[8,668]	[646]	[3,786]	[4,882]	[918]	[1,347]	[1,363]	[530]	[11%]	[1,254]	[48%]	[652]	[32%]
Hopi Res. (AZ)	8,439	637	3,676	4,763	904	1,317	1,315	502	10%	1,227	48%	644	33%
Kaibab Res. (AZ)	229	9	110	119	14	30	48	28	23%	27	36%	8	14%

Table 3 - Continued

AREA, AGENCY, RESERVATION, & STATE	TOTAL	YEARS OF AGE			LABOR FORCE STATUS, 16 YEARS OLD & OVER								
					UNABLE TO WORK		EMPLOYED			NOT EMPLOYED, ABLE TO WORK			
		65 & Over	Under 16	16 & Over	Students	Others	Total	Earn $7000 +		Total		Seeking Work	
								Number	% of Col. 4	Number	% of 7+10	Number	% of 7+12
	(1)	(2)	(3)	(4)	(5)	(6)	(7)	(8)	(9)	(10)	(11)	(12)	(13)
PHOENIX - Continued													
Papago Agency	[17,651]	[916]	[5,708]	[11,943]	[891]	[2,865]	[6,147]	[2,563]	[21%]	[2,040]	[25%]	[1,257]	[17%]
Gila Bend Res. (AZ)	760	26	272	488	52	131	218	82	17%	87	28%	60	22%
Papago Res. Sells (AZ)	10,610	660	3,363	7,247	604	1,751	3,542	1,466	20%	1,350	28%	707	17%
San Xavier Res. (AZ)	6,281	230	2,073	4,208	235	983	2,387	1,015	24%	603	20%	490	17%
Pascua Yaqui F. O. & Res. (AZ)	616	33	264	352	29	25	80	58	16%	218	73%	130	62%
Pima Agency	[10,025]	[390]	[4,698]	[5,327]	[684]	[1,837]	[1,889]	[848]	[16%]	[917]	[33%]	[467]	[20%]
Ak-Chin (Maricopa) Res. (AZ)	433	17	204	229	25	69	75	30	13%	60	44%	30	29%
Gila River Res. (AZ)	9,592	373	4,494	5,098	659	1,768	1,814	818	16%	857	32%	437	19%
Salt River Agcy. & Res. (AZ)	3,364	158	1,242	2,122	400	536	726	416	20%	460	39%	230	24%
San Carlos Agcy. & Res. (AZ)	5,967	287	1,913	4,054	690	1,330	1,229	882	22%	805	40%	255	17%
Truxton Canyon Agency	[2,149]	[110]	[839]	[1,310]	[164]	[293]	[507]	[275]	[21%]	[346]	[41%]	[264]	[34%]
Camp Verde (Yav.-Apa.) Res. (AZ)	516	45	198	318	30	111	143	110	21%	34	19%	31	18%
Havasupai Res. (AZ)	475	22	175	300	32	49	137	27	10%	82	37%	55	29%
Hualapai Res. (AZ)	1,017	38	406	611	96	119	190	106	18%	206	52%	157	45%
Payson (Tonto-Apa.) Res. (AZ)	66	2	30	36	0	10	13	10	L	13	50%	13	50%
Prescott (Yav. Pres.-Ap) Res. (AZ)	75	3	30	45	6	4	24	22	L	11	31%	8	12%
Uintah & Ouray Agency	[1,962]	[79]	[748]	[1,214]	[120]	[179]	[446]	[290]	[24%]	[469]	[51%]	[89]	[17%]
Skull Valley Res. (UT)	72	3	30	42	10	11	14	10	L	7	L	8	L
Uintah & Ouray Res. (UT)	1,890	76	718	1,172	110	168	432	280	24%	462	52%	86	17%
Utah-Paiute F. O.													
Paiute Indian Tribe of Utah	312	18	84	228	23	39	89	63	28%	77	46%	48	35%
Western Nevada Agency	[5,272]	[341]	[1,768]	[3,504]	[424]	[339]	[1,458]	[910]	[26%]	[1,283]	[47%]	[688]	[32%]
Fallon Res. (NV)	677	42	152	525	67	34	313	125	24%	111	26%	94	23%
Fort McDermitt Res. (NV)	653	53	208	445	50	78	53	38	18%	264	83%	245	82%
Las Vegas Res. (NV)	123	4	49	74	0	22	34	34	46%	18	35%	9	21%

Table 3 - Continued

AREA, AGENCY, RESERVATION, & STATE	TOTAL	YEARS OF AGE			LABOR FORCE STATUS, 16 YEARS OLD & OVER								
					UNABLE TO WORK		EMPLOYED			NOT EMPLOYED, ABLE TO WORK			
		65 & Over	Under 16	16 & Over	Stu-dents	Others	Total	Earn $7000 +		Total		Seeking Work	
								Number	% of Col. 4	Number	% of 7+10	Number	% of 7+12
	(1)	(2)	(3)	(4)	(5)	(6)	(7)	(8)	(9)	(10)	(11)	(12)	(13)
PHOENIX - Continued													
Western Nevada Agency-(Cont'd)													
Lovelock Res. (NV)	163	6	65	98	5	14	66	34	35%	13	16%	7	10%
Moapa Res. (NV)	216	9	87	129	2	0	48	46	36%	79	62%	73	60%
Pyramid Lake Res. (NV)	776	36	280	496	48	29	197	155	31%	222	53%	25	11%
Reno-Sparks Res. (NV)	603	25	201	402	52	72	199	180	45%	79	28%	38	16%
Walker River Res. (NV)	980	90	321	659	122	72	266	92	14%	199	43%	60	18%
Washoe Tribe (CA,NV)	(544)	(30)	(205)	(339)	(40)	(5)	(144)	(125)	(37%)	(150)	51%	(89)	(38%)
Carson Colony (NV)	199	16	70	129	12	1	63	55	43%	53	46%	35	36%
Dresslerville Colony (NV)	172	5	71	101	17	3	49	40	40%	32	39%	16	25%
Woodfords Colony (CA)	173	9	64	109	11	1	32	30	27%	65	67%	38	54%
Winnemucca Res. (NV)	81	3	32	49	13	3	17	3	L	16	L	0	L
Yerrington Res. (NV)	342	26	138	204	24	8	99	64	31%	73	42%	25	20%
Yomba Res. (NV)	114	17	30	84	1	2	22	14	17%	59	73%	23	51%

NOTES:

1. Figures in brackets & parentheses are non-add.

2. L means base are percentage is less than 50; no percentage shown.

Table 3 - Continued

AREA, AGENCY, RESERVATION, & STATE	TOTAL	YEARS OF AGE			LABOR FORCE STATUS, 16 YEARS OLD & OVER								
					UNABLE TO WORK		EMPLOYED			NOT EMPLOYED, ABLE TO WORK			
		65 & Over	Under 16	16 & Over	Students	Others	Total	Earn $7000 +		Total		Seeking Work	
								Number	% of Col. 4	Number	% of 7+10	Number	% of 7+12
	(1)	(2)	(3)	(4)	(5)	(6)	(7)	(8)	(9)	(10)	(11)	(12)	(13)
PORTLAND (ID,OR,WA)	52,787	2,669	18,551	34,236	3,844	6,043	11,222	8,199	24%	13,127	54%	9,266	45%
Colville Agcy. & Res. (WA)	6,090	438	1,848	4,242	187	713	865	865	20%	2,477	74%	1,461	63%
Fort Hall Agcy. & Res. (ID)	3,820	158	1,573	2,247	292	357	1,028	812	36%	570	36%	395	28%
Northern Idaho Agcy.	[2,957]	[222]	[909]	[2,048]	[395]	[421]	[814]	[651]	[32%]	[418]	[34%]	[255]	[24%]
Coeur d'Alene Res. (ID)	822	67	213	609	87	172	307	192	31%	43	12%	26	12%
Kootenai Res. (ID)	115	5	24	91	22	17	29	27	30%	23	44%	10	26%
Nez Perce Res. (ID)	2,020	150	672	1,348	286	232	478	432	32%	352	42%	219	31%
Olympic Peninsula Agcy.	[7,559]	[399]*	[2,785]*	[4,774]*	[574]*	[781]*	[2,167]*	[1,265]*	[26%]	[1,252]*	[37%]	[1,027]	[33%]
Chehalis Res. (WA)	721	43	257	464	63	53	265	171	37%	83	24%	83	24%
Hoh Res. (WA)	61	4*	22	39	0	3*	8	6*	L	28*	L	31	L
Jamestown Clallam Tribe (WA)	323	49	82	141	24	72	98	76	31%	47	32%	41	29%
Lower Elwah Res. (WA)	1,191	8	476	715	52	55	379	170	24%	229	38%	175	32%
Makah Res. (WA)	927	35	310	617	49	92	357	230	37%	119	25%	80	18%
Quileute Res. (WA)	327	4	134	193	18	48	53	38	20%	74	58%	56	51%
Quinault Res. (WA)	2,013	165	744	1,269	243	238	554	294	23%	234	30%	225	29%
Shoalwater Bay Res. (WA)	62	7	16	46	4	8	24	11	L	10	L	10	L
Skokomish Res. (WA)	1,008	40*	433*	575*	37*	112*	138*	86*	15%	288	67%	288	67%
Squaxin Island (WA)	926	44	311	615	84	100	291	183	30%	140	61%	140	61%
Puget Sound Agcy.	[16,956]	[739]	[6,151]	[10,805]	[1,731]	[1,667]	[2,903]	[1,727]	[16%]	[4,504]	[61%]	[3,681]	[56%]
Lummi Res. (WA)	2,290	165	1,097	1,193	180	290	328	278	23%	395	55%	143	30%
Muckleshoot Res. (WA)	2,227	65	1,022	1,205	94	169	341	123	10%	601	64%	449	57%
Nisqually Res. (WA)	1,257	25	535	722	54	150	163	87	12%	355	68%	355	68%
Nooksack Res. (WA)	694	47	296	398	53	41	148	95	24%	156	51%	72	33%
Port Gamble Res. (WA)	446	15	150	296	11	75	77	65	22%	133	63%	107	58%
Port Madison (Suquamish) Res. (WA)	1,784	83	212	1,572	103	232	603	428	27%	634	51%	634	51%
Puyallup Res. (WA)	5,660	196	1,878	3,782	1,132	397	735	226	6%	1,518	67%	1,477	66%
Sauk-Suiattle Res. (WA)	255	15	124	131	15	30	16	12	9%	70	81%	65	80%
Stillaquamish Res. (WA)	464	17	182	282	7	43	74	67	24%	158	68%	40	35%
Swinomish Res. (WA)	648	39	215	433	23	83	195	160	37%	132	40%	78	29%
Tulalip Res. (WA)	855	37	347	508	53	135	158	148	29%	162	51%	141	47%
Upper Skagit Res. (WA)	376	35	93	283	6	22	65	38	13%	190	74%	120	65%

Table 3 - Continued

AREA, AGENCY, RESERVATION, & STATE	TOTAL	YEARS OF AGE			LABOR FORCE STATUS, 16 YEARS OLD & OVER								
					UNABLE TO WORK		EMPLOYED			NOT EMPLOYED, ABLE TO WORK			
								Earn $7000 +		Total		Seeking Work	
		65 & Over	Under 16	16 & Over	Students	Others	Total	Number	% of Col. 4	Number	% of 7+10	Number	% of 7+12
	(1)	(2)	(3)	(4)	(5)	(6)	(7)	(8)	(9)	(10)	(11)	(12)	(13)
PORTLAND - Continued													
Siletz Agcy. & Tribe (OR)	671	26	217	454	40	43	220	142	31%	151	41%	98	31%
Spokane Agency	[2,126]	[122]	[631]	[1,495]	[126]	[208]	[644]	[472]	[31%]	[517]	[44%]	[270]	[36%]
Kalispel Res. (WA)	205	8	82	123	8	15	40	27	22%	60	60%	45	53%
Spokane Res. (WA)	1,921	114	549	1,372	118	193	604	445	32%	457	43%	225	27%
Umatilla Agcy. & Res. (OR)	1,500	75	690	810	111	190	309	170	21%	200	39%	67	18%
Warm Springs Agcy.	[2,606]	[65]	[1,017]	[1,589]	[189]	[385]	[709]	[594]	37%	[306]	[30%]	[277]	[28%]
Burns Paiute Res. (OR)	194	5	74	120	21	13	22	22	18%	64	74%	64	74%
Warm Springs Res. (OR)	2,412	60	943	1,469	168	372	687	572	39%	242	26%	213	24%
Yakima Agcy. & Res. (WA)	8,502	425	2,730	5,772	199	1,278	1,563	1,507	26%	2,732	64%	1,629	51%

NOTES:

1. Figures in brackets are non-add.
2. Asterisked numbers indicates Central Office estimates of incomplete or missing data.
3. L means base for percentage is less than 50; no percentage shown.

AREA, AGENCY, RESERVATION, & STATE	TOTAL	YEARS OF AGE			LABOR FORCE STATUS, 16 YEARS OLD & OVER								
					UNABLE TO WORK		EMPLOYED			NOT EMPLOYED, ABLE TO WORK			
		65 & Over	Under 16	16 & Over	Students	Others	Total	Earn $7000 +		Total		Seeking Work	
								Number	% of Col. 4	Number	% of 7+10	Number	% of 7+12
	(1)	(2)	(3)	(4)	(5)	(6)	(7)	(8)	(9)	(10)	(11)	(12)	(13)
Sacramento (CA)	17,861	1,259	5,845	12,016	817	1,606	3,889	2,641	22%	5,704	59%	2,976	43%
Central California Agency	[6,744]	[653]	[2,583]	[4,161]	[260]	[661]	[1,775]	[1,025]	[25%]	[1,459]	45%	[980]	36%
Alturas Rancheria	10	1	2	8	3	1	4	2	L	0	L	0	L
Benton Paiute Reservation	25	11	5	20	1	14	3	3	L	2	L	0	L
Berry Creek Rancheria	154	6	90	64	3	6	52	24	37%	3	5%	0	0
Big Pine Reservation	419	22	168	251	14	57	108	69	27%	72	40%	57	34%
Big Sandy Rancheria	129	5	75	54	4	5	22	20	37%	23	53%	15	L
Bishop Rancheria	1,006	76	274	732	78	109	362	212	29%	183	34%	160	31%
Bridgeport Reservation	81	5	22	59	1	6	25	17	29%	27	52%	24	L
Cedarville Rancheria	16	1	6	10	2	4	2	0	L	2	L	2	L
Cold Springs Rancheria	209	117	92	117	10	2	62	23	20%	43	41%	9	13%
Colusa Rancheria	44	5	15	29	2	3	18	10	L	6	25%	6	25%
Cortina Rancheria	81	67	14	67	0	3	45	25	37%	19	30%	6	11%
Coyote Valley Rancheria	216	111	105	111	0	13	46	22	20%	52	53%	36	44%
Dry Creek Rancheria	126	9	48	78	0	17	50	28	36%	11	18%	11	18%
El-Em Indian Colony	157	3	81	76	1	15	46	26	34%	14	23%	11	19%
Enterprise Reservation	18	2	5	13	0	0	4	3	L	9	L	2	L
Fort Bidwell Reservation	162	13	55	107	9	33	29	26	24%	36	55%	24	45%
Fort Independence Reservation	93	3	32	61	3	6	15	12	20%	37	71%	20	L
Grindstone Rancheria	173	5	31	142	3	13	40	26	18%	86	68%	48	54%
Hopland Band	125	9	48	77	5	31	19	3	4%	22	L	16	L
Jackson Rancheria	19	1	5	14	0	2	8	0	L	4	L	0	L
Laytonville Rancheria	177	10	68	109	12	44	29	19	17%	24	45%	24	45%
Lone Pine Reservation	204	10	92	112	10	28	40	25	22%	34	46%	29	42%
Lookout Rancheria	11	1	2	9	1	2	2	1	L	4	L	0	0
Manchester Pt. Arena Rancheria	88	5	22	66	14	22	13	6	9%	17	L	17	L
Middleton Rancheria	62	5	11	51	1	10	24	12	L	16	L	6	L
North Fork Allotment	29	8	13	16	0	4	5	5	L	7	L	0	0
Robinson Rancheria	68	5	33	35	0	18	3	3	L	14	L	12	L
Round Valley Reservation	709	36	291	418	22	67	100	41	10%	229	70%	200	67%
Rumsey Rancheria	47	1	20	27	2	11	14	8	L	0	0	0	0
Santa Rosa Rancheria	271	6	130	141	4	27	39	28	20%	71	64%	40	51%
Sherwood Valley Rancheria	173	6	49	124	18	8	60	35	28%	38	39%	16	21%

Table 3 - Continued

AREA, AGENCY, RESERVATION, & STATE	TOTAL	YEARS OF AGE			LABOR FORCE STATUS, 16 YEARS OLD & OVER								
					UNABLE TO WORK		EMPLOYED			NOT EMPLOYED, ABLE TO WORK			
		65 & Over	Under 16	16 & Over	Students	Others	Total	Earn $7000 +		Total		Seeking Work	
								Number	% of Col. 4	Number	% of 7+10	Number	% of 7+12
	(1)	(2)	(3)	(4)	(5)	(6)	(7)	(8)	(9)	(10)	(11)	(12)	(13)
Central California Agency - Cont'd.													
Stewarts Point Rancheria	204	26	59	145	0	26	95	45	31%	24	20%	12	11%
Susanville Rancheria	350	18	200	150	12	8	70	20	13%	60	46%	32	31%
Table Mountain Reservation	76	5	24	52	6	3	23	20	L	20	L	9	L
Tule River Reservation	549	13	219	330	0	0	148	97	29%	182	55%	95	39%
Tuolumne Rancheria	276	12	104	172	20	4	102	85	49%	46	31%	18	15%
Upper Lake Rancheria	133	7	66	67	0	23	32	12	18%	12	L	3	L
X-L Ranch Reservation	54	7	7	47	5	16	16	12	L	10	L	10	L
Northern California Agency	[5,275]	[204]	[1,470]	[3,805]	[236]	[255]	[828]	[674]	[18%]	[2,486]	75%	[1,057]	56%
Big Bend Reservation	106	8	26	80	2	15	11	8	10%	52	82%	5	L
Big Lagoon Reservation	7	1	0	7	0	0	1	1	L	6	L	0	0
Hoopa Valley (Square) Res.	1,816	61	590	1,226	140	90	251	226	18%	745	75%	374	60%
Hoopa Extension (Yurok) Res.	1,858	70	464	1,394	60	70	354	283	20%	910	72%	365	51%
Montgomery Creek Rancheria	19	0	10	9	0	6	0	0	0	3	L	0	0
Orleans Karok Reservation	1,192	45	298	294	10	45	156	126	14%	683	81%	273	64%
Resighini Rancheria	104	10	31	73	10	10	23	15	20%	30	57%	10	L
Roaring Creek Rancheria	36	1	11	25	2	4	8	5	L	11	L	0	0
Table Bluff Rancheria	70	6	14	56	8	6	12	2	L	30	L	30	L
Trinidad Rancheria	67	2	26	41	4	9	12	8	L	16	L	0	0
Aqua Caliente (Palm Sprgs. F.O.)	190	4	72	118	16	29	23	20	17%	50	68%	3	11%
Southern Calif. Agency	[5,652]	[398]	[1,720]	[3,932]	[299]	[661]	[1,263]	[922]	23%	[1,709]	57%	[936]	43%
Barona Reservation	301	7	133	168	21	49	64	49	29%	34	35%	20	24%
Cabazon Reservation	22	0	6	16	1	0	11	11	L	4	L	4	L
Cahuilla Reservation	148	8	51	97	2	13	28	22	23%	54	66%	15	35%
Campo Reservation	205	23	94	111	8	32	27	18	16%	44	62%	44	62%
Cuyapaipe Reservation	24	2	6	18	0	7	7	3	L	4	L	3	L
Inaja-Cosmit Reservation	10	0	3	7	0	3	3	3	L	1	L	1	L
Jamul Reservation	62	0	18	44	2	5	18	9	L	19	L	0	0
LaJolla Reservation	221	19	82	139	15	30	78	64	46%	16	17%	16	17%
LaPosta Reservation	14	0	10	4	1	0	1	1	L	2	L	2	L
Los Coyotes Reservation	161	5	46	115	12	21	33	23	20%	49	60%	49	60%
Manzanita Reservation	40	4	18	22	10	4	6	3	L	2	L	0	0

Table 3 - Continued

AREA, AGENCY, RESERVATION, & STATE	TOTAL	YEARS OF AGE			LABOR FORCE STATUS, 16 YEARS OLD & OVER								
					UNABLE TO WORK		EMPLOYED			NOT EMPLOYED, ABLE TO WORK			
		65 & Over	Under 16	16 & Over	Stu-dents	Others	Total	Earn $7000 +		Total		Seeking Work	
								Number	% of Col. 4	Number	% of 7+10	Number	% of 7+12
	(1)	(2)	(3)	(4)	(5)	(6)	(7)	(8)	(9)	(10)	(11)	(12)	(13)
Southern Calif. Agcy. - Cont'd.													
Mesa Grande Reservation	28	4	7	21	1	5	12	9	L	3	L	1	L
Morongo Reservation	743	40	215	528	82	75	183	127	24%	188	51%	120	40%
Pala Reservation	455	24	139	316	30	82	156	154	49%	48	23%	23	13%
Pauma Reservation	93	4	18	75	4	8	43	22	29%	20	32%	4	8%
Pechanga Reservation	428	38	147	281	6	86	109	91	32%	80	42%	42	28%
Ramona Reservation	3	0	0	3	0	0	2	1	L	1	L	0	0
Rincon Reservation	261	18	105	156	9	26	63	43	28%	58	48%	2	3%
San Manuel Reservation	88	1	30	58	10	12	18	13	22%	18	L	14	L
San Pasqual Reservation	347	70	99	248	8	50	45	19	8%	145	75%	25	36%
Santa Rosa Reservation	100	1	33	67	3	5	29	23	34%	30	51%	30	51%
Santa Inez Reservation	200	14	72	128	9	30	69	64	50%	20	22%	20	22%
Santa Ysabel Reservation	889	79	67	822	11	17	79	41	5%	715	90%	420	84%
Soboba Reservation	457	26	169	288	34	37	98	38	13%	119	55%	47	32%
Sycuan Reservation	70	0	29	41	5	12	18	18	L	6	L	6	L
Torres-Martinez Reservation	81	2	46	35	14	5	12	7	L	4	L	3	L
Twenty-Nine Palms Reservation	18	1	9	9	1	4	4	3	L	0	0	0	0
Viejas Reservation	183	8	68	115	0	43	47	43	37%	25	36%	25	36%

NOTES:

1. Figures in parentheses are non-add.

2. L means base for percentage is less than 50; no percentage shown.

APPENDIX

TOURISM PROJECTS

SELECTED DATA: FEDERALLY FINANCED TOURISM PROJECTS ON TWELVE INDIAN RESERVATIONS

	Opening Date	Capital Invested			
		By EDA	By Tribe	By Others	Total
Inn of the Mountain Gods, Mescalero Apache Reservation, New Mexico	July 1975	$10,165,000	$4,407,000	$2,500,000	$17,072,000
Firebird Lake, Gila River Reservation, Arizona	April 1975	2,294,000	None	None	2,294,000
Sunrise Hotel Complex, Fort Apache Reservation, Arizona	(Ski) Jan. 1971 (Hotel) Aug. 1972	5,046,000	1,000,000	454,000	6,500,000
Camel Rock Campground, Tesuque Pueblo, New Mexico	May 1977	192,000	None	44,000	236,000
Stone Lake Lodge, Jicarilla Apache Reservation, New Mexico	Dec. 1972	1,788,360	247,774	1,126,170	3,162,304
Southern Ute Tourist Center, Southern Ute Reservation, Colorado	Jan. 1972	556,000	390,000	None	946,000
Bottle Hollow Resort, Uintah and Ouray Reservation, Utah	July 1971	2,289,994	2,417,928	372,580	5,080,502
Kah-Nee-Ta Vacation Resort, Warm Springs Reservation, Oregon	July 1972	5,584,000	900,000	1,016,000	7,500,000
4 Bears Motor Lodge, Fort Berthold Reservation, North Dakota	July 1972	1,880,320	120,000	None	2,000,320
Chief Gall Inn, Standing Rock Sioux Reservation, South Dakota	July 1973	1,998,000	None	105,000	2,103,000
Crow Creek Sioux Tribal Complex, Crow Creek Reservation, South Dakota	June 1971	937,600	384,400	None	1,322,000
Radisson Inn, Grand Portage Reservation, Minnesota	July 1975	3,585,625	None	312,375	3,898,000
TOTALS		$36,316,899	$9,867,102	$5,930,125	$52,114,126

NOTE: These totals apply only to the above 12 projects. The totals for all EDA-financed tourism projects, of course, are larger.

SELECTED DATA: FEDERALLY FINANCED TOURISM PROJECTS ON TWELVE INDIAN RESERVATIONS, concl.

	Average Number of Employees	Annual Deficit*	Cumulative Deficit Since Opening*	Additional Capital Required
Inn of the Mountain Gods, Mescalero Apache Reservation, New Mexico	200	$809,466 (Year end 6/30/77)	$ 1,785,609	$ 6,950,000
Firebird Lake, Gila River Reservation, Arizona	3	$138,700 (Year end 6/30/77)	200,000	2,075,000
Sunrise Hotel Complex, Fort Apache Reservation, Arizona	100	$61,329 (11 months 3/11/77)	1,070,077	4,734,000
Camel Rock Campground, Tesuque Pueblo, New Mexico	3	Just opened	Just opened	373,000
Stone Lake Lodge, Jicarilla Apache Reservation, New Mexico	12	$144,000 (Year end 6/30/77)	609,788	1,252,000
Southern Ute Tourist Center, Southern Ute Reservation, Colorado	20	$171,000 (Year end 9/30/76)	916,560	2,515,000
Bottle Hollow Resort, Uintah and Ouray Reservation, Utah	100	$529,314 (11 months 3/31/77)	2,324,686	4,689,000
Kah-Nee-Ta Vacation Resort, Warm Springs Reservation, Oregon	209	$861,000 (Year end 12/31/76)	4,907,472	4,325,000
4 Bears Motor Lodge, Fort Berthold Reservation, North Dakota	28	$100,000 (Year end 6/30/77)	960,240	4,420,000
Chief Gall Inn, Standing Rock Sioux Reservation, South Dakota	23	$171,476 (11 months 11/30/76)	816,982	4,910,000
Crow Creek Sioux Tribal Complex, Crow Creek Reservation, South Dakota	20	$77,000 (Average per year)	668,000	661,000
Radisson Inn, Grand Portage Reservation, Minnesota	70	$409,046 (Year end 12/31/76)	757,798	3,968,000
TOTALS		$3,472,331	$15,017,212	$40,872,000

*Based on latest available figures.

Source: Harry G. Clement, The Gift That Hurt the Indians: A Report About Federally Financed Tourism on Indian Reservations, prepared by Checchi and Company for the Ford Foundation and the Bureau of Indian Affairs (Washington, D. C.: 1977), pp. 120-121.

APPENDIX C

STATUS OF NONINTERCOURSE ACT LAND CLAIMS

Connecticut

Suits filed in Connecticut seeking recovery of lands allegedly alienated in violation of the Trade and Intercourse Act are still pending for:

(1) the Schaghticoke tribe for several thousand acres of land (1975);
(2) the Western Pequot tribe (1976);
(3) the *Mohegan Tribe* v. *Zaugg* (1977); and
(4) the *Mohegan Tribe* v. *the State of Connecticut* (1977)

In the second instance legislation was passed by the Congress in 1982 but was vetoed on April 5, 1983. In the fourth instance the district court ruled that the Trade and Intercourse Act was applicable. On appeal the district court was upheld, and the Supreme Court denied certiorari. The state had contended that the Trade and Intercourse Act was not intended to apply to Indians such as the Mohegan who, it was alleged, had never resided in Indian country as defined by federal law.

Florida

In 1978 the Seminole tribe of Florida sued for 16,000 acres, and in 1979 the Miccosukee tribe sued for about 5 million acres under the Trade and Intercourse Act. On December 31, 1982, PL 97–399 (25 USC 1741) became law and completed a state settlement with the Miccosukee in which the state paid the tribe $1,000,000.

Louisiana

A 1977 suit filed by the Chitimacha tribe for 2,000 to 3,000 acres was dismissed by the district court in 1980. The Interior Department has recommended that the Department of Justice sue for 900 acres on behalf of the Chitimacha.

The Tunica-Biloxi tribe was recognized by the BIA in 1981, and the tribe has initiated negotiations for land under the Trade and Intercourse Act.

There has been no final action in either of these cases.

Maine

See chapter 5 of this book. PL 96–420 was signed by President Carter on October 10, 1980.

Massachusetts

In 1976 the Mashpee Tribe (Wampanoag) sought recovery of 17,000 acres alledgedly alienated in violation of the Trade and Intercourse Act. The courts decided the Mashpee were not an Indian tribe and therefore not subject to the act.

In 1974 the Wampanoag Tribe of Gay Head sought recovery of some 5,000 acres of land, and 1976 the Town of Gay Head voted to deed certain lands to the Indians. Some Indians have not agreed to the proposal, and final action must be approved by the state. This matter is still pending.

New York

Oneida. In 1970 the Oneida (New York, Wisconsin, and the Thomas Band Council of Ontario, Canada) sought damages for the use of 100,000 acres purchased by the state in 1795 without federal approval. Although court action has held that the lands were illegally purchased and damages are due, no formal action has been taken. In 1979 the Oneida filed another suit claiming up to 5 million acres. There has been no final action on this suit.

Cayuga. The Cayuga Indian nation claim to 64,000 acres in New York resulted in a negotiated agreement giving the Cayuga a 5,481-acre reservation and an $8-million trust fund in return for extinguishment of the 64,000-acre claim. The land was to come from a state park and national forestland. In 1980 the House of Representatives failed to pass the legislation based on the negotiation, and the Cayuga filed suit for the return of the 64,000 acres and damages. This case is still pending.

St. Regis Mohawks. The St. Regis Mohawks have claimed land, and a proposed settlement in 1980 would have given them 9,750 acres of state land and a federal trust fund of $7.5 million. No final action has been taken.

Rhode Island

Negotiations among the Narraganset Indians, the state of Rhode Island, the town of Charlestown (where claimed land was located), private landholders and representatives of the Carter administration resulted in an agreement that formed the basis for a federal statute and companion state legislation. PL 95–395, passed on September 30, 1978, provided for the extinguishment of all Narraganset Indian land claims in exchange for approximately 1,800 acres of land—900 from the state and 900 acres to be purchased at federal expense. A state corporation was created to acquire, hold, and manage the land. A settlement fund of $3.5 million was established in the U.S. Treasury to implement the act.

South Carolina

The Catawba Indian tribe claims 140,000 acres under the Trade and Intercourse Act, and a federal task force was appointed in 1978 to develop a proposed legislative settlement. There has been no agreement to date. In 1980 the Catawba filed suit for the return of 140,000 acres and damages, the case is still pending.

Virginia

The Pamunkey Indians were successful in claiming 20 acres taken without federal and state approval for a railroad right-of-way. The Southern Railway will pay the tribe $100,000 in return for the tribe's waiver of any claim for past trespass damages and for a right-of-way for ten years. After that time there would be a lease agreement. If the track were abandoned the land would revert to the Pamunkey.

Sources:
Richard S. Jones, "Indians, Land Claims by Eastern Tribes" (Washington, D.C.: Congressional Research Service, Library of Congress, Issue Brief no. 1B77040, January 15, 1981); telephone conversations with Tim Vollmann and Richard Jones, June 2, 1982.

ABBREVIATIONS

AIM	American Indian Movement
AIPRC	American Indian Policy Review Commission. This commission was established by Congress and included three senators, three members of the House of Representatives, and five Indians. The commission's *Final Report* was issued May 17, 1977.
BIA	Bureau of Indian Affairs, U.S. Department of the Interior
BLM	Bureau of Land Management, U.S. Department of the Interior
CFR	Code of Federal Regulations
EDA	Economic Development Administration, U.S. Department of Commerce
F&W	U.S. Fish and Wildlife Service, U.S. Department of the Interior
GAO	U.S. General Accounting Office
GPO	U.S. Government Printing Office
GS	U.S. Geological Survey, U.S. Department of the Interior
HHS	U.S. Department of Health and Human Services
HRC 108	House Concurrent Resolution 108, adopted August 1, 1953—frequently referred to as "the termination policy."
HUD	U.S. Department of Housing and Urban Development
IHS	Indian Health Sevice, Health Services Administration, U.S. Department of Health and Human Services
IRA	Indian Reorganization Act of 1934, 48 Stat. 984. This act authorized the organization of Indian tribes with a large degree of self-government, stopped the allotment policy, and authorized the purchase of land for Indian people.
JOM	Johnson-O'Malley Act of 1934, 48 Stat. 596, This act authorized the secretary of the Interior to enter into contracts with states or their subdivisions for education, medical attention, agricultural assistance, and social welfare for Indians.
NCAI	National Congress of American Indians
NTCA	National Tribal Chairmen's Association
OE	Office of Education, now Department of Education
OEO	Office of Economic Opportunity

OMB	U.S. Office of Management and Budget
PL 280	Statue of 1953 giving the consent of the government of the United States for any state to assume civil and criminal jurisdiction over its Indian citizens, 67 Stat. 588. PL 280 was amended in 1968 to require Indian consent, 82 Stat. 78.
PL 561	Education Amendments Act of 1978, November 1, 1978, 92 Stat. 2313
PL 638	Indian Self-Determination and Education Assistance Act, January 4, 1975, 88 Stat. 2203
PS	Park Service, U.S. Department of the Interior

NOTES

Introduction

1. Francis Paul Prucha, "Doing Indian History," in Jane F. Smith and Robert M. Kvasnicka, eds., *Indian-White Relations: A Persistent Paradox,* Papers presented at the National Archives Conference on Research in the History of Indian-White Relations, Washington, D.C., June 16, 1972 (Washington, D.C.: Howard University Press, 1976), p. 7.

Chapter 1

1. Charles A. Beard and Mary R. Beard, *The Rise of American Civilization* (New York: Macmillan, 1930), p. 11.

2. Harold E. Driver, *Indians of North America,* 2d ed. rev. (Chicago: University of Chicago Press, 1969), p. 13.

3. Wilcomb E. Washburn, *The Indian in America,* New American Nation Series, ed. Henry Steele Commager and Richard B. Morris (New York: Harper Torchbooks, Harper and Row, 1975), pp 7–10; Driver, *Indians of North America,* pp. 11–12.

4. Driver, *Indians of North America,* chap. 4 and map 3 following p. 566.

5. Douglas H. Ubelaker, "Prehistoric New World Population Size," *American Journal of Physical Anthropology* 45; 3 (November 1976), pp. 661–665.

6. Frederick Webb Hodge, ed., *Handbook of American Indians North of Mexico,* Bureau of American Enthnology Bulletin 30, 2 vols. (Washington, D.C.: Smithsonian Institution, 1912; reprinted, New York: Rowman and Littlefield, 1971), 2:814.

7. John R. Swanton, *The Indian Tribes of North America,* Bureau of American Ethnology Bulletin 145 (Washington, D.C.: Smithsonian Institution, 1952), pp. 39–40.

8. Alvin M. Josephy, Jr., *The Indian Heritage of America* (New York: Alfred A. Knopf, 1968), pp. 34–35.

9. Edward H. Spicer, *A Short History of the Indians of the United States* (New York: Van Nostrand–Reinhold, 1969), p. 11.

10. S. Lyman Tyler, *A History of Indian Policy* (Washington, D.C.: Bureau of Indian Affairs, Government Printing Office, 1973), p. vi of foreword by Rogers C.B. Morton, secretary of the Interior.

11. Saul K. Padover, ed., *Thomas Jefferson on Democracy* (New York: New American Library, Mentor Book, 1954), p. 105.

12. Tyler, *History of Indian Policy*, p. 29.

13. William T. Hagan, *American Indians*, rev. ed. (Chicago: University of Chicago Press, 1979), pp. 37–38.

14. Tyler, *History of Indian Policy*, p. 34.

15. Constitution of the United States, ARTICLE 1, SECTION 8.

16. Constitution of the United States, ART. 6.

17. Constitution of the United States, ART. 1, SEC. 2.

18. For example, the Hopewell treaty of November 28, 1785, ART. 12; the Delaware treaty of September 17, 1778, ART. 6.

19. Laurence F. Schmeckebier, *The Office of Indian Affairs: Its History, Activities, and Organization*, Institute for Government Research, Service Monographs of the United States Government no. 48 (Baltimore, Md.: Johns Hopkins Press, 1927), p. 18.

20. Hagan, *American Indians*, p. 55.

21. Ibid, p. 71.

22. Theodore W. Taylor, *The States and Their Indian Citizens* (Washington, D.C.: Department of the Interior, Bureau of Indian Affairs, 1972), p. 10 n.18.

23. Alexis de Tocqueville, *Democracy in America*, ed. Phillips Bradley, 2 vols. (New York: Vintage Books, 1956), 1:349–350.

24. Ibid., p. 349.

25. Ibid, p. 358; Hagan, *American Indians*, pp. 73–76.

26. *Federal Indian Law* (Washington, D.C.: Department of the Interior, 1958), pp. 180–199; also Hagan, *American Indians*, pp. 73–81.

27. Hagan, *American Indians*, pp. 81–85.

28. Ibid., pp. 85–86.

29. Ibid., p. 70.

30. Ibid., p. 89.

31. Ibid., p. 67.

32. Wilcomb E. Washburn, *The American Indian in the United States: A Documentary History*, 4 vols. (New York: Random House, 1973), 3:2135–2182. Washburn reprints the following: the Proclamation of 1763; Ordinance for the Regulation and Management of Indian Affairs (1786); Northwest Ordinance (1787); the Trade and Intercourse Acts of 1790, 1802, and 1834; the Trading House Act of 1806; and the Removal Act of 1830. See also Hagan, *American Indians*, p. 44, and Tyler, *History of Indian Policy*, pp. 39–40.

33. Taylor, *States and Their Indians*, p. 13.

34. Tocqueville, *Democracy in America*, pp. 356–357.

35. *Indian Affairs: Laws and Treaties*, comp. and ed. Charles J. Kappler, 7 vols. (Washington, D.C.: Government Printing Office, 1904), vol. 2, *Treaties*, p. 586.

36. Ibid., p. 1017.

37. Ibid., pp. 305–307.

38. Ibid., pp. 479–480.

39. Ibid., pp. 611–614.

40. Ibid., pp. 872–873.

41. Ibid., pp. 703–705.

42. Ibid., p. 736.

43. Ibid., pp. 843–847.

44. Ibid., pp. 1024–1025.

45. Commissioner of Indian Affairs, *Annual Report* (Washington, D.C.: Government Printing Office, 1875), pp. 16–17. See also p. 23 for a discussion of the nature of Indian sovereignty and the need for "civilization."

46. Francis Paul Prucha, *American Indian Policy in Crisis: Christian Reformers and the Indian, 1865–1900* (Norman: University of Oklahoma Press, 1976), p. 3. Prucha also has edited *Americanizing the American Indians: Writings by Friends of the Indians, 1880–1900* (Cambridge, Mass.: Harvard University Press, 1973; reprinted, University of Nebraska Press, 1978). Also see Tyler, *History of Indian Policy*, pp. 95 ff., and Washburn, *Indian in America*, pp. 233–249.

47. Prucha, *Americanizing the American Indians*, p. 6.

48. 24 Stat. 388, sometimes referred to as the Dawes Act. See D. S. Otis, "History of the Allotment Policy," U.S. Congress, House, Hearings on H.R. 7902, 73rd Cong., 2d sess., 1934, pt. 9. A recent book makes Otis's work readily accessible: D. S. Otis, *The Dawes Act and the Allotment of Indian Lands*, ed., Francis Paul Prucha, Civilization of American Indian Series vol. 123 (Norman: University of Oklahoma Press, 1973). Under the Allotment Act the president was authorized at his discretion to have any reservation or portion of a reservation surveyed and allotted to individual Indians. To keep the Indian from disposing of his land, the title was to be held in trust by the United States for twenty-five years or longer if the president thought advisable. Surplus lands on a reservation after allotments had been made could be purchased by the government through negotiation with the tribe, subject to ratification by Congress. The purchase price was to be held in trust, and the interest was for the sole use of the tribe concerned, subject to appropriation by Congress. See also the Burke Act, 34 Stat. 182.

49. Commissioner of Indian Affairs, *Annual Report*, (Washington, D.C.: Government Printing Office, 1887), p. viii.

50. A recent study by Leonard A. Carlson, *Indians, Bureaucrats, and Land: The Dawes Act and the Decline of Indian Farming*, Contributions in Economics and Economic History no. 36 (Westport, Conn.: Greenwood Press, 1981), concludes that the Allotment Act had a negative impact on Indians' becoming self-sufficient farmers, which was not anticipated by the reformers who supported the act. In most instances the Indian tribes prior to the Allotment Act had a workable system of individual land assignments, which were treated as private property. Before allotment there was a good start in many Indian communities toward individual farming and ranching. Carlson's economic analysis points up that the allotment of land made it easier to sell or lease land. At the same time it made coordinated actions by the tribe or by all Indians in a group more difficult. Carlson concluded that an Indian with an allotment would lease the land to non-Indians and work for a wage to maximize his resources. In other words, the incentives for Indians to work their land themselves were greater before than after allotment. Thus, in Carlson's view, the objective of the reformers to help the Indians become self-sufficient farmers was in part defeated by a flawed understanding of the incentives involved before and after allotment. The Allotment Act did not markedly bring about greater intermixing of non-Indians and Indians, nor did it greatly stimulate acculturation. It did provide a vehicle for the transfer of land from Indians to non-Indians.

51. 7 Stat. 159.

52. 43 Stat. 253.
53. 42 Stat. 208.
54. Tyler, *Hisory of Indian Policy*, pp. 112–115.
55. Lewis Meriam and others, *The Problem of Indian Administration*, Institute for Government Research, Studies in Administration (Baltimore, Md.: Johns Hopkins Press, 1928).
56. Tyler, *History of Indian Policy*, p. 114 n.16.
57. Pursuant to Senate Resolution 79, *Congressional Record*, 70th Cong., 1st sess., February 2, 1928, p. 2368, and subsequent continuing resolutions.
58. Meriam, *Problem of Indian Administration*, pp. 16–18, 22–23, 35–50, 462–466.
59. Ibid., p. 7.
60. Tyler, *History of Indian Policy*, p. 118.
61. Meriam, *Problems of Indian Administration*, p. 22.
62. 48 Stat. 984.
63. Commissioner of Indian Affairs, *Annual Report* (Washington, D.C.: Government Printing Office, 1933), pp. 69 and 109.
64. Lawrence C. Kelly, "John Collier and the Indian New Deal: An Assessment," and Kenneth R. Philp, "John Collier and the Controversy Over the Wheeler-Howard Bill," in Jane F. Smith and Robert M. Kvasnicka, eds., *Indian-White Relations: A Persistent Paradox* (Washington, D.C.: Howard University Press, 1976), p. 171 and p. 227.
65. 10 Stat. 1159; *Indian Affairs*, vol. 2, *Treaties*, p. 677.
66. Board of Indian Commissioners, *Annual Report* (Washington, D.C.: Government Printing Office, 1899), pp. 18–19.
67. Commissoner of Indian Affairs, *Annual Report*, (Washington, D.C.: Government Printing Office, 1917), p. 3.
68. U.S. Senate, 78th Cong., 1st sess., June 11, 1943, Report 310.
69. U.S. House, 78th Cong., 2d sess., December 23, 1944, Report 2091 pursuant to H.R. 166, p. 2.
70. U.S. Senate, Post Office and Civil Service Committee, *Officers and Employees of the Federal Government*, Hearings on Senate Resolution 41, 89th Cong., 1st sess., 1947, pp. 130, 253–259, 556–568, 576, 578.
71. Hoover Commission, *Social Security, Education, and Indian Affairs: A Report to the Congress by the Commission on Organization of the Executive Branch of the Government* (Washington, D.C.: Government Printing Office, March 1949), p. 63.
72. Commissioner of Indian Affairs, "Annual Report," 1951, in Department of the Interior, *Annual Report* (Washington, D.C.: Government Printing Office, 1951), p. 353.
73. U.S. House, 82d Cong., 2d sess., December 15, 1952, Report 2503. See Taylor, *States and Their Indian Citizens*, pp. 56–58 for more detail.
74. Memorandum to Commissioner Louis R. Bruce on termination, October 13, 1969, BIA files.
75. Bureau of Indian Affairs, "List of Terminated and Restored Tribes, Branch of Tribal Relations," February 15, 1982.
76. Munroe E. Price, "A Moment in History: The Alaska Native Claims Settlement Act," *UCLA-Alaska Law Review* 8:89 (1979), p. 94.
77. Taylor, *States and Their Indian Citizens*, pp. 40–47.
78. Price, "A Moment in History," pp. 94–95.
79. Taylor, *States and Their Indian Citizens*, pp. 108–109, footnotes.

80. See, for example, Harry C. Clement, *The Gift That Hurt the Indians,* Report prepared for the Ford Foundation and the Bureau of Indian Affairs (Washington, D.C.: Checchi and Company, August 1977); also, Alan L. Sorkin, *American Indians and Federal Aid* (Washington, D.C.: Brookings Institution, 1971).

81. U.S. House, *Indian Resources Development Act of 1967,* Hearings before the Subcommittee on Indian Affairs on H.R. 10560, 90th Cong. 1st sess., July 13–14, 1967.

82. U.S. Congress, Legislative Resolution No. 37, April 16, 1969.

83. President Lyndon B. Johnson, "The Forgotten American," the president's message to the Congress on goals and programs for the American Indian, March 6, 1968; President Richard Nixon, preelection statement, 450 Park Avenue, New York, September 22, 1968, and message to Congress, July 8, 1970. All of the above are summarized in Taylor, *States and Their Indian Citizens,* Appendix G, pp. 197–201.

84. September 22, 1968, New York City.

85. December 18, 1971, 85 Stat. 688.

86. 88 Stat. 77.

87. Pl 93-638, January 4, 1975, 25 U.S. Code (USC) 450.

88. 25 Code of Federal Regulations (CFR) 54.

89. November 1, 1978, P.L. 95-561, Title 11—Indian Education.

90. For an excellent summary of Indian policy issues since 1945 see Raymond V. Butler, "The Bureau of Indian Affairs: Activities Since 1945," *Annals of the American Academy of Political and Social Science* 436, (March 1978), pp. 50–79.

91. American Indian Policy Review Commission, *Final Report,* 2 vols. (Washington, D.C.: Government Printing Office, 1977), 1:4. The author's views on the preliminary report are included in vol. 2 of the *Final Report,* pp. 809–819.

92. 94 Stat. 1785 (Maine); 85 Stat. 688 (Alaska).

93. In 1966 Nancy Ostreich Lurie estimated that there were approximately 10 million people in the United States with some Indian blood (Nancy Ostreich Lurie, "The Enduring Indian," *Natural History Magazine* [November 1966], p. 10 ff. Since then the number undoubtedly has increased substantially.

Chapter 2

1. S. Lyman Tyler, *A History of Indian Policy* (Washington, D.C.: Department of the Interior, Bureau of Indian Affairs, 1973), p. 33.

2. Ibid., p. 46.

3. Ibid., p. 52.

4. Ibid.

5. Commissioner of Indian Affairs, *Annual Report* (Washington, D.C.: Government Printing Office, 1871), pp. 6, 191–192.

6. Board of Indian Commissioners, *The Indian Bureau from 1824 to 1924,* Bulletin no. 242 (Washington, D.C.: Government Printing Office, 1924), p. 21.

7. Theodore W. Taylor, "The Regional Organization of the Bureau of Indian Affairs" (Ph.D. dissertation, Harvard University, December 1959), p. 98.

8. 30 Stat. 495.

9. Laurence F. Schmeckebier, *The Office of Indian Affairs: Its History, Activities, and Organization,* Institute for Government Research, Service Monographs of the United States Government no. 48 (Baltimore, Md.: Johns Hopkins Press, 1927), p. 135.

10. Commissioner of Indian Affairs, *Annual Report* (Washington, D.C.: Government Printing Office, 1907), pp. 12–14. Commissioner T. J. Morgan had proposed this policy in 1892 (see the *Annual Report* for 1892, p. 9).

11. 42 Stat. 208.

12. Schmeckebier, *Office of Indian Affairs*, pp. 143–269.

13. Ibid., pp. 270–292.

14. Ibid., pp. 333–398.

15. Ibid., pp. 300–332.

16. Ibid., pp. 310–311.

17. Lewis Meriam and others, *The Problem of Indian Administration*, Institute for Government Research, Studies in Administration (Baltimore, Md.: Johns Hopkins Press, 1928), pp. 27 ff. and throughout the report.

18. Taylor, "Regional Organization," Part 2, chapters 2 and 3, particularly fn 16 on p. 217.

19. Theodore W. Taylor, *The States and Their Indian Citizens* (Washington, D.C.: Department of the Interior, Bureau of Indian Affairs, 1972), p. 59.

20. Ibid., p. 33. Usually agencies struggle to keep functions. In this instance the BIA was pushing the transfer and the Public Health Service was resisting.

21. Ibid., chapters 3 and 4.

22. Ibid., pp. 157–158.

23. Sam Adams, "Statement on Organizational Overview," BIA Division of Management Research and Evaluation, December 1981.

24. 28 Stat. 986.

25. Theodore W. Taylor "Realty Personnel Study" (Prepared for the Bureau of Indian Affairs, May 16, 1977).

26. U.S. Comptroller General, *Report to the Chairman, Committee on Interior and Insular Affairs, House* (Washington, D.C.: General Accounting Office, September 10, 1981).

27. Federal Grant and Cooperative Agreement Act of 1977, 92 Stat. 3.

28. Members of the Senate Select Committee on Indian Affairs asked the General Accounting Office to make a cost comparison of Assistant Secretary Kenneth Smith's proposals. These committee members were concerned about the proposed closing of some of the area offices and asked the BIA to hold up the reorganization until the GAO's review could be completed. The GAO was also asked to determine the effects of the Smith proposal on cost effectiveness, services, maintenance of trust responsibilities, and self-determination policies. Assistant Secretary Smith was reported to be upset over what he called Capitol Hill interference (*The Shoban News* 4:10 [March 10, 1982], published weekly, Fort Hall, Idaho).

Chapter 3

1. Raymond V. Butler, "The Bureau of Indian Affairs: Activities Since 1945," *Annals of the American Academy of Political and Social Science* 436 (March 1978), pp. 50–79.

2. "There shall be in the Department of the Interior a Commissioner of Indian Affairs," 42 Stat. 1180 (1923); 60 Stat. 939 (1946); Snyder Act, 42 Stat. 208; Indian Reorganization Act, 48 Stat. 984; Indian Self-Determination and Education Assistance Act, 88 Stat. 2203; and other statutes.

3. *The United States Government Manual 1981/82*, Office of the Federal Register, National Archives and Records Service, General Services Administration

(Washington, D.C.: Government Printing Office, revised May 1, 1981), pp. 309–320.

4. U.S. Department of the Interior, *Departmental Manual,* chap. 130, sec. 2.1.

5. Unless otherwise noted, the data in the rest of this chapter are from BIA budget submissions to Congress for fiscal years 1980, 1981, 1982, and 1983 plus personal interviews with appropriate officials.

6. Executive order, December 16, 1882.

7. 88 Stat. 1712.

8. 94 Stat. 929.

9. 70 Stat. 986; 77 Stat. 471.

10. See, for example, Harry G. Clement, *The Gift That Hurt the Indians,* Report about federally financed tourism on Indian reservations prepared for the Ford Foundation and the Bureau of Indian Affairs (Washington, D.C.: Checchi and Company, August 1977); also Alan L. Sorkin, *American Indians and Federal Aid* (Washington, D.C.: Brookings Institute, 1971).

11. *Forbes,* November 9, 1981, p. 108 ff.

12. Bureau of Indian Affairs, "Budget Justification for FY 1982" (January 1981), pp. 89–90.

13. "the collection of all construction costs against any Indian-owned lands within any Government irrigation project is hereby deferred, and no assessments shall be made on behalf of such charges . . . until Indian title thereto shall have been extinguished" (47 Stat. 564).

14. Of this land 41,856,465 acres are tribally owned, and 10,033,480 acres are individually owned. See Table 1.1 for summary.

15. Bureau of Indian Affairs, "Budget Justification FY 1981," p. 104.

16. Ibid., p. 97.

17. Theodore W. Taylor, *The States and Their Indian Citizens* (Washington, D.C.: Department of the Interior, Bureau of Indian Affairs, 1972), p. 66.

18. Department of Health and Human Services, "Budget Justification for FY 1982" (1982), pp. 110–111.

19. Dr. R. C. Kreuzburg, Indian Health Service, telephone conversation.

20. Richard S. Jones, *Federal Programs of Assistance to American Indians,* Report prepared for the Select Committee on Indian Affairs, U.S. Senate, by the Congressional Research Service (Washington, D.C.: Government Printing Office, June 1981), pp. 215–220.

21. Department of Justice, *Legal Activities* (Washington, D.C., 1981), p. 15.

22. Jones, *Federal Programs,* p. 221.

23. Department of Justice, *Legal Activities,* p. 15.

24. Table, "Indian and Native American Employment and Training Program Funded Under the Comprehensive Employment Training Act," received from EDA Indian Desk August 24, 1981.

Chapter 4

1. Bureau of Indian Affairs, "Information About the Indian People," October 1980.

2. 25 Code of Federal Regulations (CFR) 54.7; 43 Federal Register (FR) 39361, September 5, 1978.

3. 437 U.S. Supreme Court Decisions (US) 634, 1978.

4. 68 Stat. 863, August 27, 1954; 25 U.S. Code Annotated (USCA) 677. "Full-blood means a member of the tribe who possesses one-half degree of

Ute Indian blood and a total of Indian blood in excess of one-half" (25 USCA 677).

5. A Report of the U.S. Commission on Civil Rights, *Indian Tribes: A Continuing Quest for Survival* (Washington, D.C.: Government Printing Office, June 1981), p. 165 (hereafter cited as Civil Rights Commission Report 1981). Because of the perceived inadequate land base for many Indians SEC. 5 of the Indian Reorganization Act (25 U.S. Code [USC] 465) authorized the secretary of the Interior to buy land for Indian tribes. From 1936 until 1950 the total amount appropriated for this purpose was approximately $6 million (see Theodore W. Taylor, "Report on Purchase of Indian Land and Acres of Indian Land in Trust 1934–1975" [Prepared under contract with the Bureau of Indian Affairs for the American Indian Policy Review Commission, May 1976]).

6. Commissioner of Indian Affairs, *Annual Report* (Washington, D.C.: Government Printing Office, 1949), p. 339. Also see 25 USC 403a through 403c.

7. For a discussion of the IRA see Clyde K. Kluckhohn and Robert Hackenberg, "Social Science Principles and the Indian Reorganization Act," *Indian Affairs and the Indian Reorganization Act, The Twenty Year Record,* ed. William H. Kelly, from a symposium held in conjunction with the fifty second annual meeting of the American Anthropological Association, Tucson, Arizona, December 30, 1953 (Tucson: University of Arizona, 1954), p. 32 ff.

8. See, for example, the constitutions and bylaws of the Tulalip tribes of Washington, approved Janaury 24, 1936, and the Oglala Sioux tribe of the Pine Ridge Reservation, South Dakota, approved Janaury 15, 1936. The Oglala Sioux provision that the tribal council shall appropriate tribal funds, levy taxes, promulgate and enforce ordinances, etc., subject to the review or approval by the secretary of the Interior is cited by Monroe E. Price, *Law and the American Indian: Readings, Notes and Cases,* Contemporary Legal Education Series (New York: Bobbs-Merrill Co., 1973), p. 717.

9. Ibid., pp. 718–719.

10. Merrion v. Jicarilla Apache Tribe, U.S. Supreme Court, decided January 25, 1982.

11. Memorandum from Patricia Simmons, tribal relations specialist, to the chief of the Branch of Tribal Relations on the organizational status of federally recognized Indian entities, July 21, 1981. Indian includes within its meaning Eskimos and Aleuts as well as Indian tribes, bands, villages, groups, and pueblos.

12. Mary Shepardson, "Navajo Ways in Government," *American Anthropology Association Memoir 96* 65:3, pt. 2 (June 1963), pp. 70–117, quoted in Price, *Law and the American Indian,* p. 713.

13. Ibid.

14. Ibid., pp. 713–715. For one view of the recent tribal chairman, Peter MacDonald, see Jeff Gillenkirk and Mark Dowie, "The Great Indian Power Grab," *Mother Jones* (January 1982), pp. 18–49.

15. United States v. State of Washington, 384 F. Supp. at 312 (1970).

16. Oliphant v. Suquamish, 435 US 191 (1978).

17. *Justice in Indian Country,* ed. Carrie Small (Oakland, Calif.: American Indian Lawyer Training Program, January 1980), p. 1.

18. 25 CFR 11.1 lists the groups; also 25 CFR 11.2.

19. 25 CFR 11.1.

20. Civil Rights Commission Report 1981, pp. 156–157.

21. U.S. House Committee on the Judiciary, *Department of Justice Appropriation Authorization Act FY 1982, Committee on the Judiciary,* 97th Cong., 1st sess., May 19, 1981, H.R. 97–105, pp. 6–9.

22. *Indian Courts and the Future,* Report of the National American Indian Court Judges Association (NAICJA) Long Range Planning Project; Judge Orville N. Olney, project director; David H. Getches, project planner/coordinator; prepared under BIA contract (Washington, D.C.: Government Printing Office, 1978), pp. 46–47 (hereafter cited as NAICJA Report).

23. Civil Rights Commission Report 1981, chap. 5, details the problems.

24. Ibid., p. 165. PL 83–280 (67 Stat. 588) was passed on August 15, 1953, and titled "An act to confer jurisdiction on the states of California, Minnesota, Nebraska, Oregon and Wisconsin with respect to criminal offenses and civil causes of action committed or arising on Indian reservations within such states and for other purposes." As amended, the act authorized other states to assume criminal and civil jurisdiction over Indians on reservations if the Indians concurred.

25. Oliphant v. Schlie, 544 F. 2d 1007, 1113 (9th Cir.) (1976).

26. Ibid.

27. For a non-Indian view of Indian law and order see C. Herb Williams and Walt Neubrech, *Indian Treaties, American Nightmare* (Seattle, Wash.: Outdoor Empire Publishing, 1976); also Samuel J. Brakel, *American Indian Tribal Courts: The Costs of Separate Justice* (Chicago: American Bar Foundation, 1978).

28. Oliphant v. Suquamish, 435 US 191 (1978).

29. Civil Rights Commission Report 1981, p. 166; United States v. Winans, 198 US 371 (1905).

30. Washington v. Confederated Tribes of the Colville Indian Reservation, 100 S. Ct. 2029 (June 10, 1980).

31. Glen A. Wilkinson, John W. Cragun, and Robert W. Barker, "Review of Development in Indian Law in the Courts," October 1, 1979 through October 10, 1980, (Oct. 27, 1980), and October 1, 1980, through September 15, 1981, (Oct. 11, 1981), Prepared for the National Congress of American Indians (Washington, D.C., annually, mimeographed), 1979–1980, p. 3. (hereafter cited as Wilkinson, Review with appropriate dates).

32. Merrion v. Jicarilla Apache Tribe, U.S. Supreme Court, January 25, 1982.

33. Santa Clara v. Martinez. 436 US 49 (1978).

34. Dry Creek Lodge, Inc. v. Arapaho and Shoshone Tribes, 623 F. 2d. 682 (1980).

35. Wilkinson, "Review," 1979–1980, p. 17, and 1980–1981, p. 9.

36. Ibid., 1979–1980, p. 19.

37. 49 U.S. Law Week (USLW) 4296 (March 24, 1981).

38. Wilkinson, "Review," 1980–1981, p. 2.

39. Montana v. United States, ibid., 1980–1981, p. 5.

40. Ibid., 1979–1980, pp. 26–27, and 1980–1981, p. 15a.

41. American Indian Policy Review Commission, *Final Report,* 2 vols. (Washington, D.C.: Government Printing Office, 1977), 1:180. (hereafter referred to as AIPRC *Final Report*).

42. Ibid., p. 181.

43. 25 USC 1301.

44. Price, *Law and the American Indian,* pp. 742–743, gives content.

45. Civil Rights Commission Report 1981, pp. 30–31; Santa Clara v. Martinez.

46. PL 95–608, November 8, 1978.

47. *BIA Profile* (Washington, D.C.: Government Printing Office, 1981), p. 5.

48. NAICJA Report.

49. Ibid., pp. 54–103; Samuel J. Brakel, *American Indian Tribal Courts* (Chicago: American Bar Association, 1978), pp. 91–111.

50. NAICJA Report, p. 43.

51. Ibid., p. 44.

52. Brakel, *American Indian Tribal Courts*, p. 103.

53. NAICJA Report, p. 113 and p. v.

54. Brakel, *American Indian Tribal Courts*, p. 9.

55. Civil Rights Commission Report 1981, especially pp. 167–175; NAICJA Report, entire report.

56. PL 93–638, January 4, 1975, 25 USC 450 (hereafter cited as PL 638).

57. 68 Stat. 674.

58. Bureau of Indian Affairs, "Budget Justification FY 1982" (January 1981), p. 52.

59. AIPRC *Final Report*, 1:307; letters from tribes to author; and Theodore W. Taylor, *The States and Their Indian Citizens* (Washington, D.C.: Department of the Interior, Bureau of Indian Affairs, 1972), p. 256.

60. Letter to tribal chairmen, October 30, 1981.

61. Letter from Jerry R. Levi, chairman, November 25, 1981.

62. "Lt. Governor Anoatubby Gives the Financial Status of Tribe," *Chickasaw Times* 10:5 (September–October 1981), p. 3.

63. Letter from Harry Laffoon, vice chairman of the tribal council, November 6, 1981.

64. Letter from Orville C. Langdeau, chairman, February 8, 1982.

65. Letter from Phillip Martin, chairman, November 25, 1981.

66. Letter from Robert W. Trepp, director of government policy and research, November 5, 1981.

67. Letter from Daniel Peaches, state representative in the Arizona legislature from the Navajo Reservation, February 2, 1981. Several phone calls to Sam Pete's office at the reservation did not result in my receiving a copy of the Navajo budget.

68. Letter from J. Harley Nicholas, tribal governor, December 17, 1981.

69. Cynthia Chick, "The Zuni Tribe—Past, Present, and Future", *Native American News* (Administration for Native Americans) (May 1981). Two letters to Governor Robert Lewis and a personal request in Washington, D.C., did not result in a response. Several years ago when the *Navajo Times* published the Navajo budget, reporters asked Governor Lewis for his budget and he refused, indicating that the situation at Zuni was different than at Navajo.

70. AIPRC *Final Report*, p. 21.

71. 94 Stat. 1785, sec. 6(b) (4).

72. AIPRC *Final Report*, p. 179.

73. Ibid., p. 314.

74. Ibid., p. 315.

75. Ibid., p. 306.

76. Alan L. Sorkin, *American Indians and Federal Aid* (Washington, D.C.: Brookings Institution, 1971), pp. 67–68.

77. AIPRC *Final Report*, p. 305.

78. Sorkin, *American Indians*, pp. 70–71.

79. Bureau of Indian Affairs, Office of Trust Responsibilities, "Annual Report of Indian Lands and Income from Surface and Subsurface Leases" (Washington, D.C., September 30, 1980). The BIA did not want to give out this information

and tried to avoid doing so under the Freedom of Information Act, exemption 4, which "protects secrets and commercial or financial information obtained from a person and privileged or confidential." Jack H. Taylor, a newspaper reporter for the *Daily Oklahoman,* argued that the information in question for individual tribes was generated exclusively within the government and therefore did not qualify under exemption 4. The U.S. District Court for the District of Columbia, to which Taylor took the case, held that although the information for the surface and subsurface income figures had come from the tribes, the Interior Department had "failed to make an adequate showing that its release would cause the kind of harm necessary to justify their Exemption 4 claim." (Civil Action no. 80–1834, June 19, 1981). The court also held that trust fund income reports were generated within the government and, even if they had come from outside, the Interior Department had failed to make a case that their release would cause sufficient harm to qualify under exemption 4. This finding was upheld on appeal. As a result of this case the BIA furnished me with the above report at my request. The BIA also provided summary figures on interest income from trust funds and trust fund receipts. However, the Division of Program Development and Implementation requested that I submit a formal request for data related to specific tribes. The reason given for the divisions's reluctance to provide specific information was that doing so would place the tribes at a disadvantage in business negotiations because the other party could know the details of the tribe's finances. The BIA also has had the policy of not giving out information concerning individual tribes, referring queries to the tribes themselves. The district court apparently did not agree with these arguments. In a letter to tribal leaders dated May 25, 1982, Assistant Secretary Smith notified them of this decision and stated: "In this litigation the Department received only limited assistance from the National Tribal Chairmen's Association, and no specific Indian tribes actively participated in the litigation until the District Court's adverse decision was appealed." Smith continued that the case "demonstrates that tribes must become involved if the Government is to prevail in this type of litigation in the future."

80. Sorkin, *American Indians,* p. 81.

81. Harry G. Clement, *The Gift That Hurt the Indians,* a Report about federally financed tourism on Indian reservations prepared for the Ford Foundation and the Bureau of Indian Affairs (Washington, D.C.: Checchi and Company, August 1977), pp. 96–97.

82. Interviews with Gordon Evans and Larry Schneider, BIA specialists, August 1981.

83. Clement, *Gift That Hurt the Indians.*

84. Ibid., pp. 120–121. See Appendix B for specific data on these twelve projects.

85. Sorkin, *American Indian,* pp. 81–86.

86. Ibid., pp. 87–90.

87. AIPRC *Final Report,* p. 307.

88. Price, *Law and the American Indian,* p. 174.

89. AIPRC *Final Report,* p. 139.

90. William Schaab, Albuquerque tribal attorney, quoted by Price, *Law and the American Indian,* pp. 635–636.

91. Ibid., p. 636.

92. AIPRC *Final Report,* p. 15.

93. Price, *Law and the American Indian,* p. 673.

94. *Indian Tribes as Governments,* Analysis of the governing institutions of selected Indian tribes funded by the John Hay Whitney Foundation (Washington, D.C.: American Indian Lawyer Training Program, 1975), p. 3.

Chapter 5

1. U.S. Congress, Senate Report 96-957, 96th Cong., 2d sess., September 17, 1980, p. 12. This report deals with authorizing funds for the settlement of Indian claims in the state of Maine and was to accompany S. 2829. The history of the Maine litigation is found on pp. 12–14.

2. 4 Stat. 730.

3. 388 F. Supp. 649, 667 (D. Me. 1975). See also, Francis J. O'Toole and Thomas N. Tureen, "State Power and the Passamaquoddy Tribe: 'A Gross National Hypocrisy,'" *Maine Law Review* 23 (1971), pp. 1–39.

4. Joint Tribal Councils of Passamaquoddy Tribe v. Morton, 528 F. 2d 370 (1975).

5. Richard S. Jones, "Indians: Land Claims by Eastern Tribes" (Washington, D.C.: Congressional Research Service, Library of Congress, Issue Brief no. 1B77040, January 15, 1981), p. 5.

6. Recommendation to President Carter, under the letterhead Kilpatrick, Cody, Rogers, McClatchey, and Regenstein, Atlanta, Georgia, July 15, 1977, signed by William B. Gunter.

7. *Congressional Record,* House, 95th Cong., lst sess., March 1, 1977, H1533.

8. American Indian Policy Review Commission, *Final Report,* 2 vols. (Washington, D.C.: Government Printing Office, 1977), 1:608, 609 (hereafter referred to as AIPRC *Final Report*).

9. Act of August 13, 1946, 60 Stat. 1949.

10. AIPRC *Final Report,* 1:609.

11. Tim Vollmann, "A Survey of Eastern Land Claims: 1970–1979," *Maine Law Review,* 31:5 (1979), pp. 14–15.

12. 348 U.S. Supreme Court Decisions (US) 272, 1955. Vollmann, "A Survey," p. 15; see also AIPRC *Report,* pp. 606–609.

13. Maine, *Public Laws 1980,* Chapter 732, "An Act to Implement the Maine Indian Claims Settlement," sec. 31.

14. Note from Peter Taylor, special counsel, Select Committee on Indian Affairs, received in April 1982.

15. Press release, the White House, October 10, 1980.

16. Vollmann, "A Survey," p. 15.

17. See Appendix C for the status of other aboriginal land claim cases based on alleged violation of the Trade and Intercourse Act.

Chapter 6

1. For the health, education, and welfare fields see, for example, Joseph A. Califano, Jr., *Governing America* (New York: Simon and Schuster, 1981).

2. Interview with Ronald P. Andrade, executive director of NCAI, and Annette Traversie Bagley, editor and legislative coordinator, November 26, 1981.

3. PL 95-328 (92 Stat. 409), July 28, 1978.

4. As indicated in Chapter 1, of the 1,418,000 Indians counted in the 1980 census only 52 percent had any relation with the BIA. The other 48 percent

received most of their governmental services from the state and federal government in the same manner as other citizens. Even many Indian groups that did have some connection with the BIA received many services through the state. When the fact that 90 to 95 percent of Indian education is provided by the states (for both reservation and nonreservation Indians) and the high ratio of state provision of law and order and other services to Indians are considered, the estimate that states furnish 80 to 85 percent of the government services received by Indians seems reasonable.

5. American Indian Policy Review Commission, *Final Report*, 2 vols. (Washington, D.C.: Government Printing Office, 1977), 1:5. The Senate Select Committee on Indian Affairs has sought to further this objective by introducing legislation in the sessions since 1977; for example, S. 563, *Tribal-State Compact Act of 1981*, 97th Cong. lst. sess., February 24, 1981.

6. Telephone conversation with Raymond Butler, Division of Social Services, March 8, 1982.

7. Theodore W. Taylor, *The States and Their Indian Citizens* (Washington, D.C.: Department of the Interior, Bureau of Indian Affairs, 1972), particularly pp. 89–106. Theodore W. Taylor, *American Indian Policy* (Mt. Airy, Md.: Lomond Publications, in press) describes current state programs in more detail.

8. As of January 1982 forty-one states had responded by letter or telephone to the letter sent by Kenneth Payton, acting deputy assistant secretary for Indian affairs (operations), October 16, 1981, to the governors of the fifty states. Those that had not responded were Alabama, Connecticut, Georgia, Kentucky, Massachusetts, New Jersey, Pennsylvania, Vermont, and West Virginia. Not all information received could be included because of space limitations.

9. J. Leiper Freeman, *The Political Process: Executive Bureau–Legislative Committee Relations* (New York: Random House, 1965).

10. Statement of Garrey E. Carruthers, assistant secretary of the Interior, land and water resources, before the Senate Select Committee on Indian Affairs, 97th Cong., 2d sess., in regard to S. 2114, a bill "to provide water to the Papago Tribe of Arizona, to settle Papago Indian water right claims in portions of the Papago reservations, and for other purposes," and H.R. 5118, the companion House bill, March 31, 1982.

11. Hugh Heclo, *A Government of Strangers* (Washington, D.C.: Brookings Institution, 1977).

12. Hoover Commission, *Social Security, Education, and Indian Affairs: A Report to the Congress by the Commission on Organization of the Executive Branch of the Government* (Washington, D.C.: Government Printing Office, March 1949), administrative recommendation no. 8, p. 69, of the Indian affairs section of report.

13. Dennis Drabelle, *Washington Post*, May 28, 1978, p. C-3.

14. Harold Seidman, *Politics, Position, and Power: the Dynamics of Federal Organization*, 3d ed. (New York: Oxford University Press, 1980), p. 134.

Chapter 7

1. Alvin Toffler, *Future Shock* (New York: Bantam Books, 1971).

2. Wilcomb E. Washburn, *The Indian in America*, New American Nation Series, ed. Henry Steele Commager and Richard B. Morris (New York: Harper Torchbooks, Harper and Row, 1975), pp. 258–260.

3. Dan Cushman, *Stay Away Joe*, 4th ed. (Great Falls, Mont.: Stay Away Joe Publishers, 1968) is a fictional account of an extended Indian family indicating various stages of acculturation among the different members. Harry James, *Red Man, White Man* (San Antonio, Tex.: Naylor Co., 1958) relates incidents based on actual happenings to a variety of people told as the story of a Hopi returning to Hopi country after seven years in the Navy during World War I. Other titles include Hal Glen Borland, *When Legends Die* (New York: J. B. Lippincott, 1963), and Thomas Berger, *Little Big Man* (New York: Dial Press, 1964).

4. GAO study quoted in American Indian Policy Review Commission, *Final Report*, 2 vols. (Washington, D.C.: Government Printing Office, 1977), 1:317 (hereafter cited as AIPRC *Final Report*).

5. AIPRC, "Tentative Final Report," March 4, 1977, chap. 7, p. 20.

6. AIPRC *Final Report*, 2:817.

7. Ibid., 1:5–6.

8. Monroe E. Price, *Law and the American Indian: Readings, Notes, and Cases*, Contemporary Legal Education Series (New York: Bobbs-Merrill Co., 1973), pp. 635–636.

9. Don Harris, *Washington Post*, April 11, 1982, p. A3. The same article reported that the Justice Department had rejected Arizona's attempt to draw new legislative boundaries because the San Carlos Apache were split among three districts and the Apache objected.

10. Price, *Law and the American Indian*, p. 303.

11. Ibid., p. 84.

12. Ibid., p. 3.

13. Ibid., p. 105.

14. Ibid.

15. Letter to Kenneth Smith February 1, 1982; response from Kenneth Smith May 18, 1982. I had already written to the 100 largest tribes, and the few replies are reported in Chapter 4. Many of these letters were followed up by personal telephone calls to the tribal chairmen or the business managers of reservations. In the case of Warm Springs, where Assistant Secretary Smith had been business manager and a member of the tribal council, I sought Smith's help, made two telephone calls to the reservation, and wrote two letters; no information was supplied.

16. AIPRC *Final Report*.

17. Lewis Meriam and others, *The Problem of Indian Administration*, Institute for Government Research, Studies in Administration (Baltimore, Md.: Johns Hopkins Press, 1928).

18. AIPRC *Final Report*, 1:4.

19. Ibid., pp. 4 and 5.

20. Letter from Daniel Peaches February 2, 1982, in response to letter to 100 tribal chairmen and a follow-up letter to Sam Pete in Navajo Chairman Peter MacDonald's office at Window Rock.

21. Meriam and others, *Problem of Indian Administration*, p. 99; Theodore W. Taylor, *The States and Their Indian Citizens* (Washington, D.C.: Department of the Interior, Bureau of Indian Affairs, 1972), p. 59.

22. National Association of Counties, *American County Platform and Resolutions 1981-1982* (Washington, D.C., July 14, 1981), p. 203.

23. Ibid., pp. 203–204.

24. Edward H. Spicer, *A Short History of the Indians of the United States* (New York: Van Nostrand–Reinhold, 1969), pp. 249–250.

25. Taylor, *States and Their Indian Citizens*, pp. 182–183, for 1970 census figures of Indians in Standard Metropolitan Statistical Areas.

SELECTED BIBLIOGRAPHY

Brophy, William A., and Aberle, Sophie D. *The Indian: America's Unfinished Business.* Report of the Commission on the Rights, Liberties, and Responsibilities of the American Indian. Norman: University of Oklahoma Press, 1966. A very informative discussion of American Indian values, government, and interface with the non-Indian society, the meaning of reservation, the role of the BIA, Indian law, and economic development. An earlier report by the same commission, *A Program for Indian Citizens,* was published by the Fund for the Republic, Albuquerque, N. M., January 1961. Members of the commission were W. W. Keeler, principal chief of the Cherokee tribe and then executive vice-president of Phillips Petroleum Company; Karl N. Llewellyn, professor of jurisprudence, University of Chicago; A. M. Schlesinger, professor of history, Harvard University; Charles A. Sprague, the *Oregon Statesman;* and the chairman, O. Meredith Wilson, president of the University of Minnesota. William A. Brophy, former commissioner of Indian Affairs (1945–1948), was the first executive director of the commission. Dr. Sophie D. Aberle (Mrs. Brophy) succeeded Mr. Brophy in this position. From 1935 to 1944 she served as superintendent of the United Pueblos Agency, Bureau of Indian Affairs.

Cohen, Felix S. *Handbook of Federal Indian Law, with Reference Tables and Index.* Washington, D.C.: Government Printing Office, 1942. Reprinted, Albuquerque: University of New Mexico Press, 1972. See also entries for *Federal Indian Law* and Bernard Strickland for revisions of Cohen's *Handbook.*

Collier, John. *Indians of the Americas.* New York: W. W. Norton, 1947. Collier was commissioner of Indian Affairs longer than any other commissioner.

Driver, Harold E. *Indians of North America.* 2d edition, revised. Chicago: University of Chicago Press, 1969. Presents a comparative description and interpretation of Native American cultures, including maps showing various characteristics.

Federal Indian Law. Washington, D.C.: Department of the Interior, 1958. A revision and updating of Felix Cohen's *Handbook* reflecting the views and policies of the 1950s.

Hagan, William T. *American Indians.* Revised edition. Chicago: University of Chicago Press, 1979. This is a brief, readable and perceptive history of the relations between the Indians and the United States, including the clash of cultures and the relationship of this clash to the mainstream of American history.

Hodge, Frederick Webb, ed. *Handbook of American Indians North of Mexico.* Bureau of American Ethnology Bulletin 30. 2 vols. Washington, D.C.: Smithsonian Institution, 1912. Reprinted, New York: Rowman and Littlefield, 1971.

Hoover Commission. *Social Security, Education, and Indian Affairs: A Report to the Congress by the Commission on Organization of the Executive Branch of the Government.* Washington, D.C.: Government Printing Office, March 1949. This report includes the commission's recommendations and minority reports on Indian policy and reflects the diverse views often posed in Indian policy considerations.

Josephy, Alvin M., Jr. *The Indian Heritage of America.* New York: Alfred A. Knopf, 1968. Presents the archaeology, ethnology, and history of the tribes and cultures of the Indians of North and South America from prehistoric times to the present day.

Indian Affairs: Laws and Treaties. Compiled and edited by Charles J. Kappler. 7 vols. Washington, D.C.: Government Printing Office, 1904. Volume 2, *Treaties.* McNickle, D'Arcy. *Native American Tribalism: Indian Survivals and Renewals.* New York: Oxford University Press, 1973.

Meriam, Lewis, and others. *The Problem of Indian Administration.* Institute for Government Research, Studies in Administration. Baltimore, Md.; Johns Hopkins Press, 1928. A survey of the economic, social, educational, health, and other conditions of the American Indians, with a view of what remained to be done to improve services and help the Indians adjust to the prevailing civilization.

Miller, George Frederick. *A Wild Indian.* Washington, D.C.: Daylion Co.; printed by Mt. Vernon Publishing Co., 1942. Published anonymously. Miller was one of seven supervisors of Indian education in 1929. His novel reflects the Indian-agent relationship and presents a description of Indian school operations, the vagaries of policy changes and directives from Washington, and the frustration of the field personnel with Washington's attempts to upgrade services. Many parallels can be seen between this description of the 1920s and 1930s and the situation today.

Prucha, Francis Paul. *American Indian Policy in Crisis: Christian Reformers and the Indian, 1865–1900.* Norman: University of Oklahoma Press, 1976. Prucha has also written about the trade and intercourse acts, Indian policy in the 1840s, and Andrew Jackson's Indian policy. Prucha is the author of *United States Indian Policy: A Critical Bibliography,* Bibliographical Series, Newberry Library Center for the History of the American Indian. Bloomington: Indiana University Press, 1977.

"Report of the Committee on Indian Affairs." Mimeographed. Washington, D.C.: Commission on Organization of the Executive Branch of the Government (Hoover Commission), October 1948. A 345-page study by Charles J. Rhoads, John R. Nichols, Gilbert Darlington, and George A. Graham, chairman, on which the conclusions of the majority report of the Hoover Commission were based. It is a thorough review of Indian programs and discusses the relationships of Indian tribes, states, and the federal government.

Schmeckebier, Laurence F. *The Office of Indian Affairs: Its History, Activities, and Organization.* Institute for Government Research, Service Monographs of the United States Government no. 48. Baltimore, Md.: Johns Hopkins Press,

1927. A detailed look at the functions and organization of the then Office of Indian Affairs.

Smith, Jane F., and Kvasnicka, Robert M., eds. *Indian-White Relations: A Persistent Paradox.* Papers presented at the National Archives Conference on Research in the History of Indian-White Relations, Washington, D.C., June 16, 1972. Washington, D.C.: Howard University Press, 1976.

Sorkin, Alan L. *American Indians and Federal Aid.* Washington, D.C.: Brookings Institution, 1971. An analysis of the effectiveness of federal aid programs.

Spicer, Edward H. *A Short History of the Indians of the United States.* New York: Van Nostrand–Reinhold, 1969. A good short history with some different materials than Hagan's work.

Steiner, Stan. *The New Indians.* New York: Harper and Row, 1968. A view of the "red power" movement.

Strickland, Bernard, et al. *Felix S. Cohen's Handbook of Federal Indian Law.* Charlottesville, Va.: Michie Bobbs-Merrill, 1982. The most recent updating of Cohen's *Handbook,* done by Interior contract with the New Mexico School of Law and Board of Editors. Funding was provided by both the Department of the Interior and private foundations.

Swanton, John R. *The Indian Tribes of North America.* Bureau of American Ethnology Bulletin 145. Washington, D.C.: Smithsonian Institution, 1952. A description of tribes and groups about 1650 organized according to the boundaries of the present states.

Taylor, Theodore W. *The States and Their Indian Citizens.* Washington, D.C.: Department of the Interior, Bureau of Indian Affairs, 1972. Discusses the services transferred to the states and to the tribes by the federal government and state organizations concerned with Indian affairs. Includes survey of tribal attitudes and 1970 census data on the location of Indians. Traces federal policy as it pertains to transferring BIA functions to tribes and to states.

Tyler, S. Lyman. *A History of Indian Policy.* Washington, D.C.: Department of Interior, Bureau of Indian Affairs, 1973. A perceptive review of the history of Indian policy to 1972. Has a very complete bibliography of Indian materials to date of publication.

Washburn, Wilcomb E. *The Indian in America.* New American Nation Series, ed. Henry Steele Commager and Richard B. Morris. New York: Harper Torchbooks, Harper and Row, 1975. This is the most recent general review of Indian history and Francis Paul Prucha says "in many respects the best."

Watkins, Arthur V. "Termination of Federal Supervision: The Removal of Restrictions over Indian Property and Person." *Annals of the American Academy of Political and Social Science* 311 (May 1957):47–55.

INDEX OF NAMES AND SUBJECTS

INDEX OF INDIAN TRIBES AND GROUPS

About the Book and Author

The Bureau of Indian Affairs
Theodore W. Taylor

Landmark legislation, such as the Indian Self-Determination and Education Assistance Act of 1975, as well as increasing federal subsidies for Native Americans, growing demand for the energy resources located on the 50 million acres of Native American lands, expanding numbers of Native Americans and their interest groups, devastating reservation unemployment, and other factors have in the last decade radically changed the environment in which the Bureau of Indian Affairs (BIA) operates. This book presents an up-to-date description and analysis of the BIA, including its missions, organization, functions, administration, problems, and decision-making and -implementing processes. Attention is given, too, to the often friction-laden interactions of the BIA and other governmental units (among them the Department of the Interior, Office of Management and Budget, Congress, the courts, Indian Health Service, and tribal, state, and local governments) with each other and with Indian interests. Abundant tables provide information on such topics as the 1980 Indian population and land by state, BIA budgets, and agricultural and mineral production on Indian lands.

Dr. Taylor examines the current operations of the Bureau under the Reagan administration and explores possible policy decisions that will affect Native Americans as well as non-Indian citizens. The book includes a foreword by Phillip Martin, chief of the Mississippi Band of Choctaw Indians and president of the National Tribal Chairmen's Association.

Theodore W. Taylor, former deputy commissioner and assistant to the commissioner at the BIA, was a professorial lecturer in public administration at George Washington University and is now a consultant and writer on Indian affairs.